# Legal
# Handbook
# for
# Educators

# Legal Handbook for Educators

Patricia A. Hollander, J.D.

Westview Press/Boulder, Colorado

Copyright © 1978 by Westview Press, Inc.

Published in 1978 in the United States of America by
   Westview Press, Inc.
   5500 Central Avenue
   Boulder, Colorado 80301
   Frederick A. Praeger, Publisher

Paperback edition published in September 1980 by Westview Press, Inc.

Library of Congress Cataloging in Publication Data
Hollander, Patricia.
   Legal handbook for educators.
   Includes case index.
   1. Educational law and legislation—United States.
I. Title.
KF4119.H64          344'.73'07          77-26092
ISBN 0-89158-420-X
ISBN 0-86531-073-4 pbk


Printed and bound in the United States of America

## Legal Handbook for Educators

Patricia A. Hollander

A welter of new laws, newly applied laws, and judicial decisions has altered the character of educational instruction and administration; in many respects, the nature of the faculty member's and administrator's legal responsibility has undergone a drastic change. At a time when grave risks exist in the failure to follow legally defined procedures, it no longer suffices to do what one thinks is best. Educators must become aware of the new legal mandates that affect them.

This handbook provides a succinct overview of the kinds of legal issues that now face educators daily. It is a practical guide, alerting educators to areas of legal concern, informing them of possible legal remedies, and making recommendations to assist in preventing litigation. "Do's and don'ts" are used to highlight these recommendations in concrete terms. After a brief historical orientation to some of the basic legal concepts in education, Ms. Hollander discusses "legally loaded" everyday situations. Implementation of due process and other required legal procedures, such as timely notice and avenues of appeal, are considered in relation to employment practices, admission of new students, and treatment of students on campus.

With its practical orientation and substantive content, the handbook is intended for an audience at all levels of the educational range, including those who have little or no background in legal matters. In addition to serving as a general reference, it has also proved highly useful as a text for courses in higher education, law, and public administration.

Patricia A. Hollander, general counsel to the American Association of University Administrators since 1972, has served as the director of the program in law and social science, Survey Research Center, State University of New York at Buffalo, and as visiting professor at the University of Virginia, where she taught a doctoral course on legal aspects of college administration. Ms. Hollander is a member of the American Bar Association and the New York and Missouri bar associations, as well as the National Association of College and University Attorneys and the National Organization on Legal Problems. She also maintains an office in Washington for consulting on law and education and writes a regular column on "Recent Court Decisions" for *Communique*, a quarterly publication of the AAUA.

*To Ed and Pete*

# Contents Summary

# Detailed Contents

*xi*

# Preface

A growing number of new laws, regulations, and court rulings are having a major impact on education today. This book provides an overview of the legal mandates that educators must be aware of if they are to avoid legal pitfalls while carrying out their responsibilities. The questions raised here are answered in terms of prevailing judicial decisions, statutes, and regulations. Some questions have been answered differently by several courts, and opposing viewpoints may ultimately be resolved through appeals to the Supreme Court. The questions and answers are always in a state of flux; constitutions are susceptible to new interpretations by the courts, legislatures pass new laws, and new legal arguments may be more persuasive than current ones. Therefore, although the legal information in this book alerts educators to contemporary and developing issues, it cannot be definitive in all situations. Consultation with legal counsel is usually advisable in specific cases.

This handbook is organized to provide an introduction to current legal concerns, such as due process. Its principal aim is to be a practical guide for educators—alerting them to areas of legal concern, informing them of possible legal remedies, and making recommendations to assist them in preventing litigious confrontations.

The book begins with a brief historical orientation to some of the basic legal concepts in education. It moves on to "legally loaded" everyday situations confronting educators. Recent court cases and laws are used to illustrate issues. With its substantive material and its practical orientation, it is hoped that this handbook will be equally useful as a textbook in courses and workshops in education and education law.

I would like to express my gratitude to those who assisted me in preparing this handbook. My husband, Dr. Edwin P. Hollander, an experienced teacher and administrator, gave willingly of his time to read and comment on the manuscript. Dr. Raymond G. Hunt, director of the Survey Research Center, State University of New York at Buffalo, provided welcome support. The National Association of College and University Attorneys offered the cooperation of its highly competent staff and access to its fine collection of materials on legal issues affecting higher education. I thank law students Donnalynne Natoli and Henry Langer for their legal research and critical comments, and Arlene Hartzberg and Barbara Laboch, who typed the manuscript. I would also like to express my appreciation for the sustaining encouragement lent by the Board of Directors and members of the American Association of University Administrators.

*P. A. H.*
*November 1977*

# Legal Handbook for Educators

# 1. New Legal Concepts in Historical Perspective: An Introduction

This chapter begins by highlighting a few new legal concepts that have had an impact on all educational institutions in some fashion. It then concentrates on the basic rights and responsibilities of administrators, faculty, and students, the legal differences between private and public educational institutions, and the legal structure of educational systems. Recommendations appear at the end of the chapter.

A major impetus for writing this book was the 1975 U.S. Supreme Court decision in *Wood* v. *Strickland*. It held that officials at public educational institutions could be personally liable for actions they knew or should have known deprived students or colleagues of well settled constitutional rights. Many educators had no knowledge of this decision; some paid little attention to it because it was a five-to-four decision. However, even such a divided opinion clearly signaled that attention was being turned to a historically unique personal injury in the field of education—the intentional constitutional tort. Numerous cases have cited *Wood* since 1975. Generally, courts have found that constitutional rights have been violated. But the courts have been reluctant to find that the constitutional right involved was so well settled at law that personal liability should be assessed against individual educators. As the law becomes more well settled, of course, reluctance to award personal damages may decrease.

The *Wood* decision reinforced my belief that all educators, public and private, should be encouraged to become more familiar with new laws, regulations, and court decisions in order to review their own policies and procedures and try to avoid unnecessary loss of time and money responding to legal claims. Their efforts are much better spent, in my opinion, in getting on with the educational endeavor. Indeed, educators have the opportunity of using constitutional, contract, and other legal requirements as teaching tools. This may not make compliance with regulations and judicial decisions any more palatable or less time consuming, but it may move some of the cost of

*1*

complying onto the benefit side of the ledger. A dean of academic or student affairs or a school principal or teacher who sets up and operates a disciplinary system that meets legal due process standards is providing an invaluable educational experience.

Education has become a major focus of litigation in the United States today. Courts have been confronted with unprecedented questions regarding the basic educational, academic function itself. Students and parents have challenged the quality of the education being offered, for example. This has occurred at elementary, secondary, and college and university levels, resulting in calls for competency-based educational policies. Experimental research involving recombinant DNA and nuclear energy has been challenged on grounds of safety and morality. Lawsuits have involved employment problems related to the institution's role as employer. Faculty and administrators have raised countless questions, ranging from the institution's right to lay off employees in times of financial exigency to matters of compliance with equal employment opportunity laws and regulations. Rights to due process relating to academic as well as employment matters also have been asserted as never before by students, faculty, and administrators.

The impact of all this litigation on individual educators and on educational institutions has increased dramatically in the last several years. In addition to the *Wood* decision, public institutions were hit hard by the Supreme Court's 1976 decision in *Fitzpatrick* v. *Bitzer*. It held that public institutions were not shielded by Eleventh Amendment immunity from payment of money damages in those instances where Congress specifically legislated that states could be so penalized. The court found that Title VII of the Civil Rights Act of 1964 provided for exactly that kind of penalty against public treasuries. Therefore, states have become liable for payment of back pay, just like private employers.

Private institutions, too, are being sued more frequently. Using the theory that a contract exists between students or employees and the institution, suits have alleged breach of contract as the basis for seeking remedies for claims involving academic or employment matters.

The traditional distinctions between public and private institutions still exist, of course. At private institutions the relationship between the institution and its students and staff is largely a contractual one. At public institutions, the relationship includes obligations relating to constitutional rights as well as to contract rights. Public institutions are affected by sunshine laws, nondiscrimination statutes, requirements of due process, and possible personal liability for depriving persons of constitutional rights.

Some blurring of the private-public distinction has developed. Court decisions have found that particular private institutions are involved in state action because of the amount of public funding and regulation involved. These institutions then must be aware of their students' and staff's constitutional rights. Also, private institutions that receive federal financial assistance are obligated to abide by federal nondiscrimination laws affecting educational and employment practices, such as Title IX of the Education Amendments of 1972 or Title VII of the Civil Rights Act of 1964.

Educators at higher education institutions often have thought of themselves as having quite different concerns than educators at elementary and secondary schools, and vice versa. Today, this is true only in a limited sense. In the realm of law, there are many more similarities than dissimilarities. All educators are affected by new laws and legal concepts regarding accountability for quality and regarding financial exigency, rights of handicapped persons, and safety and health.

## NEW LEGAL CONCEPTS AFFECTING EDUCATION

Openness and fairness are salient characteristics of the new legal concepts which affect trustees, superintendents, school board members, institutional administrators, faculty members, and other education officials today. The objection may be raised, of course, that these concepts are hardly new. True. The newness is the specific language in various recent statutes and court decisions recognizing and extending the legal definitions of honesty and justice. Clear legal imperatives now exist to deal with students and professional colleagues openly and fairly. A number of new enforcement procedures and remedies also exist. They include sanctions by the federal government, such as withdrawing federal funds and contracts. There are also sanctions through the courts, such as injunctions to expunge records, orders to provide hearings or to reinstate students or personnel, and awards of money damages against institutions and individual officials, sometimes personally.

### Full Disclosure

Consumerism has appeared in the academic marketplace. Requirements for truthful advertising of educational services is one form consumerism takes. For example, students today have a right under regulations such as those of the Guaranteed Student Loan Program to have full disclosure of information about academic programs, faculty, financial costs, and placement possibilities for certain vocationally oriented programs of study, such as medicine, law, and nursing, *before* they take a loan for tuition.

Sunshine laws in all states require that public decisions be made in open meetings and public records be open to public scrutiny. All public educational institutions are affected by these sunshine laws, as are those private institutions engaging in state action because they receive a substantial amount of state funding or regulation. Courts are being asked to determine which institutional bodies are covered, i.e., governing boards, presidents, superintendents, principals, faculty. Another question is what constitutes a meeting.

Are informal as well as formal meetings covered? Is secret balloting still permitted?

## Fair Practices and Nondiscrimination

Fair practices in recruitment, admissions, treatment, and employment, as well as nondiscrimination in dealing with students and employees, are surely among the most legislated of academia's concerns. Age, sex, race, color, national origin, and religion—and more recently, physical and mental handicaps—are all subjects of civil rights laws that have an impact upon educational institutions. Such laws will be treated more fully in later chapters.

## Financial Exigency

Proof of bona fide financial exigency has led most courts to permit institutions to implement proposals for reorganization and retrenchment which affect such matters as faculty tenure, contract renewals, and compensation, as well as student admissions and tuition rates. These issues are discussed in Chapters 3 and 5.

## Due Process

Due process to protect constitutional rights must be afforded by all public educational institutions. A significant example is that students have been found to have a property interest in their public education, and therefore they cannot be deprived of it by disciplinary suspensions or expulsions without due process. This results from the Fourteenth Amendment to the U.S. Constitution, which provides that no state shall deprive a person of life, liberty, or property without due process. If no due process is provided, students may seek legal redress.

Equal protection under the Fourteenth Amendment must be given student organizations at public institutions. Homosexual student groups, for instance, have litigated successfully their right to be recognized on an equal basis with other student groups.

## Class Actions

A class action is a legal procedure whereby a lawsuit may be filed against an institution or person by a plaintiff on behalf of a whole "class" of persons who have suffered the same injury. This mechanism permits redress in many situations where suit by an individual plaintiff would be too costly and impractical.

## Computers

Computers have added a number of new dimensions to the academic scene. Protecting privacy of material which has been programmed and stored in computers is one kind of problem; an example would be the abuse of student and personnel records.

Quite another use of computers is found in class action lawsuits. Previously, a class might have been decertified by a court on the basis of the onerous burden of identifying the individual members of the class and the amount of damages due to each. Today, with basic information available on the school's computer, that task is relatively simple. In *Samuel* v. *University of Pittsburgh* (1976) just such a situation arose when a class consisting of female married students was permitted to recover damages against the university for its improper assessment of them at the out-of-state tuition rate rather than the resident rate. This case is discussed further in Chapter 3.

## SOURCES OF BASIC RIGHTS AND RESPONSIBILITIES

Legal bases for rights and responsibilities of persons in educational institutions stem from a number of clearly defined sources. Among these are (1) constitutions (federal and state), (2) statutes and executive orders (federal, state, and local), (3) contracts between the parties, (4) professional standards recognized by the parties, (5) policies of governing boards, schools, and departments, and (6) handbooks setting forth rules affecting students, faculty, and administrators.

### Constitutions

The federal and state constitutions are sources of basic rights for all persons in public institutions. The First, Fourth, and Fourteenth Amendments to the U.S. Constitution, for instance, are familiar sources of constitutional rights relevant to public educational institutions.

The First Amendment was involved in the landmark of *Tinker* v. *Des Moines Independent School District* (1969). It reiterated that students do not leave their constitutional rights at the schoolhouse door. This case involved public school students' First Amendment rights to freedom of expression. The U.S. Supreme Court found that students had First Amendment protection to express their feelings about the Vietnam war by wearing black armbands to school. The Court said in *Tinker* that to interfere with such a basic constitutional right the school would have to show that the wearing of the armbands "materially and substantially" interfered with the requirements of appropriate discipline at the school. The test of proving "material and substantial" interference was not met by the school in the *Tinker* case.

The Fourth Amendment protection against unreasonable search and seizure often is invoked by students as a bar to searches of their school lockers or dormitory rooms. It also protects against invasions of privacy.

The Fourteenth Amendment protects persons against loss of life, liberty, or property by action of government officials without due process of law. It is relied upon often by faculty and administrators as well as by students. When an employment contract exists at a public school, it is a property right protected by the due process clause of the Fourteenth Amendment. Therefore, notice and hearing are required. The case of *Perry* v. *Sindermann* (1972) had to do with a nontenured teacher's Fourteenth Amendment right to due process when his alleged property right to continued employment was in jeopardy. The Supreme Court held that a form of de facto tenure arose from an implied contract created by language in institutional publications, a statute, and by the behavior of the parties. Such tenure could arise from an explicit written contract as well.

Public school administrators also have Fourteenth Amendment due process protection of their contractual rights. In one case, a board of trustees attempted to terminate the services of a college president during the term of his contract without due process. The court held in *Hostrop* v. *Board of Junior Colleges* (1975) that notice and hearing were required in such a deprivation of a property right.

*Responsibilities arising from constitutional rights.* Responsibilities go along with constitutional rights. Obviously, if one person has a right to due process, another person has the responsibility to provide it. That responsibility has become a particularly heavy one. Personal liability for damages now may be assessed against educators at public schools who do not meet the responsibility of knowing when constitutional rights exist and making sure they are not violated. The doctrine of sovereign or absolute immunity of the state formerly protected educational officials against personal liability when acting in good faith. However, *Wood* v. *Strickland* (1975) held that the formerly acceptable subjective test of good faith—that is, believing sincerely that one is acting in good faith—is no longer enough. An objective test of good faith also now must be met, and it requires officials to protect those clearly established and well settled constitutional rights about which they *know* or *should have known*.

This means that if an educator knew or should have known that actions taken would violate a student's clearly established constitutional rights, such violation may result in personal liability to the educator. For instance, public school students may have a constitutionally protected property right to education granted by a state. Therefore, if a student is to be deprived of that right, by suspension or expulsion from school, due process is required (*Goss* v. *Lopez*, 1975).

Moreover, educators who fail to provide due process in similar situations to faculty members or administrators may be personally liable for damages, also.

Lawsuits alleging such personal liability often rely upon a statute known as the Civil Rights Act of 1871, 42 U.S.C. Sec. 1983. It is important to emphasize that a review of cases affected by *Goss* and *Wood* indicates that courts have found situations in which constitutional violations took place; however, the courts generally have been unwilling to find that the pre-existing law was so clear that damages properly could be assessed against school officials personally. Due process will be discussed further in Chapter 2.

### Statutes

A list of federal statutes that have an impact upon educational institutions will be found in Appendix A. Statutory law is the source of many rights and responsibilities of persons at educational institutions.

A variety of laws create or affect rights and responsibilities in the academic setting. These laws often are a response to abuses of various kinds. They usually mandate that a set of standards or regulations for action or behavior be developed, that methods of enforcing the regulations be generated, and that a set of remedies be provided when violations of the regulations occur.

Title IX of the Education Amendments of 1972, for example, is a statute passed as a response to the practice of sex discrimination in educational institutions in admissions, treatment of students, and employment of females. After Title IX was passed, regulations were developed that set forth in detail how the requirement for sexually nondiscriminatory practices could be met. Enforcement of Title IX regulations was made the responsibility of the U.S. Department of Health, Education, and Welfare (HEW). Remedies for violations of Title IX include possible loss of federal funds by the institution.

Such laws often are challenged. Title IX's coverage of sex discrimination in the employment of women by educational institutions was challenged in the case of *Romeo Community Schools* v. *HEW* (1977). The court ruled that the statute did not authorize HEW to adopt regulations governing employment practices at federally financed educational institutions, but only regulations governing admissions and similar academic and disciplinary treatment of students. The decision is limited to the area of that court's jurisdiction, and the decision is being appealed by HEW.

The Civil Rights Act of 1871, 42 U.S.C. Sec. 1983, mentioned earlier, provides in part that any government official who deprives a person of certain constitutional rights without due process may be sued personally for damages. This right to sue has become the basis for much of the litigation against educators at public institutions. The institution itself, as an entity, cannot be sued under this act.

### Contracts between the Parties

Contracts of enrollment relating to students and contracts of employment relating to staff are two principal contractual relationships in educational institutions. These contracts may be in a formal written form or may be made up informally of statements made by recruiters or printed in catalogs and relied upon by students or staff. Assuming that the parties to a contract, whatever its nature, have created a binding agreement, the courts will enforce it, or may assess damages for its breach, or perhaps both.

A contract of enrollment may be found to exist between the institution and the student with regard to criteria for admissions, amount of tuition, or quality of courses taught, depending upon statements appearing in the catalog.

Chapter 3 will consider the theory that the criteria for admission set forth in a catalog may become part of the terms of an enrollment contract between the candidate for admission and the school. If the institution uses criteria other than those stated in the catalog, such as being a relative of an alumnus, the candidate may sue either for specific performance of the contract (i.e., consideration for admission on the basis of the advertised criteria), or money damages for breach of contract, or both. Under some circumstances, the claim for damages may be made against both the institution and the individual officials involved (*Steinberg* v. *University of Health Sciences, Chicago Medical School,* 1976).

Employment contracts may exist between an institution and its faculty members, its administrators, and even students it employs. The institution may contract with its employees on a one-to-one basis or on a collective basis, as in the case of unions which serve as the collective bargaining agent for employees.

One of the most troublesome matters regarding employment contracts is determining whether a contract is a term contract, which begins and ends on specific dates, or whether it contains a promise of renewal or continued employment. A typical example would be the contract of a nontenured faculty member. If the contract is for a specific term—that is, has a given starting date and termination date—the obligations of both parties end on that final day. No reasons need be given for nonrenewal since there is no expectation of continued employment. However, if the term contract requires notice of nonrenewal and notice is not given, or if tradition at the institution is such that renewal is assumed if notice of nonrenewal is not given, then the courts may decide that there is evidence of an explicit or implied contract promising reemployment or may award damages for failure to give proper notice. Termination may result in a suit for breach of contract, reinstatement, back pay, and damages. Further consideration is given to contracts of enrollment and employment in later chapters.

## Professional Standards

Professional organizations such as the American Association of University Administrators (AAUA) and the American Association of University Professors (AAUP) have developed and adopted statements of professional standards. If such standards are recognized informally by actual practice or are formally adopted by the parties, they may form the basis for defining and enforcing rights and responsibilities. Formal adoption of a set of professional standards is sometimes accomplished by language in the "Policies of the Board" or a similar document which refers to the professional standards and indicates that the parties are operating under them.

Professional standards may require one year's notice of nonrenewal, for instance. If no such notice were given, and the evidence presented showed that the parties recognized informally or were operating formally under the standards of the profession, a violation of these standards could be charged, providing a legal ground on which to seek redress.

Appendix B contains both the 1975 "Professional Standards for Administrators in Higher Education" of the American Association of University Administrators, and the "1940 Statement of Principles on Academic Freedom and Tenure," with 1970 interpretive comments, of the American Association of University Professors and the American Association of Colleges as published in the 1977 edition of the *AAUP Policy Documents and Reports.*

## Policies of Governing Boards

Administrative bodies which are given the power to govern an institution or system must develop policies by which that institution or system is to function. These bodies may be boards of regents, boards of trustees, school districts or boards, or departmental committees. The policies often provide the framework for managing the institution or system. They set forth how the organization or system will be structured and what its goals are, and they provide broad guidelines to be implemented by subordinate bodies. It is noteworthy that these policies and their implementing regulations may create legal rights and responsibilities for persons within the institution or system.

## Handbooks of Rules Affecting Students, Faculty, and Administrators

Handbooks usually provide detailed rules which are designed to carry out the policies of the institution. Legal rights and responsibilities can arise readily from the rules set out in a handbook.

Student handbooks usually address such academic matters as grading policies as well as such nonacademic activities as general student conduct on campus or time, place, and manner of distributing student publications. More will be said about student handbooks in Chapter 4.

Faculty and administrators' handbooks also provide rules relating to both academic and nonacademic matters. Most take great care, however, not to impinge on rights to academic freedom. For instance, detailed rules regarding subject matter to be discussed in a course generally are not set forth; but rules may provide a minimum number of times per semester that a teacher must meet a class. Rules regarding sabbatical leave and sick leave also may be included. Further matters concerning faculty and administrators' handbooks are dealt with in Chapter 6.

## LEGAL DISTINCTIONS BETWEEN PUBLIC AND PRIVATE INSTITUTIONS

*Legal distinctions lead to differing legal obligations.* The relationship between a public institution and its students and staff relies heavily on a concern with protection of constitutional rights. By contrast, the relationship between a private institution and its students and staff rests largely on a concern with the law of contract.

Public institutions must meet two sets of obligations: those created by federal and state constitutions, and those created by other means such as contracts or statutes. Private institutions, on the other hand, must meet only contractual or statutory requirements, and are not usually subject to constitutional mandates such as the Fourteenth Amendment requirements for due process and equal protection.

*Public schools must protect constitutional rights.* The case of *Dixon* v. *Alabama State Board of Education* (1961) reaffirmed that the actions of public institutions, such as public schools and state universities and colleges, are to be included under the Fourteenth Amendment's due process mandate. The court held that "due process requires notice and some opportunity for a hearing before a student at a tax-supported college is expelled for misconduct." The court went on to say that "only private associations have the right to obtain a waiver of notice and hearing before depriving a member of a valuable right . . . [and] that waiver must be clear and explicit. . . . [The] relations between a student and a private university are a matter of contract."

Similarly, a public school student who has a constitutional property right to an education under a state statute cannot be deprived of that right by suspension or expulsion without due process (*Goss* v. *Lopez*, 1975). Furthermore, a nontenured public school faculty member who proves that he or she has an expectation of renewed employment has a constitutional property right in that promise of continued employment and cannot be terminated without due process (*Perry* v. *Sindermann*, 1972).

*Private schools abide by contractual rights.* A private institution's obligations are quite different from those of a public institution; they are limited to whatever contractual agreement the parties have made lawfully.

As noted before, students may view themselves as parties to a contract for the purchase of education. This legal concept rests on the argument that an implied or express contract exists between the student and the educational institution. Though the parties may not have signed a written document setting forth the duties of each, there exists an implied agreement that in exchange for the student's payment of fees and costs, the institution will provide an education to the extent it can do so in good faith. Written terms of the contract can be said to be found in various documents, such as the college catalog, the admissions form, the student handbook, policies of the board of trustees, and various rules and regulations. Statements made by authorized recruiters also may be part of the contract. Further discussion of such contractual rights appear in Chapters 3 and 4.

*Private schools are affected by statutes.* Private institutions do not have absolute freedom, however, in matters affecting students, personnel, or curriculum. It is true that much of the Fourteenth Amendment does not apply to private schools because it limits only "state action." *Shelly* v. *Kraemer* (1947) stated that the Fourteenth Amendment "erects no shield against merely private conduct however discriminatory or wrongful." However, private schools that receive federal aid are affected by nondiscrimination laws of various kinds, including certain civil rights statutes forbidding discrimination based upon race, color, national origin, ethnic background, religion, and sex.

Also, private institutions are subject to statutes such as the Civil Rights Act of 1866, 42 U.S.C. Sec. 1981, which affects admissions by requiring that blacks be afforded the same right that whites enjoy to make and enforce contracts. In effect, Section 1981 permits private schools to exclude students and enforce curriculum only on the basis of racially neutral principles. In 1976 the U.S. Supreme Court held that 42 U.S.C. Sec. 1981 prohibits private segregated schools from refusing to admit blacks who are otherwise qualified, solely because of race. Such a practice violates the act by denying blacks the same right to make and enforce contracts as is enjoyed by whites (*Runyon* v. *McCrary*).

Private conduct also is affected by statutes relating to employment, such as Title VII of the Civil Rights Act of 1964—which prohibits discrimination in employment based upon race, color, religion, sex, or national origin—and the Age Discrimination in Employment Act of 1967.

Additional consideration of the impact of such statutes on practices affecting students and employees appear in Chapters 3, 4, 5, and 6.

*Private schools may voluntarily meet Constitutional standards.* Private institutions may voluntarily agree to meet certain constitutional standards by developing appropriate policies and procedures and including them in the school's catalog, written policies, or handbooks.

Many private institutions have taken the position that as educators of persons who will be living and functioning within our form of government, it is part of the institution's educational obligation to operate under basic constitutional mandates and so "teach by doing."

*The definition of public and private institutions involves questions of public control and public funding.* An institution generally is deemed to be a public institution when there is a significant amount of (1) public control over it and (2) public funding supporting it.

Public control or regulation includes substantial control by elected or appointed government officials of the way persons are named to the governing board or the way policies of the institution are set and implemented.

Public funding is significant amounts of direct financial support to the institution from public tax monies. Public institutions, of course, may receive gifts of monies or services from private sources.

Private institutions can receive some public funds; but close legal questions arise when the balance shifts too much in a private school toward public funding and public control.

*Tests of public funding and public regulation, used to determine whether private schools may be involved in state action, are not clearly defined.* The test to determine state involvement in private educational institutions rests upon proof of sufficient public funding and public regulation. What evidence constitutes such proof is at present a difficult question to answer.

In *Burton* v. *Wilmington Parking Authority* (1961), for example, the Supreme Court said "only by sifting facts and weighing circumstances can the non-obvious involvement of the State be determined." The conduct complained of was segregation in a private restaurant. Although it was leased by the state of Delaware to a private individual, the restaurant was located in a state-operated parking building. The Court found that these circumstances constituted a significant involvement of the state in private conduct, and held that the segregation in the restaurant violated the Fourteenth Amendment.

*Examples of private schools found involved in "state action."* In *Hammond* v. *University of Tampa* (1965) private conduct in the form of discrimination in admissions was found to be state action because the establishment of the university "was made possible by use of a surplus city building and the use of other city land leased for the University's purposes."

If a private institution accepts federal financial assistance for the construction of its building, it is then subject to the regulations of the federal agency administering that financial assistance (*Flanagan* v. *President and Directors of Georgetown College,* 1976).

Also, the National Collegiate Athletic Association (NCAA) has been found to act "under color of state law" by providing organized, competitive athletic activities that otherwise would be provided by the state. The NCAA, a private, voluntary association, therefore must meet constitutional standards such as due process and equal protection in its activities (*Wiley* v. *National Collegiate Athletic Association,* 1976).

*A private institution may become a public institution.* Public institutions are founded by virtue of a state constitution or a legislative act, are controlled by public officials, and are funded by public money. Public institutions may also accept gifts from private sources. Private institutions generally are established by private individuals, are controlled by private boards or individuals, and are supported principally by private funds. Private institutions may receive some monies from state or federal governments; but if a private institution receives substantial amounts of money from governmental sources or becomes controlled by elected or appointed public officials, it may lose its "private" character and become an arm of the state. In such a situation, the institution is required to meet the same constitutional standards as public institutions, for example, in providing due process for students.

A 1974 federal district court decision gave a succinct statement of what evidence one court used to determine that a private institution had become a public institution. In *Isaacs* v. *Board of Trustees of Temple University* (1974), the court said:

> It is conceded that, prior to the mid-1960's, the university was, both in law and in fact, a private institution whose actions were beyond the scope and reach of the Fourteenth Amendment. With the passage of the Temple University–Commonwealth Act of 1965, however, the university's relationship to the state underwent a significant change. . . . It designated the university as an instrumentality of the state, incorporated it as a state-related institution into the state's system of higher education, changed its name, reorganized its board of trustees, authorized the legislature to set fee and tuition schedules for all full-time students, gave the university access to state funds for capital development, made the university accountable to the state for the public money it received, empowered the university to issue tax-exempt bonds, and subjected the university to annual reporting and auditing requirements. . . .

*Examples abound of insufficient governmental involvement in private institutions to constitute "state action."* Courts generally take the position that more than just funding with public monies must be present in order to constitute "state action." Strong evidence of public control of the conduct of the affairs of the institution must exist also. In finding that funding alone is not enough, courts have commented:

> The fact that the Federal Government contributes funds to the University, by itself, is insufficient to show the exercise of influence on University decision-making or the encouragement of specific policies (*Spark* v. *Catholic University*, 1975).

> Only when the state becomes, to some significant extent, involved in the conduct of the affairs of a private institution can that conduct be classified as state action and thus run afoul of the Fourteenth Amendment (*Ascherman* v. *Presbyterian Hospital of Pacific Medical Center, Inc.,* 1974).

> ... factors were not of the nature, kind, or degree necessary to support "state action" (*Blouin* v. *Loyola University*, 1975).

> Complaint [fails because it] omits any allegation of state support or approval of the [private] University's discriminatory conduct. (*Cohen* v. *Illinois Institute of Technology*, 1975).

The following is a partial list of governmental activities found to be insufficient to constitute "state action":

1. Tax exemption
2. Governmental financing of university buildings
3. Student loans and awards
4. Public services to the community
5. Federal revenue from grants, contracts, and student aid, in varying amounts, such as 25 percent or 12.5 percent
6. FCC license to operate a radio station and TV station
7. State's ex-officio membership on the board of administrators; state property transferred to board.

The question often is asked whether a meaningful legal difference still exists between private and public educational institutions, especially in view of the extensive public funding of many private schools and programs. The answer to that question appears to be "yes"—rather emphatically, in fact.

The courts continue to be cautious and quite selective when testing for sufficient state involvement in the regulation or funding of private institutions to find whether private conduct constitutes "state action." In most instances, in fact, courts find insufficient state involvement in the actions or funding of the institution for purposes of the institution's having to meet constitutional standards.

*Other differences between private and public institutions involve method of establishment, nature of charter, taxability, and exercise of eminent domain.* These differences involve the following considerations: (1) The charter of a public institution may be altered by the state, whereas the charter of a private institution is a contract protected by Article 1, Section 10, of the U.S. Constitution. Such a charter cannot be amended, altered, or repealed unless the state has specifically reserved to itself the right to so act. (2) Public institutions are not subject to taxation, but private institutions are, unless they have been specifically exempted. (3) Eminent domain may be exercised by public institutions but not by private institutions. (4) Whether institutions are public or private radically affects the functions, duties, and rights of educators.

In summary, basic distinctions between the two types of institutions emanate from how each was established, how it is controlled, and how it is funded. It is essential that educators be informed about the differences between public and private institutions in order that they fully understand the difference in their own legal responsibilities and rights.

*Private colleges in New York are now officially designated as independent.* In 1977, the New York State Education Law was amended to change the designation of "private institutions of higher education to "independent" institutions of higher education. New York may be the first state to take such action.

The term "independent" is thought to be a more useful one since it may subsume all institutions which, though private and church-related, are in fact independent and eligible to receive public financial aid. In the past, the term "private" included both independent church-related institutions and those religiously dominated sectarian institutions that were not eligible for public financial aid. Public aid to church-related institutions is considered in Chapter 7.

## LEGAL STRUCTURE OF EDUCATIONAL SYSTEMS

### Legal Structure of Educational Systems Determines Who Has Control of Funds

How does a particular educational institution fit into the general legal structure of the state, county, or other political subdivision? Elementary and secondary schools usually operate under the jurisdiction of school districts that have been set up by the state legislature. It is important, therefore, that educators in elementary and secondary schools understand where the legal power resides with regard to the operation and financing of their school. Institutions of higher education, too, are established and funded by operation of law. It is important to know whether an institution is a public institution or a private institution, and to know whether it is incorporated. Without such basic information, educators may find it difficult to determine their functions, duties, and rights.

### Elementary and Secondary Schools: Express and Implied Powers

School districts normally are set up by state statutes. Over the years the language in such statutes usually has been refined to set forth clearly what the express powers of a school district are. Additionally, courts routinely have held that school districts have implied powers to carry out the duties and functions set forth in the statute and implied from the express powers (*Lindsay* v. *White*, 1947).

Elementary and secondary schools do not have as many problems interpreting the power to control as do higher education institutions. School districts having mechanisms for community participation, however, often do have such problems because it is very difficult to formulate a successful way to share power with a community group.

### State Universities

State universities are usually public corporations established by either a constitutional or legislative act. About half the states refer to higher education in their constitutions. When a state university is formed under constitutional authority, the constitutional provisions may give the state university a governmental status equal to that of the legislature. This situation exists in nine states where the state constitution gives the state university autonomous status. As a constitutionally autonomous entity, the university is not directly responsible to either the legislative or executive branches of state government, but it is equal to them.

However, most states set up their universities as corporations that are accountable to and subject to control and direction by the legislature of the state. The state may require the university to report directly to it, or there may be a state agency through which the university reports indirectly to the legislature.

At issue is who controls the supervision and funding of the university— the board of trustees of the university or the state legislature? In constitutionally autonomous state universities, the board of regents or trustees has the full authority over general supervision and direction and control of all expenditures from university funds. However, where public universities have been set up by the legislature to report directly to the legislature or a state agency, as in most states, the university's board of trustees or regents is ultimately accountable to the legislature for such decisions.

Obviously, to function effectively within the organization, an educator needs to know the type of state university for which he or she is working. Such knowledge is particularly essential when the university must report to a state agency which then reports to the legislature. In those cases, university boards of trustees are often in conflict with state auditors or other state agencies regarding how the university should operate, both on a day-to-day basis and in the long run.

*Control of constitutionally independent state universities compared to those dependent upon legislatures: express and implied powers.* The principle difference between state universities which are constitutionally independent of the legislature and those which were created by and are dependent upon the legislature is the degree of freedom the board of trustees has to operate the university without intervention by the legislature. In the case of a constitutionally independent state university, the board of trustees or regents has complete freedom, in the absence of fraud, to supervise, direct, and expend university funds without intervention by the legislature.

Michigan has a constitutionally autonomous state university. The Michigan Constitution provides that "the board of regents shall have the general supervision of the university, and the direction and control of all expenditures from the university funds." Challenges to the independence of the Michigan board of regents have been raised over the years by the legislature or by private citizens. A specific instance was a dispute regarding the establishment of a department of homeopathy at the university. The culmination of the legal attack was the case of *Sterling* v. *Regents of the University of Michigan* (1896). In that case, the court confirmed the independence of the university from the legislature in these terms:

> The board of regents and the legislature derive their power from the same supreme authority, namely the constitution. . . . They are separate and distinct constitutional bodies, with the power of the regents defined. By no rule of construction can it be held that either can encroach upon or exercise the powers conferred upon the other.

However, most state universities are not constitutionally independent of the legislature. They have been created by the legislature to be directly subordinate to it or indirectly subordinate through a state agency such as a state department of administration, finance, or personnel. The more common relationship between a state university and a state legislature is one in which the legislature controls the university. Numerous controversies have arisen regarding interpretation of the legislature's powers versus the powers of the university's board of trustees. University officials often accuse legislatures or state agencies of acting beyond the powers delegated to them in university matters. Likewise, legislatures and state officials complain that university trustees and officials act beyond the express or implied powers given to them.

The degree of conflict between universities and legislatures is not great with regard to a university's exercise of express powers to act, because such express powers usually are quite specifically spelled out. However, with respect to the implied powers given to universities, there has been ongoing and continuous disagreement.

State legislatures have taken both flexible and inflexible attitudes toward implied powers. For example, a challenge was made to the power of the Board of Trustees of the University of Arkansas to accept a site for a hospital from the state hospital board and to construct a building there (*Lindsay* v. *White*, 1947). The court found that in the normal legal interpretation of the powers of trustees, "In addition to the powers conferred in specific words by the terms of the trust, the trustee has such powers as are necessary or appropriate to carry out the purposes of the trust" (Restatement of Trust Sec. 186). In other words, the court struck a balance between the university officials' power to carry out their basic duties and the legislature's power to have ultimate control of the direction and operation of the university. For a court to hold otherwise would in effect substitute the legislature's judgment for that of the university officials on a day-to-day basis, which clearly is an unwieldy and impractical situation. Conflict is virtually built in to those situations where legislatures appropriate funds on a line item basis. There is recurrent dispute in such arrangements about whether the legislature is substituting its own judgment for university officials' judgment.

Among the most important powers delegated to universities by legislatures or state constitutions is the power to raise funds, either through the issuing of revenue bonds or the pledging of funds by private citizens. Courts generally have upheld the borrowing of money for education-related purposes such as the issuance of securities to construct dormitories or parking lots or to maintain and operate an educational television station (*State ex Rel. Curators of the University of Missouri* v. *Neill*, 1966; *Turkovich* v. *Board of Trustees of the University of Illinois*, 1957). Funding is discussed further in Chapter 7.

## RECOMMENDATIONS

### New Legal Concepts

The increase in litigation involving educators and their institutions has reached the point where serious efforts must be made to stem the flow. Too much time and money are being lost defending suits. Preventive measures must be taken. These include attempting to stay current regarding new laws, regulations, and court decisions. Institutional policies and procedures require regular and knowledgeable review in order to assure compliance with legal requirements.

Each educational institution will find it helpful to develop some sort of procedure to provide it with current information concerning new laws, regulations, and relevant court decisions. Obviously, subscriptions to various educational news services and publications are one means of accomplishing this. Membership in professional associations that provide updating services are important, as well. Educators are to be encouraged in their individual attempts to be well informed regarding legal matters. For example, two of the most litigious areas of education law at the present time involve equal opportunity in education and employment, and maintenance of safe and healthful working conditions at the place of employment. There have been numerous suits alleging discrimination in recruiting, admission, and treatment of students, as well as in recruiting, hiring, promotion, and termination of staff. In all probability, most such suits could have been avoided by reasonable compliance with the relevant equal opportunity laws and regulations. Costs in time and money to prevent the possibility of such claims in all likelihood would have been a good deal less than the costs of defending claims and expending monies in payment of court awards of damages, back pay, and similar remedial actions.

Measures of other sorts are needed as well. Institutions should be encouraged, for example, to testify at legislative hearings before a law is voted on. They should take advantage of the comment period offered by the government as regulations are being proposed to implement new laws. Frivolous lawsuits filed against an educator or institution should be fought strongly.

Ideally, the posture of an institution would be to participate in legislative decision making to the fullest extent possible. Laws should be complied with, of course, after they are passed. However, poorly regulated laws require feedback from institutions to governmental agencies. Claims made and suits filed which an institution or educator feel are unjustified should be resisted through legal procedures whenever possible.

### Basic Rights and Responsibilities

Institutions are well advised to develop, with assistance of legal counsel, appropriate written documents such as policies for governing boards and handbooks for students, faculty, and administrators. Mutual understandings with regard to academic and employment relationships between the institution and its various constituencies should be reduced to writing whenever possible. These should eliminate many misunderstandings that ultimately find their way into courts for settlement.

## Legal Distinctions between Public and Private Institutions

Institutions which believe themselves to be private institutions should periodically review that status. If, for instance, it is found that there has been a sharp increase in the amount of public funding at a private institution, it would be wise to consult legal counsel to determine whether the institution may be reaching a point where there may be sufficient evidence for a court to find the institution involved in "state action."

Private institutions need to be reminded that a number of civil rights laws apply to them if they receive federal financial assistance. Appendix A may help private institutions to determine which such federal laws affect them.

## Legal Structure of Educational Systems

It is essential that administrators and other educators become familiar with the power structure and funding structure of their own institutions and systems. Such information may be of strategic importance, and lack of information may cause massive and long-lasting consequences. If, on the other hand, the legal structure and power system are fully understood, information and influence may be applied properly and the goals of the institution moved forward in an expeditious and appropriate fashion.

# 2. Due Process and Personal Liability; Other Legal Liability

This chapter is divided into two sections. The first considers important recent changes in the risk of personal liability for educators who violate constitutional rights of students or colleagues. The second takes up more common forms of liability, such as breach of contract, negligence, and defamation.

## DUE PROCESS AND PERSONAL LIABILITY

Two 1975 Supreme Court decisions have had great impact on education law. The first ruled that where a state extends to students the right to an education, a legitimate entitlement to a public education is created. It must be recognized as a constitutional property interest protected by the due process clause. Some kind of due process must be provided by the public institution if that protected interest is placed in jeopardy, as by suspension or expulsion. The Court said:

> It would be a strange disciplinary system in an educational institution if no communication was sought by the disciplinarian with the student in an effort to inform him of his defalcation and to let him tell his side of the story in order to make sure that an injustice is not done (*Goss* v. *Lopez*, 1975).

The second case ruled that an educator may be liable *personally* for damages "if he *knew or reasonably should have known* that the action he took within his sphere of official responsibility would violate the constitutional rights" of the person affected (emphasis added). In that case the Court also said:

> an act violating a student's constitutional rights can be no more justified by ignorance or disregard of *settled, indisputable* law on the part of one entrusted with supervision of students' daily lives than by the presence of actual malice [emphasis added] (*Wood* v. *Strickland*, 1975).

Similar constitutional property or liberty rights may exist regarding faculty and administrators at public institutions, as will be discussed shortly.

Thus, it has become essential that educators know as much as possible about settled, indisputable law on constitutional rights, and how to provide due process when such rights are at risk.

## What Is Due Process?

"Once it is determined that due process applies, the question remains what process is due" (*Morrissey* v. *Brewer*, 1972). Due process, in simplest terms, is fair play. It is a set of legal procedures used to protect individual rights from governmental actions. However, due process is not one particular set of procedures; it is a flexible concept. "The interpretation and application of the Due Process Clause are intensely practical matters" (*Goss* v. *Lopez*, 1975). "The very nature of due process negates any concept of inflexible procedures universally applicable to every imaginable situation" (*Cafeteria Workers* v. *McElroy*, 1961).

Determining what process is due in a given setting requires a court to take into account the individual's stake in the decision at issue, as well as the state's interest in the particular procedure for making the decision. The student's interest in disciplinary cases, for example, is to avoid unfair or mistaken suspension or exclusion from the educational process, with all of its unfortunate consequences. The institution's interest is that the particular procedures required not be prohibitively costly or interfere with the educational process. A balance needs to be struck between the institution's mission and the person's rights.

Courts have tended to be cautious in suggesting specific due process procedures for use in educational settings. The U.S. Supreme Court said in a case holding unconstitutional, under the First and Fourteenth Amendments, Arkansas statutes forbidding the teaching of evolution in public educational institutions:

> Judicial interposition in the operation of the public school system of the Nation raises problems requiring care and restraint. . . . By and large, public education in our Nation is committed to the control of State and local authorities" (*Epperson* v. *Arkansas*, 1968).

*Two key elements of due process are notice and hearing.* As early as 1863, one finds a decision stating, "Parties whose rights are to be affected are entitled to be heard; and in order that they may enjoy that right they must first be notified" (*Baldwin* v. *Hale*). In 1975, in *Goss* v. *Lopez*, the Supreme Court said: "At the very minimum, therefore, students facing suspension and the consequent interference with a protected property interest must be given *some* kind of notice and afforded *some* kind of hearing."

*Due process for suspensions of ten days or less.* Specifically, with regard to disciplinary suspensions of ten days or less imposed upon public high school students, the Court in *Goss* v. *Lopez* (1975) held that due process would be achieved by the following procedure:

1. The student should be given oral or written notice of the charges, that is, a statement of what the student is accused of doing.
2. If the charges are denied, the student should be given an explanation of the evidence the authorities have and an opportunity to present his or her side of the story for consideration and verification.
3. Notice and hearing should procede suspension except in emergencies involving danger to persons or property or disruption of the academic process, in which case the student may be removed immediately from school and a hearing follow within a reasonable time, such as seventy-two hours.

Hypothetically, due process in a public school suspension could be met by a school official's stopping a student in the hall and telling the student that she has been charged with spiking the punch at the dance in the gym the evening before in violation of school regulations. If the student denies the charges, the school official may say that there is evidence that the student was seen spiking the punch by a parent chaperoning the dance. The student might respond that on the evening before, she was maid of honor at her brother's wedding and she arrived home with her parents at one o'clock in the morning. This story is easily verified and, if it is true, the matter may be closed. Due process has taken place.

Thus, the definition of due process in many cases is very simple, and involves procedures that most educational institutions already have in place. Most *Goss*-type cases arise when students are suspended or otherwise disciplined without notice of the charges or without first being allowed to tell their side of the story. Minimal notice and hearing standards, the Court says, require explaining the charges to the accused persons, that is, stating the reasons for their being suspended or expelled and describing what the evidence is against them. It does not mean the accused persons have to see documented proof, but they must be informed of the kind of evidence there is. Second, the accused persons should have the opportunity to rebut the evidence and tell their side of the story for consideration and verification.

What is being described here is essentially "fair play," not making a final decision before all the facts are known. It is analogous to scholarly investigation of a hypothesis, that is, proposing a hypothesis and then doing research and collecting evidence before coming to any conclusion. It should be a process familiar to all educators.

*Impact of the* Goss *case on involuntary transfer cases at public schools.* A public school district's involuntary transfer of students from one school to another for disciplinary reasons involves significant property and liberty rights that cannot be denied without application of due process procedural safeguards. In a recent Pennsylvania case about the disciplinary involuntary transfer of a public school student, the court found that "disciplinary transfers bear a stigma of punishment . . . [and that] any disruption of a primary or secondary education is a loss of educational benefits and opportunities. Realistically, many if not most students would consider a short suspension a less drastic form of punishment than an involuntary transfer" (*Everett v. Marcase*, 1977).

The *Everett* case is instructive in that the parties to the suit, with assistance from the judge, entered into a consent decree which set forth the following minimum due process standards for a *Goss*-type hearing in situations involving involuntary, disciplinary lateral transfers:

1. Pupils must be given some kind of notice and hearing.
2. Parents may bring to the hearing a representative of their choice who may be an attorney. However, there is no constitutional right to legal counsel which would permit indigent parents to obtain, at public expense, appointed counsel.
3. "The School Board shall have the right to designate the place and personnel to conduct the hearings, provided no principal or other person recommending a lateral transfer, nor anyone under their supervision, shall serve as a hearing officer." The court pointed out that the hearing officer could be a superior of the principal, for example someone from the school superintendent's office.
4. Due process in this situation shall consist of two steps. The first step is the informal hearing before the principal, who has the authority to order a lateral transfer. The second step, should such transfer be ordered, is a formal hearing before an appropriate hearing officer. The court found that due process does not require a third-step hearing or right of appeal.
5. "A transfer prior to final hearing, in the absence of an emergency situation, would appear to violate the due process prescribed in *Goss*-type suspensions." Thus, the court found, a pupil has a right to continue attending a school pending final determination of the transfer.

*Impact of the* Goss *case on disciplinary expulsion cases at public schools.* Severe penalties (that is, penalties more severe than suspension of ten days or less) in student disciplinary cases usually trigger due process of a more complex sort. In addition to notice of charges, an explanation of the evidence, and an opportunity for the student to tell his or her own version of what happened, the following often are considered essential: (1) legal representation, (2) witnesses, (3) confrontation and cross-examination of witnesses for the charging party, (4) compulsory production of witnesses, (5) warnings about privileges, or self-incrimination, (6) application of principles of former or double jeopardy, (7) making a record of the proceedings, and (8) review of decision. These requirements come vey close to the elements of federal criminal due process jurisprudence.

The object, then, is to try to reach a balance between the right of the accused to due process and the right of the institution to maintain reasonable levels of personnel and financial costs in providing appropriate due process.

*Selecting impartial decision makers.* It is well established that a biased decision maker is constitutionally unacceptable, and that our system of law has always endeavored to prevent even the possibility of unfairness (*Goldberg* v. *Kelly*, 1970).

What evidence do courts use to determine whether one would be biased as a decision maker? A recent case, *Hortonville Joint School District No. 1* v. *Hortonville Education Association* (June 1976), is instructive. In general, the courts have said that the person who brings the charges should not be the decision maker. But one would not be disqualified merely for being familiar with the facts, nor even if one had taken a public stand on a policy issue related to the dispute. The courts would disqualify as an impartial decision maker one who has a financial or personal stake in the outcome or personal hostility toward those being judged. The Supreme Court has noted also that allowing a decision maker to review and evaluate his or her own recommendation or decisions raises problems about objectivity.

However, evidence about possible impartiality is sometimes tangled with other offsetting legal concepts, as in the Hortonville, Wisconsin, case. There the school board and the teachers held negotiations but failed to reach agreement on a union contract. The teachers, contrary to Wisconsin law, went on strike. The school board then, acting according to state law, gave notice to the teachers, held a disciplinary hearing, and terminated the striking teachers' employment. The teachers sued, claiming among other things that the school board, having served as negotiators, was not sufficiently impartial to discipline them, thus depriving them of due process.

The U.S. Supreme Court in the *Hortonville* decision held that "the school board members did not have such a personal or official stake in the decision to dismiss the teachers as would disqualify them, on due process grounds, from making that determination; that mere familiarity with the facts of the case gained by the school board in the performance of its statutory role as negotiator did not disqualify it as the decisionmaker in the instant case; and that due process did not guarantee teachers that decision to terminate their employment would be made or reviewed by a body other than the school board."

Thus the Court found that the record contained no evidence to support the teachers' contention that the board members had a personal or official stake in the dismissal decision sufficient to disqualify them. The school board was found to be qualified to serve as the impartial decision maker to terminate striking teachers even though the school board earlier had been the negotiating party with whom the teachers failed to reach agreement, and it was that failure that resulted in the illegal strike. The Court found no conflict between the school board's two statutory duties—namely, to participate in collective bargaining negotiations and to make policy decisions such as this one as part of its responsibility for governing the school district. The Court commented that the legislature had placed the balance of power between the board and the teachers where it was; should voters not agree with the present arrangement, they could so indicate by their votes at the next election of legislators and school board members.

### When Is Due Process Required?

*Procedural due process is required when certain actions are taken by persons deemed to be government officials.* Constitutional rights exist for persons enrolled or employed at public institutions. The First Amendment to the U.S. Constitution, for instance, protects the right of students, faculty, and administrators to exercise free speech and expression. An early First Amendment case involved the disciplining, without due process, of high school students who exercised their right to oppose the Vietnam war by wearing black armbands to school. This was the case of *Tinker* v. *Des Moines Independent Community School District* (1969). The Supreme Court upheld the students' rights to this mode of free speech. More will be said about this case in Chapter 4.

The First Amendment also protects a public institution's faculty and administrators who choose to express their opinions on various matters, for example on school bond issues. The case of *Pickering* v. *Board of Education* (1968), in which the Supreme Court held in favor of such a faculty member, is considered in Chapter 6.

In both of these cases, persons' substantive constitutional rights were threatened by "state action." Therefore, procedural due process, in the form of notice and hearing, was held to be essential before penalties could be assessed.

The Fifth and Fourteenth Amendments to the U.S. Constitution guarantee that no person shall be deprived by government action of life, liberty, or property without due process of law.

State actions are defined as those taken by officials of federal, state, or local governments. This category may include trustees, board members, superintendents, principals, administrators, and faculty and other staff at public educational institutions when such persons are acting within the scope of their official duties. As previously noted, some private schools may qualify as being involved in state action depending on the amount of public regulation or funding involved.

*Public institutions: students' liberty and property rights.* The due process clause of the Fourteenth Amendment forbids arbitrary deprivations by state officials of a student's constitutional liberty right, that is, the student's right to his or her good reputation, name, honor, and integrity. In the 1975 *Goss* case, an Ohio statute gave public school principals authority to suspend public school students for misconduct for up to ten days without a hearing of any kind. The U.S. Supreme Court held that such a statute is unconstitutional. The Court ordered that the affected students' records be expunged of the misconduct charges which, if left recorded, could seriously damage the students' reputations as well as interfere with their later educational and employment opportunities.

Public school students' property rights to a public education also were discussed in the *Goss* case. The Court held that "having chosen to extend the right to an education to [such students], Ohio may not withdraw that right on grounds of misconduct, absent fundamentally fair procedures to determine whether the misconduct has occurred, and must recognize a student's legitimate entitlement to a public education as a property interest that is protected by the Due Process clause. . . ."

Procedural due process was another principal concern in *Goss*. Having found that public school students' substantive constitutional liberty and property rights could not be abrogated without due process, the Court then described what kinds of procedural due process must be offered to a student in situations of either mild or severe sanctions, such as suspension and expulsion.

*Public institutions: faculty and administrators' liberty and property rights.* Faculty and administrators, similarly, are not to be deprived by the government of liberty (reputation) or property (employment) without due process of law.

An individual's reputation and good name are "liberty" in the view of the courts. Generally, there is protection against government officials making arbitrary or capricious remarks which would "seriously damage" one's reputation and standing (*Board of Regents* v. *Roth*, 1972). More will be said about the definition of "serious damage" as it relates to faculty and administrators in Chapter 6. At this point it suffices to say that "the *Roth* Court held that a nontenured teacher who simply is not rehired by a public university could not claim to suffer sufficient reputational injury to require constitutional protections" (*Goss*, 1975). However, if the state makes a charge against the teacher which may seriously damage his or her standing and association in the comunity and may foreclose his or her freedom to take advantage of other employment opportunities, then "serious damage" is involved and due process is required (*Roth*, 1972).

The courts view a contract of employment at a public institution as a property right. A tenured faculty member, of course, has a property right in the contract of continuing employment which cannot be placed in jeopardy without due process. A nontenured faculty member has a property right in the currently existing term contract during its life.

What of the nontenured faculty member who alleges that he or she has been promised reemployment at the conclusion of the term? In *Perry* v. *Sindermann* (1972) the Court found evidence that the policies and practices of the college supported the allegation of an implied expectation of continued employment. The Court's decision, then, was that a person is entitled to due process when there exists a promise of reemployment, either express or implied. The matter of nontenured faculty contracts is discussed further in Chapter 4.

Administrators often are employed without a contract and are subject to the pleasure of the person or body that hired them. If, however, an administrator at a public institution does have a contract of employment, the same principles apply as in the case of faculty contracts. In *Hostrop* v. *Board of Junior College District* (1972), a college president was dismissed without a hearing during the term of his employment contract. The court found that his property interest in his employment contract entitled him to Fourteenth Amendment due process rights. Because these due process rights had been violated, he was entitled to recover damages against the board that dismissed him.

*Due process obligations of public and private institutions depend upon whether educators at a particular institution are defined as government officials.* Due process is fair play by government officials. At public educational institutions, where administrators and sometimes faculty members act as government officials, due process is mandatory when constitutional rights are at stake.

At private institutions, by contrast, due process in such matters is voluntary. Private institutions are required, however, to abide by contractual agreements and by statutes which may provide for due process. Private institutions also may wish to implement due process simply because they view it as essential in any institution training persons to live within our form of government. Also, as noted earlier, some private institutions have been judged by courts to be sufficiently controlled and funded by government that their actions are deemed "state actions."

## What Legal Remedies Are Available for Denial of Due Process?

The Civil Rights Act of 1871, 42 U.S.C. Sec. 1983, forms the basis for many lawsuits in which individuals seek redress from state officials for violation of constitutional rights as well as for violation of various statutory rights. It reads:

Every person who, under color of any statute, ordinance, regulation, custom, or usage, of any State or Territory, subjects, or causes to be subjected, any citizen of the United States or other persons within the jurisdiction thereof to the deprivation of any rights, privileges or immunities secured by the Constitution and laws, shall be liable to the person injured in an action of law, suit in equity, or other proper proceedings for redress.

The definition of "persons" under this statute includes state officers, agents, and representatives. In educational institutions, the term "person" may cover people such as trustees, school board members, presidents, superintendents, principals, and other administrators, as well as faculty members. Notably, the educational institution or similar governmental entity itself is not deemed to be a "person" under this act.

Individuals may seek redress at law or in equity. Thus, actual, compensatory, and punitive money damages may be sought for unfair disciplinary practices or for unjustly lost employment. Individuals also may seek declaratory relief adjudging a statute to be unconstitutional. Injunctive relief may be sought to expunge student or faculty records of damaging information.

Impressive examples of remedies sought under Section 1983 were found in two 1975 Supreme Court decisions mentioned earlier, *Goss* v. *Lopez* and *Wood* v. *Strickland*. *Goss* was a public high school suspension case, and *Wood* was a public high school expulsion case. The legal principles of these cases apply, however, to all levels of public educational institutions.

The *Goss* case was a class action suit brought by nine suspended high school students against various administrators of the Columbus, Ohio, public school system seeking nonmonetary relief: (1) a declaration that the Ohio statute permitting suspensions without a hearing was unconstitutional, and (2) an order enjoining the officials to remove the references to the suspension from the students' records. The Supreme Court found the statute and implementing regulations to be unconstitutional. The requested injunction was duly granted, and administrators were ordered to remove all references to such suspensions from the students' records. No money damages were sought.

In the *Wood* case, two expelled high school students filed suit against individual members of the school board, two school administrators, and the Special School District of Mena, Arkansas. The suit sought, in addition to declaratory relief and an injunction, compensatory and punitive money damages. Specifically, the relief sought by the students in *Wood* was: (1) compensatory and punitive money damages against all named school officials, including damages sought against individual officials personally, (2) injunctive relief allowing the students to resume attendance, (3) an injunction against the school officials from imposing any sanctions as a result of the expulsion, (4) an order restraining enforcement of the challenged regulation, (5) declaratory relief as to the constitutional invalidity of the regulation, and (6) expunction of any record of their expulsion.

The U.S. Supreme Court sent the case back to the court of appeals for further hearing to determine whether the students were denied procedural due process. By that time, the students, who were tenth-graders at the time they filed suit, had graduated from high school with their class. The court of appeals found that the students had been denied procedural due process and ordered their records cleared of the charges. The court of appeals then remanded back to the district court the evidenciary question of whether the school officials had acted in good faith in order to determine the issue of personal liability (*Strickland* v. *Inlow*, 1975).

The *Wood* case has had an important effect upon later cases alleging personal liability of educators.

### Personal Liability for Violating Constitutional Rights

*Personal liability of public administrators and educators is affected by the new definition of good faith immunity set forth in* Wood v. Strickland. Under the doctrine of sovereign immunity, state officials acting within the scope of their authority had been clothed in absolute protection against lawsuits as a matter of public policy. Statutes and court decisions have gradually modified that absolute immunity to a qualified immunity in many instances.

In 1974 in *Scheuer* v. *Rhodes*, for example, a lawsuit for damages was brought by parents and students at Kent State University against the president of the university, the state governor, and state national guardsmen. The Supreme Court held that instead of absolute immunity for these officials, there was qualified immunity. The Court said, "It is the existence of reason-

able grounds for the belief formed at the time and in light of all the circumstances, coupled with good faith belief, that affords a basis for qualified
immunity of executive officers for acts performed in the course of official
conduct." The Court returned the case to the district court to hear evidence
to determine whether the state officials had acted reasonably, within their
discretionary powers, and in good faith. Only if the evidence so determined
would the qualified immunity protect the officials. The district court heard
the case in 1975, and the jury found that the evidence did so determine. The
officials were exonerated from liability. However, a rehearing of this case
has recently been ordered to allow presentation of additional evidence.

Similarly, in 1975 in *Wood* v. *Strickland*, the Supreme Court found that
school board members had not an absolute but a qualified good faith immunity from damages under the 1871 Civil Rights Act.

In the past, administrators and faculty relied upon the absolute
sovereign immunity of the state as a defense against personal liability in lawsuits such as those alleging unfair school discipline. Under the old test, absolute immunity protected an official from liability if the actions were taken in
good faith and nonmaliciously to fulfill official duties. Now, however, the
new test includes in the concept of good faith the additional duty on the
part of the official to know the "unquestioned constitutional rights" of
students, teachers, or administrators.

The Supreme Court in *Wood* came to deal with the definition of good
faith immunity because the district court and the court of appeals, in earlier
hearings of the case, had disagreed on its definition. The district court had
instructed the jury that a decision for the students had to be premised upon a
finding that the officials acted with malice in expelling them. The district
court defined "malice" as meaning "ill will against a person—a wrongful act
done intentionally without just cause or excuse." The court of appeals disagreed. It held that specific intent to harm wrongfully was not a requirement
for the recovery of damages, and that "it need only be established that the
defendants [officials] did not, in the light of all the circumstances, act in
good faith. The test is an objective, rather than a subjective one."

*Wood* continued to recognize the common-law tradition and public
policy which accorded public officials a qualified good faith immunity from
liability for damages under Section 1983, assuming, of course, that no malice
is involved. However, the Supreme Court was dissatisfied with the prevailing
definition of good faith.

*New test of qualified good faith immunity.* How then did the Supreme Court
in *Wood* define good faith immunity? The Court found that the appropriate
qualified immunity standard necessarily contained elements of both a "subjective" and an "objective" test of good faith. The Court stated that "the

official must himself be acting sincerely and with the belief that he is doing right" (the subjective test of good faith), "but an act violating a student's constitutional rights can be no more justified by ignorance or disregard of settled, indisputable law on the part of one entrusted with supervision of students' daily lives than by the presence of actual malice" (the objective test of good faith). The actual language of the Supreme Court's holding in *Wood* is:

> Therefore, in the specific context of school discipline, we hold that a school board member is not immune from liability for damages under Sec. 1983 if he *knew or reasonably should have known* that the action he took within his sphere of official responsibility would violate the constitutional rights of the student affected, or if he took the action with the malicious intention to cause a deprivation of constitutional rights or other injury to the student [emphasis added].

The Court went on to note specifically that "such a standard" of conduct for school board members does not impose "an unfair burden" upon a person voluntarily "assuming a responsible public office requiring a high degree of intelligence and judgment for the proper fulfillment of its duties." Nor does the Court see the standard to be an "unwarranted burden in light of the value which civil rights have in our legal system. Any lesser standard would deny much of the promise of Sec. 1983."

The Court emphasized that it was not saying that school board members are "charged with predicting the future course of constitutional law," a reiteration of its position stated in *Pierson* v. *Ray* (1967). Rather, the Court apparently was saying in *Wood* that educators now are charged with knowing pre-existing "settled, indisputable law."

The *Wood* Court stated further that a "compensatory award will be appropriate only if the school board member has acted with such an impermissible motivation or with such disregard of the student's clearly established constitutional rights that his action cannot reasonably be characterized as being in good faith."

*How much money in damages has been awarded by courts for personal liability?* Courts have been reluctant to find that pre-existing constitutional law is so settled and indisputable that officials are liable personally. In those cases where personal liability has been found, the amounts assessed in damages would be nominal, such as one dollar, unless proof exists of actual injury (*Carey* v. *Piphus*, 1978). Three cases illustrate damages where actual injury was proved.

First, a lower court decision in 1975 indicated how one court computed money damages. In that case, *Endress* v. *Brookdale Community College*, the judge found that Endress was terminated three days before she would have gained tenure. This action, the judge felt, was in retribution for an editorial she had written for the college newspaper in which she accused the chairman of the board of trustees of a "conflict of interest in regard to an award of a contract to purchase teaching equipment from a company headed by the chairman's nephew."

In *Endress* the lower court judge concluded that the college and six trustees "did violate the plaintiff's First Amendment rights" involving free speech and freedom of the press. He went on to point out that "punitive damages are absolutely necessary to impress people in authority that an employee's constitutional rights cannot be infringed." The lower court judge awarded punitive damages of $10,000 each against the college president and six trustees, plus $10,000 compensatory damages, plus $10,000 in lawyers' fees, and $14,121 in compensation for lost salary—a grand total of just over $104,000 in damages and lawyers' fees.

However, in 1976 the lower court's ruling in *Endress* was appealed. The appellate court substantially modified the lower court's decision. It reduced the punitive damages against the president to $2,500, reversed the punitive damages against the six trustees (some of whom were not present at the decision-making meeting and others who merely routinely rubber-stamped the president's recommendation), reduced the compensatory damages to $2,500, and eliminated the award of attorneys' fees. Endress was ordered reinstated with tenure, and she was entitled to back pay estimated at $19,000 per year for two years.

The second case, the 1975 Kent State case known as *Scheuer* v. *Rhodes*, was tried before a jury at the lower court level after an earlier U.S. Supreme Court hearing on a technical issue. The plaintiffs sued the former Kent State University president, the former state governor, the adjutant general of the Ohio National Guard, and individual officers and guardsmen, seeking to hold them personally liable for the deaths of four students and the wounding of nine other students, by depriving them without due process of their constitutional right to life and liberty. Plaintiffs sought about $45 million in actual and punitive damages. The jury trial of the thirteen separate cases lasted fifteen weeks during the summer of 1975 and finally resulted in the jury's finding insufficient evidence to support the allegations. All twenty-nine defendants were exonerated. In September 1977, an appeal for another hearing was granted. The date for that hearing has yet to be set.

In the third case, in June 1977, a U.S. district judge ordered a university president personally to pay $5,000 in punitive damages for "pernicious insensitivity" to a faculty member's First Amendment right to free speech. The untenured faculty member had been quoted in three articles on homosexuality printed in city and student newspapers. The university president decided not to renew his contract in December 1975. The judge said that a teacher cannot be fired for his public statements unless the institution demonstrates that the statements impeded the performance of his duties or disrupted the operations of the institution. The court found no such evidence in this case and ordered the teacher reinstated for the 1976-1977 academic year. Because that year had ended, the university was ordered to pay the teacher $12,454, representing his salary for 1976-1977, plus $10,000 in compensatory damages. The university president was ordered to pay the teacher $5,000 in punitive damages. As of this writing, the university had not decided to appeal (*Aumiller* v. *University of Delaware*, 1977).

### Possible Defenses against Personal Liability

*Defense of following advice of legal counsel.* Can administrators and faculty defend themselves in cases charging violations of constutional rights on the grounds that their counsel had assured them that their actions were legal? Exoneration from liability would be claimed on the basis of the affirmative defense of due diligence.

"No," said an appellate court to such a defense in *Tillman* v. *Wheaton-Haven Recreation Association* (1975). This was a case on remand from the Supreme Court. It involved personal liability of the directors of a public community swimming pool. With advice of counsel they had unlawfully discriminated against black applicants for membership in violation of the 1866 Civil Rights Act.

The court in *Tillman* said due diligence is not a defense in such a case since "due diligence has its genesis in the law of negligence." This cause of action is not based on negligence but is based on an intentional tort. The court also pointed out that to accept "the argument that a corporate official may violate Sections 1981 and 1982 with impunity because he exercised due diligence by relying on advice of counsel about the meaning of the law should severely restrict the application of these statutes."

*Defense afforded by U.S. Supreme Court decisions.* Two 1976 cases have caused reflection on former assumptions about liberty and property rights. The first case, *Paul* v. *Davis* (1976), did not involve educators, but the principle could apply as well to them. The plaintiff, Mr. Paul, was a shopper apprehended by a store security guard who placed him under arrest for alleged shoplifting. Paul pleaded not guilty and the case was filed away with leave to reinstate. No trial took place. Seventeen months later, still without any trial, the sheriff's department published a poster of mug shots of "active shoplifters" that included the plaintiff's picture. It was distributed to approximately 800 merchants. All of this occurred without a trial or the presentation of proof. Shortly after, the charge was dismissed. In the meantime the plaintiff's employer confronted him with the poster, and his job seemed in jeopardy —whereupon the plaintiff sued the sheriff, claiming damage to his reputation that is, to his right to liberty.

When the *Paul* case reached the Supreme Court, the decision was against the plaintiff. The Court found that the distribution of the poster did not deprive him of any "liberty" or "property" rights, largely for the reason that in the Court's view (a new and, it is to be hoped, aberrant view, judging from the strong dissenting opinion), reputation alone, apart from some more tangible interests such as employment, does not implicate any "liberty" or "property" interests sufficient to involve the protection of the due process clause. The Court went on to say that to establish a claim, more must be involved than simply defamation by a state official. Also the Court found no state law on which to found a right. The Court implied that had the plaintiff brought a claim in state court for defamation of character, he probably would have been successful, because "imputing criminal behavior to an individual is generally considered defamatory *per se*, and actionable without proof of special damages."

The dissenting opinion in *Paul* was in sharp disagreement with the notion that the criminal "active shoplifter" label would not affect plaintiff sufficiently. The long dissent concluded by pointing out that "Our precedents clearly mandate that a person's interest in his good name and reputation is cognizable as a 'liberty' interest within the meaning of the Due Process Clause, and the Court has simply failed to distinguish those precedents in any rational manner in holding that no invasion of a 'liberty' interest was effected in the official sitgmatizing of respondent as a criminal without any 'process' whatsoever."

The second case, *Bishop* v. *Wood* (1976), is a very similar case involving an alleged property right in employment. A city policeman was dismissed. Under all of the old definitions, he would have had a property right to continuing employment under the language of the city ordinance. However, the Court found that the city ordinance could be interpreted in two different ways: either to confer or not to confer a right to continuing employment. It emphasized that property interests in employment are not created by the Constitution but must be decided by reference to state law. The Court went on to support the lower courts' interpretation of the ordinance as not conferring continued employment, thereupon finding that there was no property right which required due process. Nor was damage to his reputation found.

An eminent authority on constitutional law, Howard Mann of the Faculty of Law and Jurisprudence of the State University of New York at Buffalo, has commented that these two decisions may be a reaction by the

Supreme Court against bringing issues to the federal level that more properly should have stayed at the state level. The federal courts have pointed out that they cannot provide a forum to remedy every administrative personnel error. Legislation to provide redress in state courts may be forthcoming; indeed, some remedies at lower levels already exist. For example, there are states that presently have administrative procedures acts that provide due process procedures. Therefore, it well may be that these rulings by the Supreme Court are a kind of pressure to force provision for redress at the state level. In a larger sense, however, one is still unaware of what the long range effect of these two recent decisions will be.

*Defense of unavailability of settled criteria by which to measure reasonableness of lack of knowledge of constitutional rights.* In June 1976, a court of appeals said that it was not confident by what criteria to measure the reasonableness of school officials' lack of knowledge of due process requirements. It suggested that in developing such criteria courts were required to take into account three kinds of evidence. First, a court must inquire into the status and responsibility of each individual official: e.g., should trustees be held responsible for the same level of knowledge of constitutional rights as college presidents or commissioners of education? Second, it must determine what was the relative availability of legal counsel to each individual official (*Skehan* v. *Board of Trustees of Bloomsburg State College* [Pa.], 1975). (But also recall *Tillman* v. *Wheaton-Haven Recreation Association* [1975], in which raising the defense of having taken advice of counsel in a similar case was held inapplicable.) Third, it must determine what was the relative certainty of the legal issue of clearly established constitutional rights.

## Unsettled Constitutional Law

A number of cases illustrate the unsettled nature of some areas of law regarding what are clearly established constitutional rights. These decisions generally rely on the determination that the law at the time the officials acted was questionable and not settled or undisputable. This is in keeping with the notion in *Wood* that officials cannot be held liable for "unforeseeable constitutional developments." However, they can be held liable for knowing preexisting law.

These cases of official immunity from damages include *Shirley* v. *Chagrin Falls Board of Education* (1975), in which a teacher was forced to resign in her fifth month of pregnancy. The official's liability for damages was precluded on the basis of qualified immunity due to the unsettled law on constitutional rights in this area. Other similar cases were *Hutchinson* v. *Lake Oswego School District No. 7* (1975), another case involving failure of a board to grant sick leave to a pregnant teacher; *Bertot* v. *School District*

*No. 1, Albany Co., Wyoming* (1975), involving discharge of a teacher in violation of her First Amendment rights and immunity found on the basis of special interrogatories returned by jury at trial finding good faith; and *Jagnandan* v. *Giles* (1976), involving resident alien students who had been required to pay nonresident tuition fees. All these cases revolved around a finding of unsettled law or good faith.

*Athletics and unsettled constitutional law.* Not long ago, a court departed from precedent and found that the opportunity to participate in athletics is a constitutional property right requiring due process. In *Regents of University of Minnesota* v. *National Collegiate Athletics Association* (1976), three basketball players had been accused of infractions of NCAA rules. They were cleared of the charges after university due process hearings. The university refused, then, to suspend the players. The NCAA took the position that the university's due process board had made a faulty finding. The NCAA imposed a general probation on all the university's athletic teams because of the university's refusal to suspend the three players. The court held that the opportunity to participate in intercollegiate basketball is a property right entitled to due process guarantees. The reasons given by the court for this decision were two: first, that such participation may lead in some situations to a very remunerative professional basketball career, and second, that it is an important part of the student athlete's educational experience. The court ordered the NCAA to lift its probation on the teams and the NCAA appealed. The appellate court reversed the lower court and allowed the probation to stand. It also sent the case back to the trial court for further deliberation August 2, 1977. One issue appears to be that if due process is required, who shall supply it and what shall it be. A suggestion has been made that the NCAA establish its own due process board.

*Homosexual organizations and unsettled constitutional law.* First Amendment protection has been sought and found in courts by homosexual student groups. Gay Liberation student groups usually become involved in litigation when they seek to be recognized by an institution as a formal student organization eligible to use the institution's facilities for business and social meetings. A number of institutions have attempted to refuse to recognize such groups with wide-ranging reasons for refusal. "Protecting the campus environment from what the board has determined to be detrimental and anti-social influences" was the reason given by Virginia Commonwealth University in *Gay Alliance of Students* v. *Mathews* (1975). A higher court, however, judged that reason insufficient to overcome the First Amendment right of students to decide for themselves whether to join an organization. The university was ordered to recognize the homosexual organization (*Gay Alliance of Students*

v. *Mathews,* 1976).

In states where homosexual acts are illegal the decisions may be different. One initially successful refusal of formal recognition of a student homosexual group was premised on protecting students from an "association . . . likely to incite, promote and result in acts contrary to and in violation of the sodomy statute of the State of Missouri" (*Gay Lib* v. *University of Missouri,* 1976). The equal protection clause, said the court, was not meant to protect "a group presenting a clear and present danger of violation of the criminal laws of a state by comparing such a group with other groups who do not present that danger." This decision has recently been reversed because there was no evidence of illegal acts.

*Public interest research groups (PIRGs) and unsettled constitutional law.* Student-funded public interest research groups wishing to finance litigation as part of their activities have asserted First Amendment rights for protection. The Maryland Public Interest Research Group (MARYPIRG), an approved student organization at the University of Maryland, wanted to use funds from its student appropriations, received from the Student Government Association, to pay litigation expenses. The Board of Regents objected. PIRG alleged that such objection abridged PIRG's right under the First Amendment to petition the government for redress of grievances. The Board of Regents argued that a state law would be violated if the funds were so used, but the court found no evidence that such a state law existed. The court concluded that PIRG was entitled to an order enjoining the university from prohibiting or restricting the use by PIRG of student activity funds for litigation activities that it conducts to protect its interests as an organization or to enable it to gather information relating to public interest concerns affecting students at the campus (*Maryland Public Interest Research Group* v. *Elkins,* 1976). This ruling was reversed later by an appellate court which found that there was a compelling state interest sufficient to justify an exception to the First Amendment. The appellate court pointed out that MARYPIRG still would be able to litigate but would have to use non-state monies such as gifts and contributions to finance the litigation (*MARYPIRG* v. *Elkins,* 1977).

*Corporal punishment as newly settled constitutional law.* The constitutional status of students' rights regarding corporal punishment is an example of formerly unsettled disputed law which now may be settled. The Supreme Court in *Ingraham* v. *Wright* (1977) held that the Eighth Amendment protection against cruel and unusual punishment protects only those accused of crimes. It found that the Florida statute in question provided adequate protection against unjustified corporal punishment by requiring that there be consultation with the school principal and that the spanking not be degrading or unduly severe. Some states also require that another adult be present. The Court found also that no notice and hearing are required for corporal punishment of students.

Earlier corporal punishment decisions by lower courts had held otherwise. A court saw in *Baker* v. *Owen* (1975) a direct parallel to *Goss*, for "the assertion is that the North Carolina state allows corporal punishment without parental consent or procedures." Adopting the *Goss* Court's type of analysis, the North Carolina court in *Baker* continued, "The initial inquiry must be whether Russell Carl has a liberty or property interest, greater than de minimis, in freedom from corporal punishment...." Finding that the school statute itself gave such expectation, by requiring that "such punishment be reasonable and used for specific purposes only," the court in *Baker* had agreed with plaintiff that there was a need for procedural safeguards. The *Ingraham* decision, discussed above, apparently has overturned the *Baker* decision.

*Conclusions: impact of the* Goss *and* Wood *decisions on personal liability of educators.* At the present time courts appear willing to find that constitutional violations have taken place, but they seem unwilling to find that the pre-existing law was so clear that damages properly could be assessed against school officials personally, as in *Shirley* (1975).

When personal liability is found—a rare occurrence—the amount of damages assessed against an individual school official may be substantial, as in *Endress* (1976); or if no actual injury, nominal, as in *Carey* (1978).

Courts tend to give careful attention and consideration to the evidence in each case regarding the criteria by which to measure the reasonableness of the school official's lack of knowledge of due process requirements, as in *Skehan* (1976).

However, as time passes, more areas of law will be settled to the degree that evidence will support a finding of undisputed, clearly established rights, as in *Goss* and *Wood.* Education officials, then, may find more difficulty in proving the reasonableness of their lack of knowledge. They may become more vulnerable to findings of personal liability and to awards of more than nominal damages.

## Settled Constitutional Law

Are there some well settled areas of constitutional law that are so clearly established by pre-existing law that educators surely would know them and therefore should be held personally liable for their deprivation? Criteria to be used for determining such settled law might be (1) status and reputation of the court that made the decision, such as the U.S. Supreme Court; (2) source of the right, such as the U.S. Constitution or federal or state statute; (3) number of years the decision has been relied upon; and (4) fundamental commonality of the right, such as right of free speech.

Could it be agreed that most public school educators would recognize the following as violating clearly established constitutional rights?

- A rule against students wearing symbols, such as black arm bands, in nondisruptive fashion (First Amendment; *Tinker* v. *Des Moines Community School District*, 1969).
- A rule precluding a student newspaper's printing any editorial criticism of the governor or state legislature (First Amendment; *Dickey* v. *Alabama State Board of Education*, 1967).
- A rule requiring daily Bible readings (First Amendment; *Abington Township School District* v. *Schempp*, 1963).
- A rule permitting the school to distribute free Gideon Bibles (First Amendment; *Tudor* v. *Board of Education*, 1953).
- A rule requiring saluting of the flag by students whose religious convictions would be violated thereby (First Amendment; *West Virginia State Board of Education* v. *Barnette*, 1943).
- A rule permitting disciplinary suspensions or expulsions without due process (Fourteenth Amendment; *Goss* v. *Lopez*, 1975).
- A rule permitting segregation by race (Fourteenth Amendment; *Brown* v. *Board of Education of Topeka*, 1954).
- A rule permitting termination of employment without due process of administrators or faculty during the life of a term or tenure contract (Fourteenth Amendment; *Hostrop* v. *Board of Junior College District No. 515*, 1972; *Perry* v. *Sindermann*, 1972).

## Recommendations

The goal is twofold: first, an institution needs to identify as precisely as possible those specific situations where due process is required by law. Then, appropriate due process procedures for giving notice of charges and holding hearings should be put in place. Legal counsel is essential.

Due process is more likely to be required at public institutions than at private ones. Private institutions may be free from much responsibility for due process as a matter of law. However, in order to fulfill their educational purposes, they may decide that some form of due process is desirable as an example to students. Various permutations of due process may be considered, such as use of an ombudsman, fact-finder, mediator, or arbitrator.

To reiterate:

Have your attorney review and point out rules at your institution that may conflict with the constitutional rights, protected by due process, of students, faculty, administrators, and others.

Ask your attorney to recommend due process procedures for giving notice and providing hearings.

Make sure that all rules, regulations, sanctions, and due process procedures are known to persons who will be affected by them and by persons who will be enforcing them.

Follow the rules!

If unexpected situations arise, try to consult with your attorney before you act or react.

Try to anticipate problems as much as possible. Ideally, next year's problems should have been discussed with your attorney *last* year.

## OTHER LEGAL LIABILITY

This section discusses traditional, better-known kinds of liability to which educators are exposed; educators may be liable for violations of civil law (e.g., breach of contract) or of criminal law (e.g., embezzlement). Legal remedies range from money damages and correcting student or personnel files to fines and imprisonment. A brief look at the more traditional legal liabilities follows in this chapter. Additional legal liabilities are discussed at appropriate points in subsequent chapters.

### Breach of Contract

An educator who signs a contract in his or her official capacity usually is not held liable personally for a breach of that contract. Therefore, it is imperative that administrators and faculty members take care that all contracts they sign clearly indicate that such signature is that of an official of the institution rather than of the individual. The institution, then, is the liable party. Governing board members, such as school board members or members of boards of trustees, also would be protected against personal liability if they took similar precautions.

If an unauthorized person, such as a student, signs a contract on behalf of the institution, that individual is liable personally. The institution, administrators, governing body, or faculty would become liable only if, after having actual knowledge of the signing of the contract, they acquiesced in it and ratified it by accepting its benefits. For instance, if an unauthorized student signed a contract on behalf of the institution for the purchase of a new typewriter, and upon delivery the institution kept and used the typewriter, the institution then would be liable for the price of the typewriter.

At both public and private institutions, the relationship between the institution and its students may be based on the legal theory of contract of enrollment. Students may claim their contracts of enrollment were breached by failure to provide competent teaching or by failure to graduate them or grant a degree upon satisfactory completion of required courses. Similarly, the relationship between the institution and its employees may be based on the legal theory of contract of employment. Employees whose contracts of employment are breached, perhaps by suspension or termination without timely notice or by termination of a tenured contract without just cause, may bring suit on the basis of breach of their contract of employment. Legal remedies possible in these instances include payment of money damages, expunction of records, and provision of letters of recommendation. The liability generally would be the institution's. However, individual officials may be liable personally if malice is proved. Officials may avoid such suits by assuring that procedures for handling student and employee complaints are appropriate and adequate and that they are followed. Officials who disagree with a proposed action should make certain that their position is clearly on record. Enrollment and employment are discussed further in later chapters.

## Negligence

Negligence may be the basis for lawsuits that allege injury to an individual's person, property, or reputation due to the negligent act of educational officials. Basic tort law regarding negligent acts provides that reasonable care must be taken to avoid acts or omissions that reasonably may be fairly expected as likely to injure someone. An educator's actions should be those of a reasonable, prudent person under the prevailing circumstances. The duty is that of due care. No intent to injure is necessary if there is a direct proximate causal relationship between the act or omission and the injury.

What constitutes reasonable, prudent care varies greatly depending upon the circumstances. For example, the extent of the duty and degree of care required to protect students are quite different at the elementary school level, the high school level, and the higher educational institution level. Elementary school children must be supervised closely; high school students require less supervision; and college students require the least supervision. Even in the case of college students, however, a high degree of supervision would be required in extremely hazardous situations. For example, close supervision is required over the confinement of dangerous substances such as chemicals, high energy, viral substances, and microbiotic materials.

A court would determine whether the lack of proper supervision was the proximate cause of the injury. A teacher's not being present in the room when a student is injured by a piece of plaster that suddenly falls from the ceiling without warning probably would not constitute a direct cause and effect between degree of supervision and injury. This kind of unforeseen event does not constitute negligence. If, however, the teacher knew the ceiling had been damaged and was in a dangerous condition, the degree of care and supervision would be quite different. It would be commensurate with the knowledge of the possible danger in that particular setting.

Defenses to allegations of negligence include producing evidence that one had no duty of care, or showing that there was no proof of proximate cause between the lack of due care and the injury. In addition, a defense against negligence may be the contributory negligence of the injured person. Contributory negligence is an act or omission which amounts to lack of ordinary care on the part of the complaining party. This contributory negligence, along with the defendant's negligence, is the proximate cause of the injury. For example, if a teacher warns a high school class not to take seats under a leaking ceiling fixture, but a student sits there anyway and is injured, the negligence of the teacher in not roping off the seat or otherwise removing access to it is overcome by the student's contributory negligence.

Another defense against negligence may be the knowing assumption of the risk. Here none of the fault for injury rests with plaintiff, as in the case of contributory negligence. Plaintiff simply has assumed the consequences of possible injury. The fault may lie with the defendant or a third person, or it may lie with no one. That to which a person assents is regarded in law as no injury. For instance, persons working with dangerous viruses or nuclear radiation may legally assume all risk. Any injury to themselves generally is without legal remedy.

## Defamation

Defamation is the offense of injuring a person's character, fame, or reputation by false and malicious statements. Some states require proof of actual damage; others do not.

## Appropriate Criticism: Qualified Protection

An unfavorable but nonlibelous tenure recommendation prepared by a department head for use by a tenure committee would be protected by a qualified privilege. Such reports ordinarily are based upon factual material pertaining to teaching, research, and service to the community (*Petroni* v. *Board of Regents*, 1977).

## Absolute and Qualified Privilege

A recent case, *Stukuls* v. *State of New York* (1977), involved a state university faculty member who sued the acting president of the institution for libel and slander. The defaming act was the acting president's reading aloud of a letter accusing the faculty member of having attempted to seduce a female student. The letter was read to a faculty committee considering the teacher's qualifications for tenure. The truth of the assertions in the anonymous letter had never been verified, though the letter had arrived months earlier. The teacher had never actually seen the letter or heard it read or been afforded the opportunity to do so. The statements in the letter, if not true, were libelous. The teacher alleged that the acting president maliciously had taken the letter from the president's private file, had read the letter to the tenure committee knowing it had been discredited earlier, and had removed favorable student comment from the teacher's file before submitting it to the tenure committee. The teacher claimed these actions resulted in his being denied tenure. The acting president claimed that as the institution's chief executive, he was protected in taking such actions by an absolute, rather than a qualified, privilege. An absolute privilege would cover situations involving malice, but a qualified privilege would not.

The court found that an absolute "privilege exists to protect those who bear the greatest burdens of government or those to whose official functioning it is essential that they be insulated from the harassment and financial hazards that may accompany suits for damages by the victims of even malicious libels or slanders. . . . the immunity is intended for the welfare of the public and not for government employees." Therefore, only officials who are the "principal executives of state or local government or . . . entrusted by law with administrative or executive policymaking responsibilities of considerable dimension" require an absolute license to defame.

Specifically, in the case of the State University of New York, the court found that the decision-making process was vested in its trustees and chancellor. Presidents of constituent units of the state universtiy were found only to implement decisions and policies made by the trustees and chancellor. Therefore, the SUNY trustees and chancellor were found to have absolute immunity; presidents of constituent units of SUNY were not.

The court went on then to consider whether institution presidents have a qualified privilege of immunity from liability. A qualified immunity protects communications made by a public official or other person having a particular duty or interest to another person having a corresponding duty or interest. For example, the chief executive of a private or public institution would have a qualified immunity to impart relevant information to a tenure committee, even though in other circumstances such information would be slanderous or libelous. There would be no qualified privilege to pass along the information to other colleagues, who have no corresponding institutional duty or interest. A qualified privilege may be overcome only by a plaintiff who produces evidence to satisfy a jury that the comunications are false and that the defendant was actuated by express malice or actual ill will.

In the case at hand, the court held that the acting president did have such a qualified immunity. However, the court felt also that his behavior had been such that malice or ill will could be involved. The court held that the faculty member should therefore have been given the opportunity to discover the source and contents of the letter; at whose initiative its reading in fact came about; what relationship it bore, if any, to the past circulation of a rumor; what part the revelation of the letter played in the committee's recommendation and in President Jones' ultimate decision to recommend against tenure to the University; the statements which accompanied the reading of the letter, including those which tended to characterize it as fact or rumor; the extent of Dr. Corey's knowledge of its truth or falsity and his efforts, if any, to acquire that information; the practice, if one there was, with regard to the use of such letters in arriving at tenure decisions at the College; the nature of the other documents removed from claimant's file by Dr. Corey and when and why that was done; whether Dr. Stukuls was confronted with the contents of the letter and afforded an opportunity to respond to it; and such other matters as the Court of Claims in its judgment may deem appropriate.

Accordingly, the order of the appellate division was reversed and the case remitted to the court of claims for further consideration.

## Emotional Distress

A California case illustrates the damage done by defamation and intentional infliction of emotional distress on a professor who was terminated without sufficient opportunity to rebut malicious press releases issued by a dean of a state college. The situation was unusual in that the court held that the state itself was liable for tortuous conduct independent of the dean's liability. The implied jury finding of actual malice destroyed the qualified privilege of the state, prescribed by the civil code (*Toney* v. *State of California*, 1976).

## College Officials and Citizens

A college official cannot recover damages from a citizen for derogatory statements made about the official unless they are made with "actual malice" —that is, with knowledge that the statement was false or with reckless disregard of whether it was false or not (*St. Amant* v. *Thompson*, 1968).

## Public Figures and the Press

A qualified privilege protects the press in its comments about public figures unless actual malice or reckless disregard of the truth can be shown. The facts in each case determine whether there was malice. For example, no protection would exist if a publisher had serious doubts about the truth of the publication. However, negligence in reporting is not enough to establish malice or reckless disregard of the truth (*Time, Inc.* v. *Hill*, 1967).

### Breach of Fiduciary Duty

Administrators, faculty, and members of governing boards often are found to be in a fiduciary relationship to the institution. This requires that they exercise "close oversight" of the operation of the institution. Conflicts of interest are to be avoided at all costs. An administrator, faculty member, or governing board member who is in the building or construction business, for example, should consider carefully whether it is appropriate to bid on a contract for construction work at the educational institution with which he or she is connected. The best advice is to avoid even the appearance of a conflict of interest.

### Criminal Liability

Criminal intent combined with a forbidden act usually is required for an individual to be exposed to criminal liability. For example, criminal penalties are possible for violations of the Equal Pay Act, which requires employers to pay females no less than males for equal work. Criminal penalties also may be levied under the Fair Labor Standards Act, which provides for certain minimum wages and maximum hours. These penalties seldom are assessed, because a criminal intent usually is not present when an educational administrator is found violating either of these acts. It is within the realm of possibility, of course, that criminal intent could be proved by evidence that the administrator intended to do financial injury to an employee by not complying with these acts, or to convert the money intended for employees to his or her own use.

Each state has its own criminal code which sets forth what constitutes a crime in that particular state. As mentioned earlier, specific criminal intent is not always necessary. Sometimes it is implied. For example, a state criminal statute may provide for imprisonment for the mere possession of a stated amount of a controlled substance such as a drug. An educator in charge of drugs being used for research in an educational institution may be criminally liable if the inventory of drugs is found to contain more than the law permits. Educators may also be exposed to criminal liability for more ordinary crimes such as embezzlement. Crimes against persons also may be alleged, for example assault and battery or perpetration of an immoral act on a student or colleague.

### Sovereign Immunity

The doctrine of sovereign immunity, that the sovereign can do no wrong and cannot be sued by his or her own courts, is not to be relied upon to protect educators as it has in the past. Many states have legislated it out of existence for most purposes. Other states permit it in instances of ministerial acts (those which must be done by virtue of the office held) but not for discretionary acts (those which may or may not be done at the discretion of the officer). The best advice is to avoid situations of liability when at all possible. In most cases, it is imprudent to place reliance on sovereign immunity for protection.

## Insurance and Risk Management

Insurance is a must for protection against many kinds of risks. Advice should be sought from an experienced insurance broker who is familiar with the entire operation and legal structure of the particular educational enterprise. Regular review of risk management is also essential, in order that as conditions change, protection is modified correspondingly.

It is of utmost importance to point out that over the past several years a number of national educational associations, including the AAUA, have spent a great deal of time attempting to identify insurance coverage for educators who may be sued under 42 U.S.C. Sec. 1983 for alleged violations of constitutional rights. One problem that immediately arises is that such acts, if proved, are found generally to be outside the scope of employment and therefore not covered by an institution's insurance. This kind of liability is discussed in detail earlier in this chapter.

At this writing, there appear to be few insurance companies willing to cover intentional constitutional torts. Self-insurance plans of various kinds have been put in place. For example, the university system of Georgia and the state of South Carolina have generated self-insurance plans to cover risks including constitutional torts.

## Prepaid Group Legal Services Plans

Prepaid group legal services plans have developed as a possible means of handling educators' legal problems. This is true especially in instances where insurance appears not to be available.

Caution is advised in considering group legal services plans. Very few plans have been in existence long enough to have a track record showing what works and what does not. Educators have a number of specialized legal problems—in addition to the more common real estate, traffic court, and family court matters—as this book attempts to illustrate. A helpful clearinghouse of information about group legal services plans is the National Resource Center for Consumers of Legal Services, 1302 18th Street, NW, Washington, D.C. 20036. Bar associations may also have recommendations.

Prepaid group legal services plans may become very worthwhile additions to present plans designed to protect educators. However, many questions remain unanswered at this time. The National Resource Center, for example, has initiated a campaign for some sort of minimal regulation of such plans.

Readers who have information about plans that are working well are urged to share their experiences with the author.

## Recommendations

In general, educators should take care to act reasonably, with careful forethought, and without haste.

Learning to recognize potential legal pitfalls will assist in preventing them. When there is doubt as to a correct response, one would be wise to delay action until legal advice has been sought and suggestions received as to possible alternative courses of action available.

# 3. Recruitment, Admission, and Financial Obligations of Students

This chapter discusses a number of matters concerning student recruitment, admissions, and tuition which may have legal ramifications for educational institutions and for educators personally. Specifically, any of the following may serve as the basis for some form of legal redress:

- Failure to recruit or admit otherwise qualified applicants because of physical or other handicaps, race, sex, color, national origin, or religion
- Failure to disclose fully information about academic programs or costs to prospective students
- Improper use of admissions test for handicapped or minority students
- Improper use of photos of individuals in recruitment publications
- Improper practices with regard to assigning financial aid and scholarship funds, including alleged discrimination based upon sex, handicaps, or race
- Improper designation of students as nonresident for tuition purposes
- Failure to abide by explicit or implicit promises made in catalogs or by recruiters
- Improper procedures for keeping student records

Examples of actual cases will be used here to illustrate the matters at issue, and recommendations for acceptable practices will be made.

## RECRUITMENT PRACTICES

*Students have a right to a public education in most states.* A public education today generally is a right rather than a privilege. This is certainly true when a state extends to students the right to a public education by passing legislation to that effect. The state then must recognize that a student has a legitimate entitlement to that education as a *constitutional property interest* protected by the Fourteenth Amendment's due process clause (*Goss* v. *Lopez*, 1975).

Thus, the attitudes and practices of the past, regarding the recruitment, admission, and financial obligations of students, must respond to the impact of the stronger constitutional legal position of students in public institutions.

The legal relationship of students in private schools to the institution is a contractual one. Here, too, courts appear more willing than ever to make sure that students' rights under such contracts are protected (*Zumbrun* v. *University of Southern California*, 1972).

## Full Disclosure

*Full disclosure of programs and costs should be given to applicants.* Consumerism is found today in the academic marketplace, where some persons view education as an advertised product. Many laws and regulations requiring full disclosure of academic programs are said to be the result of certain recruitment practices of educational institutions. Usually mentioned are the practices of "overselling" educational wares, especially vocationally oriented programs of study, to poorly informed students who are thought of as consumers. Students who view education as a product are typical of consumers in general who react unfavorably to deceptive advertising. The true legal basis of consumerism, in fact, probably rests upon the contractual relationship between the student and the institution. That there is such a contractual relationship at private institutions is clear, as already indicated. A contractual relationship may be found as well at public institutions, in addition to the critical requirement that public institutions safeguard constitutional rights.

A number of instances of an attitude of consumerism may be cited, but one that stands out is the federal Guaranteed Student Loan Program (GSLP)* and its strong regulations for full disclosure. Similar requirements exist regarding loans to students at elementary and secondary schools. The federal government became alarmed by the growing number of defaults in repayment of loans by graduates who could not find jobs for which they had been trained. Many persons apparently were recruited to institutions offering vocationally oriented programs of study by promises of placement possibilities which were based largely upon myth rather than reality. To combat this situation, GSLP regulations were developed to try to provide facts before the student borrower took out a loan and paid his or her tuition.

Specifically, the Guaranteed Student Loan Program requires that insti-

---

*See Appendix A for further information about federal statutes mentioned throughout this book.

tutions offering clinical and vocationally oriented courses of study—notably nursing, medicine, and law—make a good faith effort to provide prospective students, prior to enrollment and payment of tuition, with a complete and accurate statement of the institution's program of study, its costs, and the qualifications of its faculty. In addition, students are to receive information about the current employment pattern of the program's graduates, such as the number who have found jobs in the profession and their average starting salaries. These placement disclosure requirements generally are not applicable to nonvocational training programs in liberal arts institutions.

Penalties for noncompliance with disclosure requirements include loss of eligibility for a number of federal loan and grant programs for both students and institutions.

## Legal Status of Catalog Statements

*Statements and course descriptions in an institution's catalog may be instrumental in creating a contract with a student.* The language in an institution's catalog has been used as the basis for breach of contract lawsuits. Such suits allege that a contract for education exists between a student and an institution, and that some terms of the contract are embodied in that catalog. Other terms of the contract may be contained in other institutional documents, such as policies of the board of trustees or the student handbook. Contracts also are said to result from oral statements or promises, including those which may be made to applicants for admission by recruiters.

Following are typical examples of suits alleging breach of contract for admission and breach of contract for providing incompetent instruction in a particular course. Other examples appear in later chapters.

*Breach of contract for admission.* An applicant for admission to a private medical school alleged a breach of contract, claiming that the school had published its qualifications for admission in its bulletin but had ignored those criteria and admitted some applicants instead on the basis of their familial relationship to trustees, faculty, or alumni. This applicant had submitted his application form with a $15 application fee. His application was rejected. He filed a class action suit seeking, among other things, an injunction against the school prohibiting it from continuing such admissions practices and requiring it to account for all application fees collected. However, he did not ask the court to order the school to admit him.

The aggrieved applicant claimed that the medical school's bulletin amounted to an invitation to applicants to make an offer to be considered for admission based on the criteria for admissions stated in the bulletin. He claimed that the school, by accepting his $15 fee, had accepted his offer and that a contract had been created. But thereafter, the applicant alleged, the medical school used different, unpublished criteria to judge the applicant for admission, and so it had breached the contract. The applicant contended that the school's decision to accept or reject an applicant was based principally on whether an applicant was related to members of the alumni, faculty, or board of trustees, and whether the applicant or his family might make financial contributions to the school. The court in this case said:

> The court agrees with the applicant's position. The applicant and the school entered into an enforceable contract: the school's obligation under the contract was stated in the school's bulletin in a definitive manner and by accepting his application fee, a valuable consideration, the school bound itself to fulfill its promises. The applicant accepted the school's promises in good faith and he was entitled to have his application judged according to the school's stated criteria (*Steinberg* v. *University of Health Sciences, Chicago Medical School,* 1976).

*Breach of contract for incompetent teaching (unsubstantiated).* A student claimed that the University of Bridgeport (Connecticut) had breached its contract with her for an education course. The student alleged that the contract was created when the university accepted her $155 tuition fee. She claimed that the contract was breached because the course content failed to fit the course description, no tests were given, no grading of work was done, and there was little or no classroom discussion or critique. The university offered evidence from other students in the course about the teacher's conduct and the content of the course. The student's complaint centered around the allegation that the university had promised at least minimally competent instruction and had not provided it. In its defense the university was unwilling to concede that a contract existed between it and the student, and it claimed that to supervise an instructor would infringe upon academic freedom.

The student sought damages in the sum of $2,500. The lower court led that her claim was unfounded, and she then appealed to a higher court. Upon appeal, the Common Pleas Court in Bridgeport, Connecticut, directed a verdict for the university. The plaintiff, therefore, was unsuccessful in both attempts to seek redress through the courts for the alleged breach of contract (*Ianniello* v. *University of Bridgeport,* 1977).

## Use of Photos in Recruitment Publications

*Invasion of privacy: Use of photos of individuals for advertising or trade.* A number of states have passed statutes regarding rights of privacy. Such statutes may provide that the use of a person's photo for advertising or trade purposes requires the person's written consent. However, incidental use of photos in news stories usually is not an actionable basis for invasion of privacy.

*Libel: injury to reputation.* Use of a person's photo that causes injury to the person's reputation may be the basis of a cause of action alleging libel.

*Lawsuit illustrates both privacy and libel concepts in use of photos.* A woman's photo appeared on the cover of a homosexual student publication at the University of Rochester (New York), a private institution. As plaintiff, she sought money damages for unauthorized use of her photo. The university asked for a summary judgment in its favor, claiming no responsibility for the acts of its student organization.

On the issue of invasion of privacy, the court held that the student publication's use of the woman's photograph without her consent did not come within the prohibition of a state statute providing a cause of action for the unauthorized use of a person's photograph for advertising or trade.

However, on the matter of liability for the publication of libelous material, the court held that a private university, unlike a public university, may be in a position to use prior restraint against the publication of libelous material in its student publications. The responsibility of a university for taking precautions against libel must accordingly await presentation of all the facts at a trial. The court therefore did not grant a summary judgment in favor of the university, but directed that the trial proceed (*Wallace* v. *Weiss*, 1975).

## Equal Opportunity Recruiting

*Equal opportunity and nondiscrimination in education are to be distinguished from integration in education and from affirmative action in employment.* Equal opportunity and nondiscrimination are passive concepts: an educational institution may simply wait for qualified females, minorities, or handicapped persons to apply for admission and then treat them without discrimination. Integration in education and affirmative action in employment, on the other hand, are active concepts; that is, an institution is required to take certain positive steps regarding its admissions or employment practices. These include recruiting and admitting, or advertising for and hiring, qualified minorities, handicapped persons, and females underrepresented in its student body or work force. More will be said about affirmative action in employment later.

*Equal opportunity to education.* Equal opportunity for persons recruited by and admitted as students to educational programs at all levels, at public and private institutions, is provided for in varying degrees and by varying means, as in the following examples. These and others appear in Appendix A.

The equal protection clause of the Fourteenth Amendment to the Constitution has served as one of the basic cornerstones for equal opportunity in education. It requires equality of treatment by the state in classifying groups of individuals. It forbids discrimination by prohibiting the state from passing legislation that favors particular persons over others in like condition. Reasonable classifications are permissible. Unreasonable classifications sometimes have included those based on race, sex, handicaps, and personal appearance, such as long hair or beards. For instance, laws classifying women as a group not permitted to be trained as lawyers or doctors, to vote, to work overtime, or to serve on juries have been held unconstitutional as violating the equal protection clause.

The Rehabilitation Act of 1973 prohibits discrimination against qualified handicapped persons in any educational program or activity receiving financial assistance from the U.S. Department of Health, Education, and Welfare.

Title VI of the Civil Rights Act of 1964 prohibits discrimination based on race, color, and national origin in any educational program or activity receiving federal financial assistance.

Title IX of the Education Amendments of 1972 prohibits discrimination based on sex in any educational program receiving federal financial assistance.

The Civil Rights Acts of 1866, 42 U.S.C. Sec. 1981, prohibits racial discrimination in making contracts; Sec. 1983 prohibits violations of a person's constitutional and statutory rights by government action without due process. Moreover, there is a possibility of personal liability for state officials who knew or should have known that their actions would deprive persons of clearly established constitutional rights.

Internal Revenue Service (IRS) regulations provide that private schools that are without nondiscriminatory admissions policies cannot qualify as organizations exempt from federal income tax.

These statutes will be discussed in relation to specific practices shortly.

## ADMISSIONS PRACTICES

### Admissions Criteria

*Admissions criteria should be applied equally to all applicants.* The legal concept that a contract between an applicant for admission and the institution may be generated from recruiters' promises or statements in an institution's catalog was discussed above in the 1976 *Steinberg* case. An institution may select almost any lawful admissions criteria it wishes, so long as the criteria are acceptable to the appropriate accrediting organization. Once settled upon, however, those criteria should be made known to all applicants and applied equally to all of them.

*Transfer students from foreign medical schools pose a serious question re-garding government influence on admissions requirements.* It has been tradi-tional in our educational system, as pointed out earlier, for courts to be reluc-tant to intrude into academic decision making. A number of medical schools now believe that the legislative arm of the federal government has reached too far into the arena of academic decision making. Congress recently voted an amendment to the Health Professions Educational Assistance Act of 1976. It requires medical schools that receive federal capitation grant payments to admit a certain number of American medical students enrolled abroad who meet certain minimal criteria. The purpose of the requirement is to facilitate, for a limited period of time, the entry into U.S. medical schools of qualified U.S. students currently enrolled in foreign medical schools. A number of medical school officials object to being forced to waive normal admissions re-quirements for such transfer students. In late summer of 1977, nine medical schools said that they would not comply with the requirements. They refused the federal subsidies they would have received.

There are a number of serious questions involved in this issue. They range from a concern that the shortage of physicians in this country may soon become an oversupply to a concern about the quality of training re-ceived in foreign medical schools. Complicating these issues are the fact that there remains a shortage of physicians in rural and inner city areas and in primary care specialties, and the fact that about half of the staff positions in American hospitals have been filled by foreign nationals trained in medical schools abroad. It is apparent, however, that the most critical issue from the point of view of American medical schools is the question of who—the aca-demic community or a legislative body—has the power to set admissions re-quirements for transfer students. For the present the question remains un-answered.

## Admissions Tests: Proposed Truth in Testing Law

The content and use of tests and test scores as criteria to judge qualifi-cations for admission to elementary, secondary, postsecondary and graduate schools is undergoing careful scrutiny as a result of several recent Supreme Court decisions. The decisions involve tests for employment, not admissions, but some of the principles laid down in these cases may be applied to tests used to determine qualifications for admission to educational institutions.

A critical question raised by these cases, for instance, is whether mere disproportionate adverse *impact* of a test on blacks is a crucial factor, or whether a racially discriminatory *intent* in using the test is required also. Or, putting the question another way, is there a constitutional violation created by the mere use of any tests which may disproportionately exclude blacks from admission, or must there also be an intent to discriminate in order that the use of the test is unconstitutional? The answer appears to depend partly on whether the claimant alleges a violation of Title VII of the Civil Rights Act of 1964, which applies only to employment, or a violation of the equal protection clause of the Constitution, which may apply to diverse situations.

To illustrate, Title VII prohibits employment discrimination based on race, color, religion, sex, or national origin. A black employee challenged a test used to judge suitability for employment. The Supreme Court found that Title VII does permit employment tests; but if the particular tests or measuring procedures used have adverse or disproportionate impact upon blacks, then the tests used must be proved to be valid in predicting successful job performance. That is, any tests used should be validated to show that they measure the person for the job, not just in the abstract. Validation procedures used by companies have generally been closely examined by courts since this decision (*Griggs* v. *Duke Power Co.*, 1971). Tests that rely on correlations with subjective evaluations of supervisors have been questioned. Tests for entering employees, said to evaluate later promotability, have also been challenged.

The Supreme Court held later, however, that the *Griggs* ruling is an interpretation of Title VII only, and is not a requirement of the equal protection clause of the Constitution. The Court then went on to hold that, in cases alleging violation of the equal protection clause, while "disproportionate impact is not irrelevant . . . it is not the sole touchstone of an invidious racial discrimination forbidden by the Constitution" and that "a racially discriminatory *purpose*" is a necessary element of the requisite "invidious quality" of unconstitutional discrimination (emphasis added). The Court found acceptable a written test used by the District of Columbia Police Department even though a greater proportion of blacks failed the test than members of other racial or ethnic groups. No intent to discriminate against blacks was found (*Washington* v. *Davis*, 1976).

Statutes that may be relied on in cases concerning admissions testing conducted in educational institutions include Title VI of the Civil Rights Act of 1964, which prohibits racial or ethnic discrimination in education; Title IX of the Education Amendments of 1972, which prohibits sex discrimination in education; the Civil Rights Act of 1866; 42 U.S.C. Sec. 1981 of the Civil Rights Act of 1871, which prohibits racial discrimination in the making of contracts; and 42 U.S.C. Sec. 1983 of the same act, which prohibits denial of constitutional rights and other statutory rights by government officials without due process, and which may result in personal liability.

*A federal "truth in testing law" has been proposed in Congress.* In May 1977, public concern about the use of standardized admissions and other educational tests culminated in the introduction of the Testing Reform Act of

1977 in the House of Representatives (H.R. 6776). The bill was designed to protect students and consumers without unduly burdening testing organizations and educational organizations. It would affect public and private institutions receiving federal funds. The proposed law would require all reliability and validity studies conducted by test designers to be available to the general public. It would also require testing firms to attach to any test score a prominent warning that the seemingly exact number is only an approximation of the student's performance on the test. It would require an equally prominent indication of the margin of error involved. Before taking the test, persons would be given notice of the skills to be tested and of the scoring procedures. The legal rights of the persons tested would have to be set forth. Thirty days after the test, persons tested would have access to their scores, their test, and the correct answers. The proposal would restrict dissemination of test scores and use of auxiliary codes. Penalties would be developed for improper use of tests, and testing firms would be regulated. The goal of the proposed bill is to encourage more individualized consideration of students regarding admissions as well as academic performance in general. The bill would not apply to tests used for research purposes only. Should a version of this proposed legislation become law, it would have strong impact on standardized testing throughout the academic world.

*Tests used by the federal government are undergoing review.* In June 1977, the U.S. Air Force announced that it was seeking advice on how the literacy tests it uses to select candidates may be reviewed to ensure that the tests are related to actual job performance in the Air Force rather than to reading ability in general (*Commerce Business Daily*, June 3, 1977, p. 30).

*Ability and intelligence tests.* Tests that measure ability, such as IQ tests like the Wechsler, Leiter, and Stanford Binet tests, are used often in elementary and secondary schools for various purposes. In California such tests were used to identify elementary school children for classes for the educable mentally retarded (EMR). Lawyers for black children alleged that the tests were culturally and racially biased and that the six black children they represented were wrongfully placed in EMR classes as a result of such tests. This case began in 1972. At that time evidence convinced the court that IQ testing of minority children should be banned temporarily in all San Francisco schools. In 1975, the ban was extended to the entire State of California. The case finally went to full trial in the fall of 1977. Evidence presented in the course of the trial has led observers to believe that the case will eventually go to the Supreme Court. As of this writing, no decision has been handed down (*Larry P. v. Riles*, 1977).

*Vocational aptitude tests.* High school students sometimes have been given a vocational aptitude test developed by the U.S. Office of Defense. The test is called the Armed Services Vocational Aptitude Battery (ASVAB). Two kinds of complaints have been raised regarding this test. First, the test is primarily a recruiting device for the armed services; yet students and parents often are led to believe that the main purpose of the test is general vocational guidance. Second, the quality of the test has been called into question by professionals in the field of tests and measurement. In particular, the test items have been criticized as poorly drawn, and the subtests are felt to be unreasonably difficult. Validity tests as to nonmilitary careers are said to be inconclusive and sparse. Sex differences, too, have not been taken into account, it is alleged.

Schools administering such tests may wish to review their reasons for using the tests and take a critical look at alternative tests and other methods of measuring aptitude. It is important also that requirements of applicable laws, such as the Privacy Act of 1974, be met. For example, prior to the test it may be necessary to disclose its purposes and how the data collected will be used. Informed consent of the student or parent may be required as well, as required by the 1974 Human Subjects Research regulations, if the data may be used for research.

### Admissions Committee Meetings: Sunshine Laws

Sunshine laws basically provide that public decisions shall be made in meetings open to the public. All states now have some form of open meeting statute. It is inevitable, then, that a prospective student who was rejected for admission to a public institution will claim that the decision not to admit was made in a closed meeting in violation of the state's sunshine law. The applicant may allege that violating the sunshine law voids the rejection. The matter of a claimed violation of a state sunshine law could arise at any public educational institution; it is more likely that such a suit would arise at the higher education level than at the primary or secondary level.

The threshold question would be whether an admissions committee meeting is subject to the requirements of an open meeting law. If it is, and if an applicant who is rejected at a closed meeting files suit, the question arises as to what remedy the rejected applicant would seek. Would the committee be required to review its decision regarding that particular application in an open meeting, or would the institution be ordered to admit the student?

There are few cases referring directly to this point. One informative case arose at a state law school. A group of students sued to force the dean and faculty senate to open their meetings to the public. The critical issue in the court's decision in favor of the students was who had power to make decisions. Evidence showed a specific delegation of power from the board of regents through the university president to the law school dean and the faculty senate regarding the performance of certain important governmental tasks for the university. In particular, the law school dean and faculty senate were delegated the power to control admissions and graduation requirements, curriculum and academic programs, and scholastic standards required of students. The court found that the dean and the faculty senate were indeed exercising governmental power. Therefore they were conducting the "people's business" within the contemplation of the sunshine act. The court ordered that the law dean and the law faculty open their regular faculty meetings to the public. This decision may indicate that in institutions where the faculty delegates its admissions power to an admissions committee, the meetings of that committee may well be subject to sunshine requirements. However, sunshine laws are still largely untried and untested. This particular case is simply an illustration of a future possibility (*Cathcart* v. *Andersen*, 1974).

## Discrimination in Admissions

Generally, discrimination based upon handicaps, race, sex, national origin, or religion in admission to public educational institutions has been declared unconstitutional or in violation of statutory law. There are some exceptions, as will be pointed out. These may include religious institutions, some private institutions, and public institutions below the graduate level which traditionally have been single-sex institutions.

Private schools, too, are required to meet certain nondiscriminatory statutory requirements. For instance, to be eligible for IRS exemption from federal income tax, they must maintain nondiscriminatory admissions policies.

Age discrimination in admissions has been attacked as violating the equal protection clause. Such challenges largely have failed. However, it is unlawful to discriminate because of age in employment, and this will be considered in Chapter 5.

*Racial discrimination in public educational institutions evolved from court decisions condoning "separate but equal" to those finding "separate is inherently unequal."* The first discrimination test cases of importance were based on race. Prior to 1954, the courts generally had responded to attacks on segregation that alleged a violation of Fourteenth Amendment equal protection with variations on the "separate but equal" doctrine set forth by the Supreme Court in *Plessy* v. *Ferguson* (1896). The separate but equal doctrine basically considered segregated schools and colleges to be constitutional if the tangible facilities at the schools and colleges were equal. That is, if buildings, books, teachers, and other similar tangible features of both black and white schools and colleges were substantially equal, the courts found no constitutional violation of equal protection by the laws.

Later, a number of cases successfully attacked segregated colleges at the graduate level. For example, in a case involving a public law school for blacks only, the Supreme Court found inequality in that some specific benefits enjoyed by white students at white law schools were denied to black students with the same educational qualifications (*Sweatt v. Painter*, 1950).

In 1954 the U.S. Supreme Court reversed itself and ruled that "separate educational facilities are inherently unequal" (*Brown v. Board of Education of Topeka*, 1954). It was not until the 1954 *Brown* case that the Supreme Court was asked to rule directly on the question whether segregated educational institutions with equal tangible benefits could ever be truly equal in providing "intangible" benefits. Testimony of psychologists and sociologists in *Brown* was a factor in convincing the Supreme Court that the intangible qualities of a segregated educational setting substantially flawed the education of blacks as well as whites. This consideration led the Court to find that separate educational facilities were inherently unequal.

Once the Supreme Court had found that governmentally established (de jure) segregated public educational institutions were unconstitutional, the stage was set for new major legal issues that then arose over how to implement the order to desegregate.

*Implementing racial desegregation in public educational institutions.* Three questions arose. How quickly must elementary and secondary schools be desegregated? Must higher educational institutions desegregate also? If so, how fast?

The first question that arose after the *Brown* decision in 1954 concerned the speed at which desegregation was to take place. Must desegregation be immediate, or could it be accomplished gradually over a period of time? In 1955, the U.S. Supreme Court decided the second *Brown* case, in which it set forth a time standard of "all deliberate speed" (*Brown v. Board of Education*, 1955).

A second question arose almost immediately whether the order to desegregate applied to higher education as well as to elementary and secondary education. A federal district court ruled that it applied to both. The case involved the University of North Carolina's unsuccessful contention that the *Brown* decision applied only to children but not to adults, and that therefore desegregation at the undergraduate level in institutions of higher education was not required (*Board of Trustees v. Frasier*, 1956).

Having determined that institutions of higher education must be desegregated, the Supreme Court was asked to resolve the question of whether those institutions could desegregate with "all deliberate speed" or were required to desegregate immediately. The Supreme Court held they must desegregate immediately; it ordered the University of Florida Law School immediately to consider Hawkins, a black, for admission under the rules and regulations applicable to other qualified candidates. It is interesting to note that ultimately, in 1958 after another court battle, the school finally did consider Hawkins for admission but found his qualifications lacking. He apparently was never admitted. That same year the University of Florida Law School did admit its first black student (*Florida ex rel. Hawkins* v. *Board of Control of Florida,* 1956).

*Public elementary and secondary schools are to take positive steps to overcome racial segregation.* In 1966 a court found that (de jure) governmentally established, unconstitutional segregation in elementary and secondary schools carried with it a positive duty on the part of the school officials and school districts to devise active integration plans in order to bring their policies and procedures into line with the Constitution (*United States* v. *Jefferson County Board of Education,* 1966). In 1968, the Supreme Court agreed in another case that "school officials have the continuing duty to create a unitary, nonracial system." De facto segregation, that is, segregation resulting from housing patterns, was found not to require active plans to integrate (*Green* v. *County School Board of New Kent County, Virginia,* 1968).

Lack of success in integrating elementary and secondary schools led to many lawsuits. As a result, a number of cities are now under court order to integrate their schools. Sometimes the court appoints a person or group to oversee the development and implementation of such plans. Most such integration plans involve busing of students to a different school, closing down predominantly black schools, or devising systems to attract students and their parents to enroll voluntarily in an integrated school. One method being used to accomplish the last plan is the use of so-called magnet schools. These schools are specially organized and staffed to be of particularly high quality and therefore attractive to students interested in the variety of educational programs offered.

A number of questions about court-ordered busing plans have arisen, for example a case that asked how broad a geographic area must be included in a busing plan. The Supreme Court recently held that the remedies should not be any broader than the specific constitutional violations that were found to have occurred. Thus, only if systemwide discrimination is shown, may there be a systemwide remedy. The amount of busing must be commensurate with the violations shown (*Brinkman* v. *Gilligan,* 1977).

Another question considered intent, that is, how much evidence there must be to show that the segregation was intentional. The Supreme Court said that a clear showing must be made that a school board intended to foster segregation before it can be found to have violated the Constitution (*Brennan* v. *Armstrong,* 1977).

The particular ingredients of one court-ordered integration plan in the Detroit school district were placed before the Supreme Court for review. This plan included the usual reassignment of pupils and four "educational components," consisting of a remedial reading program, in-service training for teachers involved in the program, elimination of discriminatory testing procedures, and counseling and career guidance. The Supreme Court approved the four components. It relied on the "basic rule" laid down in the 1955 *Brown* case that, in fashioning desegregation decrees, courts should follow equitable principles. In this case, the Supreme Court said,

Application of those equitable principles requires federal courts to focus upon three factors . . . [1] the nature and scope of the constitutional violation . . . [2] the decree must be remedial in nature, that is it must be designed as nearly as possible "to restore the victims of discriminatory conduct to the position they would have occupied in the absence of such conduct" . . . [3] the federal courts in devising a remedy must take into account the interest of state and local authorities in managing their own affairs, consistent with the constitution.

The Supreme Court pointed out that in including in the Detroit plan the four educational components mentioned above, the lower court had adopted specific programs proposed by a number of other school authorities, "who must be presumed to be familiar with problems and needs of a system undergoing desegregation." The Court added: "Pupil assignment alone does not automatically remedy the impact of previous, unlawful education isolation; the consequences linger and can be dealt with only by intensive measures. Speech habits acquired in a segregated system do not vanish simply by moving a child to a desegregated school."

In effect, the Supreme Court found in the situation in Detroit that the remedy had been appropriately tailored to fit the scope of the violation. The Court also found that when state defendants were guilty of discriminatory acts, as in this situation, then it is proper for the state to share in the costs of implementing desegregation plans. The state of Michigan was ordered to pay half of the costs of Detroit's integration plans (*Milliken* v. *Bradley*, 1977).

In sum, in elementary and secondary school systems a court will order an integration plan only if there is a clear showing of governmental intent to discriminate. There must also be evidence of how wide geographically the discrimination is in order to determine the amount of busing necessary. If a state is to share the costs of a city's integration plan, there must be a showing of discriminatory acts by state officials.

*Public higher education institutions also now have a positive duty to integrate racially.* The Supreme Court has held that there is a positive duty for a state to dismantle its dual system of higher education when such a system is a vestige .of de jure, governmentally established segregation. The Court also pointed out that the scope of the relief must fit the scope of the violation; and in general, enough flexibility should be given to encourage a state to set its own educational policy (*Geier* v. *Dunn,* 1972).

In addition to constitutional remedies, remedies for racial discrimination in higher education are available under Titles IV and VI of the Civil Rights Act of 1964, which involve ultimate loss of federal funding. One suit brought under the act's provisions resulted in a judge's order to HEW to assist a number of states to integrate their colleges and universities. Several attempts to produce integration plans failed. HEW has responded now by sending six states—Arkansas, Florida, Georgia, North Carolina, Oklahoma, and Virginia—new criteria for desegregating their public universities and colleges over the next five years (*Adams* v. *Califano,* 1977).

In another case, a federal district judge ordered that the predominantly white University of Tennessee–Nashville Campus be merged with the predominantly black Tennessee State University by 1980, the black university to be the surviving institution (*Geier* v. *Blanton,* 1977).

*Sex discrimination in admissions in educational institutions may be affected by state law more than by federal law.* The matter of sex discrimination in admissions requires careful examination of state law as well as federal law. Some states have passed legislation banning sex discrimination in admissions in public schools. In such instances, it is quite clear that females and males are to be treated equally in the admissions process in public schools. There is no such clarity as far as federal law is concerned.

Discrimination in admissions on the basis of sex is banned by federal law only in a specified and limited number of institutions. Only *after* admission do the major constitutional and federal statutory prohibitions against sex discrimination apply.

Unless state law prohibits sex discrimination in admissions, most single-sex public and private elementary and secondary schools, as well as private undergraduate institutions, apparently may remain one-sex institutions under federal law. However, at institutions that decide to become coeducational or already are, females and males must be treated equally after they are admitted. It is the post-admission requirements for equal treatment of females and males which is the major impact of Title IX of the Education Amendments of 1972. Equal treatment of females and males after admission will be discussed in the next chapter.

Title IX specifically prohibits discrimination in admissions on the basis of sex only in institutions of vocational education, professional education, graduate higher education, and public undergraduate higher education (other than those which have been traditionally and continually single-sex institutions). Title IX does not affect admissions at private undergraduate institutions offering first-degree professional and vocational programs. In 1975, federal legislation was enacted permitting admission of women to U.S. military academies.

Specifically prohibited by Title IX are such admissions practices as setting quotas of the number of students of either sex that may be admitted, ranking applicants separately on the basis of sex, inquiring into or applying any rule based upon marital status or pregnancy of an applicant, or setting higher admissions standards for women than for men.

In summary, Title IX prohibits sex discrimination in admissions in education programs or activities receiving federal funds at all vocational, graduate, higher education, professional, and public undergraduate schools not traditionally single-sex institutions.

The purpose of Title IX, of course, is to provide for female students substantial access to the many vocational and professional training programs available to males. Female students, therefore, may seek admission to institutions that train doctors rather than nurses, school superintendents rather than teachers, and scientists rather than laboratory assistants.

The equal protection clause of the Constitution has been thought of as a tool to eliminate sex discrimination at public elementary and secondary schools. A case on this point involved a public school district's maintenance, in an otherwise coeducational system, of two single-sex high schools that specialized in college preparatory programs. Enrollment in these schools was voluntary. The Supreme Court in an even split decision affirmed a lower court decision to the effect that the educational opportunities offered to female students and male students were essentially equal at the two schools. Therefore, there was no violation of the equal protection clause (*Vorchheimer* v. *Philadelphia School District*, 1977). The Court's even split decision does not set a legal precedent, but it does appear to support the notion that under certain circumstances the doctrine of "separate but equal" education of the sexes is permissible in public educational institutions.

The failure of means such as those just described to eliminate sex discrimination in admissions has led many persons to conclude that complete elimination of sex discrimination in admissions will succeed only through passage of the Equal Rights Amendment.

*Discrimination on the basis of physical, mental, or other handicaps.* The Rehabilitation Act of 1973, Section 504, provides regulations designed to eliminate discrimination against handicapped persons, such as blind persons, deaf persons, persons confined to wheelchairs, and mentally ill or retarded persons. The goal of the act is to provide access to the mainstream of American life for handicapped people.

Costs for special academic programs, building facilities, equipment, or personnel are to be borne by the institution that receives the financial assistance from HEW. The institution need not meet the financial obligations solely through its own funds, but may rely upon funds from any public or private source, including insurers and similar third parties. (Deadlines and other information about this new law appear in Appendix A.)

*Preschool, elementary, and secondary education: Rehabilitation Act.* Preschool, elementary, and secondary education institutions that receive funds from HEW are covered by the Rehabilitation Act regulations, which deal with both admission and later treatment of handicapped students. The provisions of the Rehabilitation Act of 1973 have been closely coordinated with those of the Education of the Handicapped Act (EHA) of 1975, as amended by Public Law 94-142. The basic requirements, common to Section 504 and to the EHA and to court cases concerning standards for the education of handicapped persons, are

- that handicapped persons, regardless of the nature or severity of their handicap, be provided a free appropriate public education,
- that handicapped students be educated with nonhandicapped students to the maximum extent appropriate to their needs,
- that educational agencies attempt to identify and locate all unserved handicapped children,
- that evaluation procedures be improved in order to avoid the inappropriate education that results from the misclassification of students, and
- that procedural safeguards be established to enable parents and guardians to influence decisions regarding the evaluation and placement of their children. (Minimum procedures include notice, a right to inspect records, an impartial hearing with a right to representation by counsel, and a review procedure.)

In sum, the new Section 504 regulations require that all qualified handicapped students receive a free, appropriate public education in the most "normal" setting possible. Regarding the admissions process, the regulations set forth evaluation requirements designed to ensure the proper classification and placement of handicapped children. Due process procedures for resolving disputes over placement of students are available to parents. HEW has said that before it will review individual placement decisions, it will pursue cases in which a pattern or practice of discriminatory placements may be involved. HEW does intend to ensure that testing and evaluation take place and that adequate opportunity for review and challenge is provided. The regulations stress, however, that if a handicapped student is so disruptive in a regular classroom that the education of other students is significantly impaired, the needs of the handicapped child cannot be met in that environment. Therefore, regular placement of that student would not be required by the regulations.

Private educational institutions that receive HEW funds may not exclude, on the basis of handicaps, a qualified handicapped person if the person can, with minor adjustments, be provided an appropriate education. Private institutions may charge more for providing an appropriate education to handicapped students than to nonhandicapped students to the extent that additional charges can be justified by increased costs.

Although the law is relatively new, several courts have heard cases involving handicapped students. A public elementary school was held in violation of the Rehabilitation Act when it excluded a minimally handicapped six-year-old child from a regular public classroom. The child suffered from spina bifida, and she had minor physical impairments, including incontinence of the bowels and a noticeable limp. The school authorities had agreed to admit the child only if her mother would accompany her to school. The parents alleged they had never had an opportunity to challenge the conditions placed upon the child's admission. Unless the mother accompanied the child to school, the school would place the child in a special classroom for physically handicapped children ages ten to seventeen, only two of whom were ambulatory and one of whom was legally blind. The court concluded that such placement of the child would be in "gross violation of state regulation," and found the school officials in violation of the Rehabilitation Act for not making the effort to include this child in the regular public classroom, even if there were some expense involved. The court also found that making such a placement decision about a child without prior written notice and accompanying procedural safeguards, including the opportunity for parents and students to be heard, is contrary to the due process clause of the Fourteenth Amendment (*Hairston* v. *Drosick*, 1976).

*Postsecondary institutions: Rehabilitation Act.* The Rehabilitation Act requires that institutions of higher education review their recruiting and admission procedures and make reasonable adjustments to permit handicapped persons to be evaluated fairly and admitted into regular academic programs even if auxiliary aids are required. The regulations specifically provide that groups of colleges may not establish consortia exclusively for handicapped students.

In brief, the purpose of the Rehabilitation Act is to provide equal access and opportunity to higher education, insofar as possible, to handicapped persons in order that they may be admitted to regular educational programs. Emphasis is to be placed on their ability to perform rather than on their handicaps or disabilities. Thus, in taking admissions tests, arrangements must be made for blind students to have access to assistance from sighted readers or Braille material, and students in wheelchairs must be provided with ramps or other means to enter the place where the test is being given. The tests themselves must be appropriate and validated, under the conditions set forth in the regulations. For instance, at the postsecondary level special provisions exist for assistance from HEW's Office of Civil Rights in locating appropriate tests.

One case involved a deaf student enrolled in graduate courses at a private college. The student, an English teacher certified in deaf education, was required by the state department of education to periodically earn additional college credit to maintain her permit to teach. The student asked the college to supply funds for an interpreter so she could participate in classroom activities. The college alleged that the student must seek redress by applying to HEW rather than by maintaining a private lawsuit. The college also feared that should it supply an interpreter, with a resultant fee of about $1,000 in this situation, it might be faced with similar financial burdens in the future. The court found that the deaf student was entitled under the Rehabilitation Act to have the college provide funds for an interpreter. The court found also that Congress intended to provide for private lawsuits for noncompliance under the Rehabilitation Act. The court expressed its sympathy for the college in this situation, which the court described as ironic. As it happens, Converse College has been in the vanguard of educational institutions that have developed programs and facilities for the handicapped. The college now finds itself in a position in which its students and benefactors may now be forced by the federal government to shoulder a substantial financial burden to provide special services for any handicapped persons who should choose to go there. The court ordered the college to find and compensate a qualified interpreter of its choosing for the purpose of assisting the student in her summer school classes (*Barnes* v. *Converse College,* 1977).

A student with a hearing disability was denied admission by a college to a program for registered nurses. The student claimed that the college had denied her equal protection of the law and had violated the Rehabilitation Act of 1973. The court felt that the evidence failed to establish a denial of equal protection of the law. It also held that the refusal of the college to admit her to the program did not constitute a violation of the Rehabilitation Act, even though her hearing disability fell within the statutory definition of "handicapped persons" (*Davis* v. *Southeastern Community College,* 1976).

*Age discrimination in the admission of students.* The consideration of age in the admission of students to elementary and secondary schools has not presented a great problem. Most states have statutes that set forth in detail the ages between which youngsters must or may attend school.

Age poses quite a different problem for institutions of higher education. Colleges and universities seldom deny admission on the basis of age to persons who are applying to undergraduate institutions. They are pleased to have the additional student, as well as the additional revenue. Generally, however, at the graduate and doctoral levels, and particularly in programs of professional education such as medicine, dentistry, and law, admissions committees often are reluctant to admit older persons. The reasons for this are several. There is a genuine concern that the older applicants will be unable to maintain a sound and satisfactory academic standard, though one would be hard pressed to find actual data to substantiate such a position. The reason given more frequently for denial of admission of an older applicant to a graduate program or professional school is that the interest of society is better served by using the limited resources available to train younger people, who probably will be able to spend a longer period of time practicing their professions and benefiting the public. A number of unsuccessful candidates for admission, turned away because of age, have resorted to the courts for assistance. In most cases, their claims were unsuccessful.

A fifty-one-year-old applicant to a doctoral program at a state university was denied admission because of her age, among other factors. She alleged that this was in violation of the equal protection clause. The court dismissed her complaint and said:

> The court finds and concludes that the use of age as a criterion for evaluation of applicants to educational programs is not in violation of the Equal Protection Guarantees of the U.S. Constitution or of any other statutory or constitutes no prohibition and is a reasonable practice in light of the limited resources available for educating persons in the field of educational psychology at the University of Utah (*Purdie* v. *University of Utah*, 1977).

In an earlier case, a candidate for admission to the School of Medicine at the University of Chicago contended that she had been denied admission on the basis of both her age and sex. Her lawsuit against the institution involved first a claim under a civil rights statute which forbade certain acts by the state without due process. The court rejected this contention on the basis that the medical school was a private institution and therefore not covered by a statute pertaining to acts by the state. The applicant also alleged that Title IX had been violated since she claimed she was discriminated against on the basis of sex. The court again found against her on the basis that Title IX provides a remedy in the form of resort to a governmental agency (HEW) for assistance, rather than to a private lawsuit. (This portion of the decision was affirmed again in 1977.) The applicant for admission finally alleged that the university was violating the Age Discrimination in Employment Act of 1967. The court again replied in the negative, commenting that the case at hand involved admission to an educational institution rather than to employment (*Cannon* v. *University of Chicago,* 1976).

On the other hand, where a state statute prohibiting age discrimination was involved, an applicant for admission to a school of medicine was more successful. A Massachusetts state statute provides:

> It shall be an unfair educational practice for an educational institution . . . to exclude, limit, or otherwise discriminate against any persons seeking admission to a program or course of study leading to a degree beyond a bachelor's degree because of age.

The applicant had been an assistant professor of biochemistry and pharmacology employed by the School of Medicine at Tufts University for four years before applying there for admission as a student. When his application was rejected, he filed a complaint with the Massachusetts Commission Against Discrimination. After investigating, the commission found that "probable cause exists for crediting" the professor's allegation that he had been denied admission because of his age. Based upon the commission's finding, the applicant filed a petition in a state court to require the college to admit him and was granted a preliminary injunction. This matter was reported in the *Chronicle of Higher Education,* August 18, 1975. The case illustrates the importance of state statutory prohibitions against age discrimination in admission to an educational program.

It is ironic that current economic exigency at many educational institutions has forced them to seek to recruit nontraditional groups of individuals. Age barriers to admissions may be broken by economic necessity faster than by laws against age discrimination.

### Special Admissions Programs

*Preferred admissions programs for relatives of alumni, faculty, and trustees.* Special admissions programs have dealt principally with minority admissions, but they also include preferred admissions programs. Such applications for admission may be encouraged with the hope that such enrollees or their families may assist with financial and other development of the institution in the future.

In the *Steinberg* case (1976), which was discussed earlier in this chapter, an applicant who was rejected by a private medical school successfully sued the school on the basis of breach of contract. As already noted, he alleged that the school published qualifications for admissions in its bulletin which it then ignored by admitting some students under different, unpublished criteria. These criteria, he contended, were that they were relatives of faculty or trustees, and that they might make financial contributions to the school. In this case, it also was alleged that these preferred candidates did not have to meet all the criteria published in the catalog. The court agreed with the plaintiff that a contract had been created between him and the school, providing for the plaintiff's application to be judged by the published criteria, and that these criteria were not actually applied.

*Admission of disadvantaged persons, including minorities.* Special programs for admission of disadvantaged persons are meant to encourage applications by individuals whose economic, cultural, or educational background have placed them at a disadvantage in the past in taking tests or achieving high grades. An admissions committee usually considers other criteria, such as experience, motivation, and competence measured by nontraditional means, in determining whether a disadvantaged applicant has the potential to succeed at the institution and beyond.

A number of institutions have sought to increase admissions of disadvantaged and minority persons by developing such special admissions programs. They have been sued by whites for using "different" admissions standards to admit disadvantaged persons, such as blacks and to reject otherwise qualified white persons. Some whites have claimed that this is "reverse discrimination" and is a violation of 42 U.S.C. Sections 1981 and 1983.

*Reverse discrimination cases.* "Reverse discrimination" is a term used to criticize the practice followed in some admissions programs which admit disadvantaged blacks or other minority applicants under standards said to be lower or in other ways different from standards that must be met by white applicants. Opponents argue that this may result in otherwise qualified white applicants being rejected solely because of race, which would be a violation of their constitutional rights.

Three cases are pertinent examples of suits filed by whites against public institutions in which the white plaintiffs complained of being damaged by reverse discrimination.

*DeFunis* v. *Odegaard* (1974) was a lawsuit filed by a rejected white applicant to the University of Washington Law School. DeFunis claimed that he was a qualified applicant who had been rejected solely because of race. He claimed that if the school had not been filling places in the entering class with "less qualified" black applicants, he would have been admitted. His contention was that this action by the state was in violation of his constitutional rights.

In the course of the various legal proceedings, DeFunis was admitted to the law school, and by the time the case was petitioned to the Supreme Court, he had graduated. The Supreme Court declared the issue moot and declined to hear the case. The constitutionality of disadvantaged minority admissions programs was therefore left unresolved.

*Alevy* v. *Downstate Medical Center of New York in Brooklyn* (1976) involved a claim that the medical school's minority admissions program constituted reverse discrimination and was unconstitutional and illegal. This minority admissions program survived the challenge. The New York State Court of Appeals ruled unanimously that the practice of giving special treatment in education and employment to minority group members was constitutional "in proper circumstances." However, the court warned that its opinion should not be interpreted too broadly.

The plaintiff had challenged the Downstate Medical Center's practice of giving minority applicants who were less qualified than white applicants a greater opportunity for admission. The school asserted that its admission practice was responsive to the medical needs of the community's large black and Puerto Rican population. The lower court had found that such a practice was permissible so long as it served the compelling interest of the state in increasing opportunities for culturally, economically, and educationally disadvantaged applicants. The lower court also felt that such disadvantages could be taken into account by admissions committees in assessing an applicant's true potential for a successful medical career. In any event, the court of appeals found that the plaintiff would not have been admitted to the school even if minority applicants had not been given preference.

*Bakke* v. *Regents of University of California* (1976) involved a white applicant who was refused admission to medical school in 1973 and 1974. The case reached the California Supreme Court. It ruled that the disadvantaged minority admissions program at the Medical School of the University of California at Davis, where Bakke had been rejected, violated the Fourteenth Amendment equal protection rights of white applicants and was unconstitutional. The program, said the court, had the effect of denying admission to some white applicants solely because of their race. Of the one hundred openings in the entering class, sixteen were set aside for disadvantaged minorities under this program.

Bakke asked the California Supreme Court to direct the medical school to admit him, but it returned the case to the lower court to determine whether he would have been admitted had there been no minority admissions program.

This case was heard by the U.S. Supreme Court during its October 1977 term. Until the Court reaches a decision, the legality of all disadvantaged minority admissions programs is clouded.

## COSTS AND FINANCIAL AID

Educational costs for students are a source of much litigation. The legal problems arise over many issues. When does an institution have the right to change its tuition rates? How are decisions made regarding resident or non-resident tuition for students? Other questions concern students' rights to have tuition refunded if they withdraw from the institution, the kinds of financial aid available, and whether students at church-related institutions may receive financial assistance from public funds. There are also matters of nondiscriminatory policies regarding the awarding of scholarships, the bases for loan eligibility, and the effect of a student's filing bankruptcy on the repayment of loans. Finally, there are several questions about whether a student must pay income tax on the financial aid received.

Business and financial aid officers of public and private institutions have much of the responsibility for handling such problems and for modifying the institution's policies and procedures as new laws and judicial rulings appear.

### Increases in Tuition

*Increases in tuition generally are sustained by courts.* Educational institutions that charge tuition, whether public or private and at whatever level, inevitably find that certain increases in costs can be managed only by increasing the amount of tuition or fees paid by the students. Courts generally sustain tuition increases. However, it goes without saying that most institutions resort to raising tuition rates with the greatest reluctance. They well know that students find it extraordinarily difficult to absorb increases in costs of their education. Particularly hard hit are those students who are in midstream, so to speak; that is, those who entered the institution under the impression that total costs would be based upon figures appearing in the institution's bulletin at the time they entered. If tuition costs rise in the midst of their educational career, they feel cheated. A number of students have filed lawsuits attempting to force an educational institution either to rescind tuition increases or to substantially modify the increases. These lawsuits have generally been unsuccessful.

A class action suit of approximately 500 medical school students was filed against George Washington University, for instance. The students contended that new, higher tuition rates had been announced which were contrary to those that had been set forth in the institution's bulletin. They argued that this was a breach of their contracts with the university. The 1974-75 bulletin of the medical school contained the following language:

academic year tuition increases have been estimated as follows: ... every effort will be made to keep tuition increases within these limits. However, it is not possible to project future economic data with certainty, and circumstances may require an adjustment.

As noted earlier, it is settled law that the relationship between a student and a private university is contractual and that the terms in a university's bulletin may become part of that contract. The court found, in this case, that the words used clearly expressed the possibility of changes in tuition rates. The broad language used in the bulletin, as evidenced by words such as "estimated," "approximate," and "projected," made the earlier printed tuition rates too indefinite to be enforced as a contractual obligation (*Basch* v. *George Washington University*, 1977).

### Nonresident Tuition Fee

*Tuition for in-state residents may be lower than tuition for out-of-state residents.* At all educational levels, public institutions that charge tuition differentiate between the amount charged bona fide residents of their own district, city, county, or state, and that charged nonresidents. In the case of elementary and secondary schools, it is quite usual for students who reside in one district, and who are given permission to attend school in another district, to be charged a special fee to cover costs. Actually, because of planning and budgetary problems, many school districts have all but eliminated the possibility of students attending schools in a district other than the one in which they reside. Even so, a number of school districts, particularly those under court order to integrate, have had to devise ways to handle costs for students who are bused from their regular school to another, sometimes across city or county lines.

*Resident status must be bona fide.* Higher education institutions have dealt with the problem of in-state versus out-of-state tuition eligibility for a number of years. Some states have passed legislation to handle most of the problems. For example, a statute may require a student to establish a bona fide domicile in the state for at least one year before he or she becomes eligible for resident tuition at state colleges and universities. Such a statute in Colorado was reviewed affirmatively all the way to the Supreme Court (*Montgomery* v. *Douglas*, 1975).

*Residency eligibility rules must be equal as to age requirements.* A state statute that allows students over the age of 21 whose parents reside outside the state to establish residency by residing in the state for one year, but that denies the same opportunity to students under 21, was found to violate the equal protection rights of the latter students. A court found that no apparent rational basis related to legitimate state objectives existed to set up the two classes of students (*Burke* v. *Raschke,* 1977).

*Residency status by emancipation depends upon law.* In another case, a student attempted to claim residency status in Florida by contending that he was an emancipated minor and could qualify as a Florida resident for tuition purposes. The court held that he had no legal capacity to establish a Florida domicile separate and apart from that of his parents, and furthermore that emancipation for the establishment of the required domicile could be accomplished only by reaching the age of majority, by marriage, or by order of a competent court. The student had to continue to pay the nonresident tuition fee (*Florida Board of Regents of the Department of Education, Division of Universities* v. *Harris,* 1976).

*Presuming irrebuttably a nonresidency status for all aliens is impermissible.* In a case involving nonimmigrant aliens, a public university was told by a court that it could not irrebuttably presume, for tuition purposes, that nonimmigrant aliens are out-of-state residents. The student involved was a nonimmigrant alien whose visa permitted entry into the United States on the basis of employment by an international organization of a member of the student's immediate family. The court said that the university had reasonable methods by which it could determine a nonimmigrant alien's domicile without irrebuttably presuming it to be out of state. The court pointed out that the university routinely makes such determinations on a case-by-case basis with regard to other students seeking to pay domiciliary tuition rates under its in-state policy. Nonimmigrant aliens should be given the same opportunity to prove residency status (*Moreno* v. *University of Maryland,* 1976).

The state of Mississippi passed a law classifying all aliens as nonresident for the purpose of charging them higher tuition and fees at state-controlled institutions of higher education. The court found this classification to be a violation of the equal protection clause of the Constitution. The statute had no provision for permitting an alien to rebut the presumption that he or she was not a bona fide resident alien (*Jagnandan* v. *Giles,* 1976).

*Residence of married students cannot be irrebuttably presumed that of spouse.* In the past it has been traditional to consider the residence or domicile of a married woman student to be that of her husband. Today, that assumption may be merely a presumption that students have the right to rebut. It is clear now that either a husband or a wife may offer proof that his or her domicile is different from that of a spouse.

Earlier it was mentioned that a former Pennsylvania statewide residency rule, stating that, for tuition purposes, the domicile of the wife was that of her husband, was declared unconstitutional. A new rule was established that the domicile of the wife was only presumed to be that of her husband. In spite of the new rule, the University of Pittsburgh continued to require resident married women students having nonresident spouses to pay nonresident tuition rates. The affected students brought a class action suit against the university and won. The court held that the students were entitled to restitution of the difference between the nonresident tuition rate they had paid and the in-state tuition rate they should have paid.

The court pointed out that the criteria to determine domicile should not be applied differentially to persons based upon marital status or sex. It directed that residency status be determined for married woman students according to the same criteria employed for single women and males. These criteria were twelve months' residence in Pennsylvania as a non-student prior to enrollment, registered to vote in Pennsylvania, licensed to drive a car in Pennsylvania, the state where the student was previously employed, if any, and the residence at the time of application and enrollment (*Samuel* v. *University of Pittsburgh*, 1976).

*Computer used to figure amount of damages.* The *Samuel* case also highlights the fact that courts have become sophisticated regarding uses to which university computers may be put. In the past, a court may have been swayed by a university's defense that it would be far too burdensome to go through its entire registration card file to ascertain residency status of a large class of persons, such as all married women students. Today, computerized registration systems make this a relatively simple task, and class action lawsuits may prevail today in circumstances where they may not have in the past. Formerly, a court might have decertified a class of persons such as those in the *Samuel* case and required each student to pursue her claim individually.

### Refund Policy

Educational institutions are required by the Education Amendments of 1976 to indicate clearly in their bulletins how their refund policy operates. Most refund procedures are founded upon a prorated basis, with the amount of the refund geared to the number of weeks the student has been enrolled. At a certain point, the student forfeits further refund. This is permitted because by then the institution has no way of admitting an additional student to replace the student who has left. Accordingly, the institution would then suffer an irreplaceable loss of revenue that is relied upon to cover its expenses for the year.

An example of a vaguely drawn refund policy in a contract of enrollment is the following:

If written notice is received on or before May 1, this agreement may be terminated. After September 1, no refund or remission of the foregoing fees for the entire college year will be made on account of absence, illness, withdrawal or removal at the request of the college or for any other reason.

The parent in this case notified the institution in August that the student would not attend. The parent acknowledged the forfeiture of the deposit he had made earlier. He then alleged that he had given timely notice to the institution and was not liable for the whole year's tuition. The trial court found in favor of the college. The appellate court asked the trial court to reconsider the decision because the contract was "susceptible of an interpretation that the September 1 deadline would be meaningless unless interpreted to permit withdrawal up to that date without further obligation to pay tuition." The court went on to say that if the college could prove a different interpretation of the language making the parent liable, the college should be asked also to submit evidence that it suffered actual damages equal to the price of the full tuition (*Cazenovia College* v. *Patterson*, 1974).

In June 1977, a New York State statute was signed into law requiring correspondence schools to refund a part of the tuition if a student drops out of a course. It is thought to be the first statute of its kind in the country. New York City's Department of Consumer Affairs already had such a regulation, which will be strengthened by the new state law.

### Financial Aid

Full disclosure and nondiscriminatory practices are prime factors to be considered in setting up and implementing financial aid programs. As mentioned earlier, the Guaranteed Student Loan Program regulations (Appendix A) require disclosure to prospective students, before tuition is paid, of accurate, complete information about all major characteristics of an institution, including the financial aid program. The new requirements apply to schools, colleges, trade schools, and other postsecondary institutions. Detailed, full information must be supplied concerning costs, refund policy, student retention rates, academic programs and courses, and career placement. Noncompliance with these requirements, or the supplying of misleading information may result in loss of eligibility for a number of federal loan and grant programs for both institutions and students.

States may have similar requirements. In June 1977, for instance, New York State passed legislation requiring that the State Commissioner of Education establish regulations to see that educational institutions make available to prospective students detailed information on costs of attending the institution, financial assistance available, and number of students who actually complete the program in which a student plans to enroll.

*State financial aid.* A survey by the National Association of State Scholarship Programs indicated that the number of students receiving state scholarship financial assistance increased from 470,800 in 1969-70 to 1,095,300 during 1976-77. According to that survey, three states—Alaska, Arizona and Nevada —offer no state grants or loans. At this writing, Arizona has been awaiting legislative authority for a planned program.

During 1976-77, only 22.4 percent of state scholarships were awarded on the basis of merit rather than demonstrated financial need. As an example, New York provides financial aid of three types. The first type is the Regents' College Scholarships, which are awarded to high school graduates based on performance on a competitive examination. The second type—the largest and most commonly granted form of financial aid—is the Tuition Assistance Award, which is noncompetitive and available to graduate and undergraduate students "enrolled in approved programs and who demonstrate the ability to complete such courses." The amount of the award depends on tuition and income. The ceiling on assistance is $600 ($1,500 for undergraduates). The third form of assistance is a student loan guaranteed by the state. A borrower meeting certain incomes restrictions is entitled to favorable interest rates and generally to an interest-free grace period of at least nine months after he or she completes or terminates a course of study. Restrictions on eligibility for participation in any of these programs generally include a modest durational residency requirement (Section 661(3), New York Education Law.)

*Resident alien students cannot be denied state financial aid.* New York State had a statutory bar against giving state financial aid or scholarships for higher education to resident alien students who decline to apply for U.S. citizenship. This statute was declared unconstitutional by the U.S. Supreme Court because it was judged to violate the Fourteenth Amendment's equal protection clause. The Court pointed out that resident aliens are required to pay full taxes so there is no real unfairness in allowing them to participate in programs to which they contribute (*Nyquist* v. *Mauclet*, 45 LW 4655, June 13, 1977).

*State tuition grants to handicapped persons must not violate equal protection clause.* The state of Virginia set up a system of tuition grants for handicapped students. It provided partial reimbursement to parents of the cost of sending a handicapped child to a private school. A court found the system impermissible since it did not provide for the equal protection rights of those handicapped children whose parents could not afford to supplement the difference between the amount reimbursed by the state and the cost of private education (*Kruse* v. *Campbell*, 1977).

*Federal financial aid.* A number of federal financial programs also assist students in paying the costs of their education. Among these are the Basic Educational Opportunity Grants, Supplemental Work-Study Program, Educational Opportunity Grants, National Direct Student Loans, the College Program, and the Guaranteed Sudent Loan Program.

*Fraud in student loan applications.* Students must be independent of parental income to be eligible for federal student aid. There has been substantial increase in the number of students who have listed themselves as independent in the last several years. According to the U.S. Office of Education, in 1973 about 14 percent of the college freshmen who applied for Basic Educational Opportunity Grants (BEOG) listed themselves as independent of parental income. By 1976, 36 percent of all BEOG applicants claimed they were independent. There is concern that many of these may be fraudulent claims.

    The federal government has proposed tightening up the definition of "independent." The new standards would require the "independent" aid applicant not to have been claimed for federal income tax exemptions by any person other than the student or the spouse for two prior calendar years, intead of one. The weeks-lived-with-parents rule would be liberalized, from two to six permitted weeks per year. The limitation of $600 per year received from parents would remain unchanged. It is hoped that the proposed change regarding tax exemption will discourage fraudulent claims.

## Scholarships

    Scholarships often originate as private gifts in the form of charitable trusts given to both public and private educational institutions. Donors sometimes attach conditions of eligibility for the scholarships which in later years become illegal, constitutionally impermissible, or unacceptable to the institution for other reasons. Courts are asked, then, to determine whether the changed conditions have so altered the original intention of the donor that the awarding of the scholarship should cease and the remaining funds should be returned to the donor or to his or her estate. Alternatively, a court may find that the intent of the donor can be carried out even though an original condition of eligibility no longer may be effectuated completely. Courts apply the doctrine of *cy pres* ("as near as") to carry out the donor's wishes as closely as possible under the new circumstances.

    For example, a charitable trust had set up scholarships for "needy, deserving boys . . . who are members of the Caucasian race and who have severally, specifically professed themselves to be of the Protestant Congregational Faith." The selection committee sought advice from a court regarding the restrictions on sex, race, and religion. The court removed the racial and sexual restrictions, but declined to remove the religious restrictions on the ground that the latter did not violate the equal protection clause (*Lockwood* v. *Killian*, 1977).

In a similar case, a trust had as its goal "to aid and assist worthy and amibitious young men to acquire a legal education." Female law students who were rejected for consideration for scholarship aid filed suit for a judicial interpretation of the trust instrument. Ultimately, the court stated that "If some ambiguities remain, the declared policy of the Commonwealth regarding equal treatment of the sexes leads the court to resolve it in favor of the female law students" (*Ebitz* v. *Pioneer National Bank*, 1977).

*Discrimination in the administration of scholarships for minority students.* Another case noted previously concerned the percentage of scholarships reserved for minority law students at a private institution. The court found a violation of the Civil Rights Act of 1964 because 60 percent of its law school scholarship funds were allocated to "minority students," who comprised 11 percent of its entering students, while only 40 percent of the scholarship funds were left for the remaining 89 percent of the entering class. The court noted that this was a discriminatory practice (*Flanagan* v. *President and Directors of Georgetown College*, 1976).

*Sex discrimination in awarding athletic scholarships may be a violation of Title IX.* Title IX of the Educational Amendments of 1972 mandates the awarding of athletic scholarships on a sexually nondiscriminatory basis. The purpose of the Title IX regulations is not to require that absolutely equal amounts of scholarship funds go to males and females, but that there be a reasonable distribution based upon the amount of interest and participation by male and female students. For instance, there may be fewer football scholarships for females than for males if an institution can show a lesser amount of interest and participation in football by females than by males.

Institutions should take care that if scholarships are to be awarded on criteria other than academic merit, those criteria should be neutral. Such criteria may include financial need or athletic skill or both. However, the norms used for assessing athletic skill may have to be different for males and females if the range of ability between the sexes differs widely due to the sex of the student. The distance that males can drive a golf ball generally may be farther than that for females. In this situation, such a norm would not be admissible in selecting candidates. Instead, it would be appropriate for females to compete against females for a golf team scholarship.

A number of sports may lend themselves to coeducational competition for scholarships, especially where the institution supports coeducational teams in noncontact sports that depend more on skill than on strength. Even in sports where strength is a factor, there occur overlaps in height, weight, and general size between the sexes. As a result, coeducational golf, tennis, swimming, and archery teams already exist at all levels of education.

### Loans and Bankruptcy

*Congress has restricted the effect of a bankruptcy discharge on insured student loans.* Increasingly, students who have borrowed money for education under federally insured student loan programs have sought discharge of the loans through bankruptcy proceedings after they graduate. In some instances courts supported such discharges, and in others they did not. The major concern has been that the continuation of loan programs would be jeopardized if discharges through bankruptcy continued. Congress now has restricted the effect of a bankruptcy discharge on insured student loans owed at the time of bankruptcy. The law excludes educational debts from discharge and bankruptcy by excepting from discharge "any educational debt if the first payment of any installment thereof was due on a date less than five years prior to the date of the petition and if its payment from future income or other wealth will not impose an undue hardship on the debtor and his dependents" (20 U.S.C. Sec. 1087-3).

Two cases illustrate problems raised in bankruptcy cases. In the first case, a court did discharge the loan in bankruptcy. Later, the student asked for a transcript of his credits to gain admission to graduate school and sued the institution when it refused to issue it. The institution claimed that its student handbook provided that a transcript cannot be released until all accounts are paid. The institution was upheld. The court said that the institution could not pursue collection of the debt because it had been extinguished. But the institution was not obliged to supply a transcript when it had not been paid for its services (*Girardier* v. *Webster College,* 1977).

In the second case, the court held that an insured student loan, received under the National Defense Student Loan Program, was not the kind of provable debt that can be discharged in bankruptcy. The reasons given by the court were that a provable debt by definition could not be the kind of loan that is cancelled if the debtor dies, becomes disabled, or teaches in specified schools. It must be a loan proved due and payable at the time of the bankruptcy (*New York* v. *Wilkes,* 1977).

### Financial Aid as Taxable Income

*Income tax must be paid by students on some forms of financial assistance.* In broadest possible terms, it is generally true that students who are still candidates working toward a degree need not pay income tax on scholarships, grants, and similar financial assistance. The reasoning behind the IRS ruling excluding such scholarships and grants from gross income is that the funds are used principally to support education and therefore benefit society as a whole.

On the other hand, students who have completed their degrees, such as new medical doctors working as hospital interns, are required to pay income tax on their stipends. The IRS's position is that these stipends constitute wages rather than scholarships or grants. Tax courts have taken the same position on payments received by postdoctoral graduate teaching fellows.

In another realm, some employers encourage their employees as a matter of policy to enroll in updating educational courses. When the employers pay the tuition for such courses, this aid does not qualify as a scholarship and must be included in taxable income by the employee. However, if the employee pays the cost of such *required* continuing education, it usually may be deducted later as a business-related expense.

The basis used by the IRS to determine whether scholarships and grants are taxable income appears to be the educational status of the student. If the student is truly a student working toward a degree, financial aid is not considered income for tax purposes. If, however, the person has graduated and has received a degree of some sort, so that his or her current status is that of an employee providing services to the institution, any money received from the employer is deemed to be a wage in compensation for such services. These wages are included in gross income for tax purposes.

This area of taxation has some other more technical features associated with it. Therefore, students or institutions who are not sure whether certain funds should be treated as educational scholarships or as wages are strongly advised to consult an attorney who knows about current IRS regulations and relevant rulings regarding them.

## RECOMMENDATIONS

The always important legal question to ask before taking action regarding students (or colleagues, for that matter) is whether the anticipated action would affect any existing constitutional, statutory, or contractual rights.

The organizational structure of the institution should be such that responsibility for all functions, including recruitment, admissions, and financial aid, is delineated clearly. Institutional support to carry out such functions is needed, as well.

### Recruitment Practices

A specific person should be identified to handle recruitment. At some institutions this function is combined with the duties of the admissions offi-cer. At others, it is handled by the resource development officer. Someone must be given responsibility to review and monitor recruitment practices, including overseeing promotional materials and bulletins. There are at least four reasons for this. First, as has been pointed out, the institution may find itself bound contractually by what recruiters say or by what is published in bulletins. Second, prospective students may have a legal right to full dis-closure of programs and costs. Third, many students drop out because a set of expectations regarding the institution were generated somehow in the stu-dent's mind which are, in fact, unreal. The disappointments that may result when the student is confronted with reality after matriculating at the institu-tion may be the basis for disappointments of various kinds, many of which may be prevented if the institution takes care to give as realistic a picture as possible to a prospective student. The student needs to be aware of the insti-tution's academic standards and the various sanctions that may result if those standards are violated. The student also should be advised of the institution's standards for behavior conduct and concomitant sanctions. In this way, pro-spective students will be better able to assess their own "fit" with the insti-tution prior to making application to it. Fourth, recruiting policies and proce-dures require careful review and monitoring to ensure that they are in compli-ance with the various equal opportunity laws.

The individual in charge of recruiting needs support of various kinds from the institution, including support of the institution's chief executive officer. Needed also is a regular input of current legal information regarding policies and practices. Such information can be obtained by subscribing to various information services, attending professional conferences and seminars, and maintaining contact with counterparts at other institutions. Access to legal counsel is important, too.

### Admissions Practices

The institution would be well advised to think very carefully about what its admissions criteria are based upon its stated mission. Once criteria have been determined, they should be published in the institution's bulletin and then carefully adhered to. They should be applied equitably to all appli-cants as fairly as possible. A number of lawsuits have been based upon the claim that admissions criteria set forth in the institution's written publica-tions were not actually followed.

Admissions tests have been challenged repeatedly in courts as not pro-viding a true and accurate prediction of successful performance of applicants whose cultural backgrounds differ from that of the population used in con-structing the tests. Some institutions have found it useful to develop addi-tional methods for collecting information about the experience and competence of applicants. These institutions may still use test scores and grade point averages to predict ability to succeed at the institution. Studies are being conducted to see whether such supplementary information provides a more accurate and valid picture of applicants' competence and probable success.

Each institution should check its own state's sunshine or open meeting law and seek legal counsel on how the law affects the operation of the institution. In particular, a decision needs to be reached whether a state's sunshine law requires the institution to open meetings of its admissions committee to the public.

Discrimination in admissions can result in serious penalties. An institution should check its admissions policies to see that applicants are not discriminated against for handicaps, race, sex, national origin, or religion, to whatever extent the law provides. Age discrimination at present is not a serious threat, but may be in the near future. A law called the Age Discrimination Act of 1975 (Public Law 94-135), prohibits unreasonable discrimination on the basis of age by recipients of federal financial assistance. At this writing, regulations have not been developed to implement this act. As soon as they are, institutions probably will be required to eliminate age as a basis for refusing to admit an applicant. The Rehabilitation Act of 1973 is the most recent nondiscriminatory act to affect educational institutions; its basic requirements are set forth in Appendix A. The essential requirement of the act is to make certain that an educational institution's programs as a whole are accessible to handicapped persons. Discrimination in admission is the basis for an enormous number of lawsuits. The institution that is successful in setting up a program to review and monitor admissions policies regarding possible discriminatory procedures and eliminating them will benefit tremendously in reduced claims filed against it.

## Costs and Financial Aid

Business and financial aid officers can contribute enormously to the institution's well-being by developing and maintaining a system of informing prospective and present students fully and accurately about financial concerns. Information regarding financial aid and costs of attending the institution should be available in written form. Care should be taken to advise students that tuition may be affected by inflation or other economic conditions relating to the institution so that the students are prepared for a possible tuition increase. If students are to be classified differently with regard to amounts of tuition due (for example resident versus nonresident students), such decisions should be made thoughtfully. The tuition refund policy should be set forth clearly and unambiguously. Full information on state, federal, and private sources of financial aid should be available to prospective and matriculated students. Scholarships should be administered in a nondiscriminatory fashion. Students who default on loans are a special problem. A number of them have been successful in having such debts discharged in bankruptcy, and some institutions are investigating the use of private collection agencies to attempt to decrease the number of bankruptcy discharges. Information as to what kind of financial aid must be declared as taxable income should be available to students.

# 4. Treatment of Students: Academic Life and Student Life

This chapter focuses on legal problems that may arise after a student has been duly admitted and enrolled. Once candidates have been recruited and admitted, the legal issues shift from those of a person outside the institution seeking admittance to those of a person within the institution and having certain legal realtionships to it. Again, in private institutions that relationship is largely contractual; in public institutions it also contains constitutional requirements. This chapter considers legal issues that have arisen over academic concerns, such as challenging the quality of teaching, getting credit for courses, being eligible to receive degrees, and being dismissed for poor scholarship. Other concerns, which may be called student life matters, also are discussed. These include a student's right to free speech and press, right to religious freedom, and right to participate in student organizations, as well as questions involving discipline, security arrangements, and dormitory life.

After matriculating, students find themselves in two kinds of roles: first, they are scholars, with concerns about academic matters; and second, they are persons, with interests in how they are treated generally as human beings. And legal problems of "academic life" are different from those of "student life."

Earlier, it was noted that courts have tended to be very reluctant to step into situations involving academic judgment, such as decisions about the quality of academic performance. They have not wished to substitute the court's judgment for that of academic experts unless pressed to do so. Traditionally, courts have supported the notion that educators, not courts, properly should be the ones to govern educational institutions. However, there are signs of a change in this attitude. If an institution arbitrarily violates its own academic rules, or fails to meet its contractual, statutory, or constitutional obligations, the balance appears to be shifting toward the rights of the injured student and toward greater willingness by the courts to intervene. With respect to student life, courts have already shown a greater willingness to exercise their judicial judgment and make determinations about policy than they have in academic life.

As scholars, for example, students expect to receive teaching of good quality, to be informed in advance as to what the grading criteria will be, and upon completion of a prescribed course of study to be promoted or graduated or to receive their degrees. They expect that their complaints about academic matters will be heard and reviewed in a reasonably fair fashion.

As persons, students may expect to exercise whatever constitutional rights they have, ranging from First Amendment rights of free speech to Fourth Amendment rights of protection against unreasonable searches and seizures.

They may expect also to participate equally regardless of race, sex, or handicaps in academic programs or extracurricular activities.

Students have a right to expect, too, that reasonable rules of behavior and conduct will be promulgated, and that only appropriate sanctions will be imposed for their violation. Furthermore, with regard to disciplinary practices, students may recognize that they are entitled to whatever due process procedures are required by law.

Administrators and faculty, as well, have the right to believe that their academic and personal rights vis-à-vis students will be respected. Faculty members expect students to attend classes and to meet the requirements of courses (assignments, papers, and exams), and students supposedly are not to cheat or plagiarize. Students who fail to meet academic standards must expect failing grades or even dismissal from the institution after whatever appropriate academic review is provided.

Administrators expect students to abide by institutional rules. The institution may regulate the time, place, and manner of other modes of expression including distribution of student publications and appearances of speakers. Violations of constitutionally permissible rules and regulations of the educational institution may result in disciplinary proceedings including appropriate due process procedures and penalties.

Sunshine laws requiring open meetings and legal requirements for access by students and parents to records also are of special concern in the contemporary educational setting.

## ACADEMIC LIFE OF STUDENTS

The general rule when a student challenges academic decisions made by educational officials is that a court may not substitute its judgment for that of educators in academic matters. However, it will determine whether a student has received equitable treatment under academic regulations reasonably drawn and fairly administered.

Setting academic standards is the right, and indeed a principal responsibility, of the academic officers of an institution. Therefore, it is not surprising that courts have been reluctant to interfere in academic decisions, and to substitute their judgments in such matters for those of academicians.

Courts usually try not to interfere with internal academic decisions such as determining grades or deciding whether a student shall be given credit for a course or has satisfied the requirements for a degree. If an institution has established and follows a reasonable set of regulations and procedures for giving grades and credits and granting degrees, and if it provides a fair review process for penalties and disagreements, courts tend to support the institutional decision as being better informed than any they could render. Courts generally have held that a student's right to continue in an academic program is a matter for the faculty to determine, assuming the faculty acts in good faith and not in an arbitrary or capricious fashion.

Instances of judicial review of academic dismissal decisions do occur sometimes, under the exceptions mentioned above relating to arbitrary and capricious actions or those taken in bad faith. In most of these legal challenges, however, students have been unsuccessful in proving bad faith or arbitrary action. A factor that works in favor of the institution in such situations is that even though a review hearing may not be required, most institutions have some form of appeals procedure available to students after an adverse decision has been made. This policy of internal review cannot help but add weight to the institution's position that a decision to dismiss, for instance, was given serious and careful consideration, presumably because the decision makers knew that an appeal was possible.

In most situations, students must have exhausted the administrative remedies available within the institution before going outside to the courts for redress. A case in point involved a student who filed a lawsuit over a failure to be granted a degree before seeking relief through the review process available at the institution (*Schwartz* v. *Bank Street College of Education,* 1976).

Academic dismissal decisions, therefore, have been viewed by courts as quite distinct from disciplinary dismissal proceedings, over which courts routinely assert the power to review to assure that appropriate procedural due process has been provided.

## Courts' Reluctance To Interfere in Academic Decisions

A typical case illustrates the rule that courts prefer not to interfere in decisions involving academic performance. A student was told that because of scholastic deficiencies in her work, she could not longer continue taking classes. The student sued, alleging bad faith on the part of the institution's officials in applying the rules and regulations of the university. She claimed a right to a hearing on the academic decision to dismiss her. Both the trial court and the appellate court found in favor of the university. The appellate court reiterated the formerly settled rules that (1) school officials have absolute discretion in determining whether a student's academic performance is adequate; (2) this discretion is limited only by the requirement that school officials not act arbitrarily or in bad faith; and the burden is upon the student to prove such motivation; and (3) a student has no right to a hearing if dismissal is for failure to meet academic standards rather than for disciplinary purposes (*LaPolla* v. *The University of Akron*, 1974).

In another pertinent case, the court held that it could not substitute its judgment for that of the faculty concerning the merits of a dissertation that was rejected. However, the court did point out that, had it been asked, it would have had authority to pass upon whether the rejection was arbitrary, capricious, or unreasonable (*Edde* v. *Columbia University*, 1957).

### Course Content and Competence of Teacher

Lawsuits have been brought against secondary schools and colleges alleging that poor teaching or weak course content caused injury to students. Such suits are based somewhat on the notion of consumerism; they perceive education as a product purchased by a student as a consumer. These cases largely have been unsuccessful thus far.

At the high school level, for example, parents of a student who graduated from high school with only a fifth-grade reading ability charged the school district with negligence. They claimed the school did not provide the student with basic reading and writing skills, thereby substantially limiting his future income. The case failed because the court found no evidence of a direct causal link between the student's lack of basic skills and the quality of teaching at the school. The court said, "The achievement of literacy in the schools, or its failure, are influenced by a host of factors which affect the pupil subjectively, from outside the formal teaching process, and beyond the control of its ministers" (*Peter Doe* v. *San Francisco Unified School District*, 1976).

At the community college level, a similar complaint was filed by eleven Des Moines Area Community College students. They filed suit alleging the college was negligent in hiring unqualified instructors and in providing inadequate instructional equipment. They sought $42,100 in damages. Their claim was denied by the court, which held that it refused "to expand the concept of negligence to include complaints arising from the area of academic education." The above-mentioned *Peter Doe* case was cited. The ruling stated that to make public schools the target of negligent education suits "would burden them and society beyond calculation" (*Des Moines Register*, March 24, 1977).

At the higher education level, a recent case, which was mentioned earlier, involved a former student who sued a university for breach of contract. She claimed that the content of a required course failed to fit the course description, no tests were given, no grading of work was done, and there was little or no classroom discussion or critique of student's work by the instructor. The student charged that the course was worthless and that she was entitled to a refund of tuition, costs, lost wages, and travel expenses. The university successfully defended itself against these charges (*Ianniello* v. *University of Bridgeport*, 1977).

In none of the above cases was the student able to prove to the court's satisfaction that the institution had not lived up to the terms of the agreement it had made them. In the future, however, cases alleging failure of the institution to meet the educational contract by not providing competent academic services may succeed. The implications of such decisions would be far-reaching.

## Grading Policies

A main concern of students is the institution's grading policy. Every institution should have written policies regarding grading procedures, including the significant issues of academic honesty and the rights and responsibilities of students, faculty, and administration.

Students should be made aware of their responsibilities regarding attending class, completing work on schedule, taking exams, and so forth. They should know what criteria are used by a faculty member to judge student work and assign grades. They should also know what sanctions may be levied against them if they are found to have cheated or plagiarized material. The policy and procedures regarding academic honesty should be clearly enunciated.

Grading policies set forth also should specify the duty of faculty to prepare grades and submit them to the administration on a timely basis for posting on student records. If grades are not completed and turned in, and if a student can show actual damages as a result (not graduating, not getting into graduate school, not getting a particular job), it is possible that the student could sue the faculty member for damages in a breach of contract action. The faculty member might also be subject to discipline or termination by the institution. If a faculty member at a public institution were found to have discriminated in grading, by being influenced by the race, sex, age, or national origin of the student, the faculty member could be liable personally for damages in a civil rights action.

The administration, too, has a responsibility to post grades with reasonable speed and care, and to maintain accurate and confidential records. Students and parents now have specific legal rights to see and to challenge information in a student's file, and to have such material kept confidential. It is important to follow the criteria for student record keeping and access set forth in the Family Educational Rights and Privacy Act of 1974, known as the Buckley Amendment.

Students should have the sense that faculty and administrators are meeting their obligations about grading, just as students are expected to meet theirs. A review and appeal procedure regarding grades should permit students to have their complaints regarding grades handled in a clearly specified way. For instance, in a case involving a student who was given a failing grade based upon the determination that the student had committed plagiarism, the court found that due process was provided to the student by virtue of the procedures made available to him for contesting the penalty imposed upon him by his professor. One member of the court commented that a student was not entitled to have a grade "corrected" by the court (*Hill* v. *Trustees of Indiana University*, 1976).

### Academic Dismissals: Students' Right to Fair Process

*Academic dismissal for marginal performance.* Successful challenges of academic decisions are rare. It would be instructive to examine several of these cases to see what legal grounds and evidence courts have relied upon when overturning an academic decision and fashioning an appropriate remedy. Most of these cases involve unusual circumstances. One case arose when a dispute occurred among the members of a faculty whether a medical student's overall performance had been only "marginal." The student had failed one of his courses in his second year. The court found it significant that the faculty for years had tried unsuccessfully to define what it meant by marginality. Accordingly, the court considered it arbitrary and capricious for the faculty to try to dismiss a student for noncompliance with a standard which the faculty had never been able to define. The court therefore ordered the school to allow the student to continue his medical studies (*Levine* v. *George Washington University School of Medicine and Health Sciences*, 1976).

*Academic dismissal involving stigma on student's future.* When academic dismissal of a student at a public institution is combined with actions that place a stigma on the student so as to foreclose future opportunities, the courts have held that the student has been deprived of a significant constitutional liberty interest and that due process is required. As a matter of equity, private schools also may wish to provide due process to students confronted with such problems.

For example, in *Greenhill* v. *Bailey* (1975), a student was dismissed from the University of Iowa College of Medicine for unacceptable academic performance. In addition to the dismissal, the school notified the Liaison Committee of the Association of American Medical Colleges in Washington,

D.C., that the student lacked "intellectual ability" or had been insufficiently prepared in his course work. The court held that this public medical school had deprived the student of a significant constitutional interest in liberty by imposing a sitgma on him through this characterization of his intellectual ability, as distinguished from his performance. This stigma, the court said, foreclosed his freedom to take advantage of other opportunities. The court likened this deprivation of one's interest in a liberty, by imposing a stigma, to the circumstances found by the U.S. Supreme Court to require due process in *Board of Regents* v. *Roth* (1972) and *Perry* v. *Sindermann* (1972). These two cases involved the question of whether due process was necessary in dismissals of nontenured faculty. They will be discussed further in Chapter 6.

A similar stigma was found in a case known as *Horowitz* v. *Board of Curators of University of Missouri* (1976). There the court found that the student had been dismissed by public medical school officials in such a manner that she would be unable to continue her medical education. Her chances of being employed in a medically related job were damaged severely, also. She had been placed on probation for poor personal hygiene, erratic attendance at clinics, and lack of rapport with patients. She was dismissed for failure to progress. Horowitz told the court that had a hearing been held, she would have explained, for instance, that her goal was to do laboratory medical research, rather than engage in the practice of medicine.

The court held in this case that such a dismissal "imposed . . . a stigma or other disability that foreclosed . . . freedom to take advantage of other employment opportunities" and was a deprivation of liberty which could not be accomplished without notice and a hearing, as in *Board of Regents* v. *Roth* (1972), mentioned earlier. The court in *Horowitz* found that the unrefuted evidence presented to it established that the student had been stigmatized in such a way that she would be unable to continue her medical education, and that her ability to return to employment in any field associated with medicine was greatly impaired. The court ordered the medical school to provide the student with a hearing before a decision-making body, where she would have an opportunity to rebut evidence used as a basis for dismissal and where all other procedural due process rights would be accorded her.

Judicial involvement in academic decisions such as these is unusual, as already indicated. This case led to a request that the U.S. Supreme Court review the *Horowitz* decision. The question presented to the Court is this: Is a medical student in a public institution of higher education entitled, as a consequence of the U.S. Constitution and its Fourteenth Amendment, to a hearing before a decision making body prior to dismissal from a medical school for deficiencies in academic performance? If the Supreme Court agrees to review the *Horowitz* decision, and if it holds that decision hearings are required in such academic dismissals, educational institutions will want to review carefully their current academic review process to bring it into conformity with the review standard set by the Court.

*Academic decision not to readmit.* In a relevant case, a former graduate student was denied, without a hearing, readmission to a doctoral program. She sued, seeking reinstatement and damages for denial of due process, among other things. The court held that a balance had to be struck between the interests of the student and the interests of the university, and it was unrealistic to require a university to conduct hearings prior to every denial of readmission. The court found that ". . . on balance, the plaintiff's procedural rights have been adequately protected by the right available to her, and other dissatisfied applicants for readmission, of an appeal to the Executive Board of the Graduate School *after* denial of readmission" (*Reiner* v. *Bidlack,* 1975).

## Credits and Degrees

*Denial of degree challenged: arbitrary procedure.* A case arose recently at New York University, a private university, where a doctoral candidate alleged that the denial to her of a Ph.D. degree was arbitrary and capricious, and that the doctoral examination proceedings were conducted in a manner contrary to established institutional rules and procedures. The university asked the court to dismiss the complaint, asserting that the court lacked jurisdiction in such a situation. The court agreed that it should not substitute its judgment for that of the university about the candidate's academic qualifications. However, the court found that it had jurisdiction to inquire whether the proceedings of the university denying the degree were conducted in a manner contrary to and in violation of the established rules and procedures of the institution. The court said:

> The doctoral candidate here does not and cannot seek review of the determination made as to the candidate's academic qualifications for the Ph.D. degree. Rather . . . the candidate claimed that the examinations were marred by hostility and abuse and that the decision on her candidacy, which followed the alleged unfair hearing, was arbitrary and capricious. Her claims in this regard, as well as her assertion of discrimination in the conduct of the examination, may or may not be valid. However, it is clear that the issues in this case cannot be determined summarily.

The court denied the university's motion to dismiss the case (*In re Press,* 1976).

*Court order to award a degree. DeMarco* v. *University of Health Sciences: Chicago Medical School* (1976) was a most unusual case. Six weeks before commencement, the medical school discovered that a student apparently had made a misstatement during the admissions process four years earlier. The school thereupon decided not to grant the student a medical degree. The lower court said it was the responsibility of the school to check out such possible misstatements "in the first weeks" after acceptance, and to take action thereon early. To act four years later would be "punitive exactment of extraordinary severity and is morally unjustifiable." Also, the court said, a contract existed between the student and the medical school under terms set forth in the college catalog. That bulletin provided for the issuance of a diploma when the student completed the academic program set forth there. The court found that when evidence establishes that a student has earned a degree, a court has the authority to compel the award of the academic degree. The court said that "withholding a diploma conferring the degree of Doctor of Medicine is a unique injury of which the courts will take cognizance." The lower court ordered the medical school to award the degree of Doctor of Medicine to the student. A state appellate court affirmed the lower court's decision. This case may be "the first time the court has ordered an institution to give a degree when the faculty has stated that, in its opinion, the plaintiff was unqualified to receive it," according to an official of the Association of American Medical Colleges.

*Power to rescind a degree.* The question whether a public university has the power to rescind a degree arose in Virginia in 1975 when it was alleged that a person who had been awarded a bachelor of science degree had altered his grade records while working in the university's computer center. The Virginia attorney general was asked for an opinion on this situation. The opinion indicated that one legal basis on which to rescind would be the principle of contract law: if a party is fraudulently induced to perform a contract, the law allows the defrauded party to rescind the agreement and obtain restoration of the benefit or property conferred by him. Due process notice and hearing would be required, of course, if the university were to decide to rescind the degree. Similarly, a doctoral degree was rescinded by the University of Florida after a due process hearing proved that the doctoral thesis had been largely plagiarized (personal communication, 1977).

Thus, it appears that a public university does have the power to resind a degree if a due process hearing proves it was acquired fraudulently.

## STUDENT LIFE

Student life activities, in particular, call attention to the degree of care for constitutional rights that is required at public institutions. The student's constitutional right is to be balanced against the public institution's right to carry out its educational mission. Private institutions must meet their contractual agreements regarding such activities and discipline, but they are not compelled, except by conscience, to recognize constitutional rights.

## Free Speech and Press

*Freedom of speech: constitutionally permissible regulations at public institutions.* Whether a public educational institution may attempt constitutionally to control individual speech or expression depends upon evidence to show that engaging in the forbidden conduct (1) would materially and substantially interfere with the requirements of appropriate discipline in the operation of the institution, or (2) would create a clear and present danger of imminent and substantive evil. Furthermore, the evidence must show that the forbidden conduct is of an active sort, such as assaults on persons or property, rather than being merely a passive protest, such as the peaceful wearing of a button containing a noninflammatory message.

Each of the cases brought under First Amendment rights essentially has been decided on the particular evidence produced to shift the balance from the individual's right of free expression to the institution's right to carry out its educational mission. It is difficult, therefore, to produce a list of cases whose circumstances can be relied upon at all times and under all circumstances to serve as examples of institutional rules that are reliable examples of either constitutional or impermissible regulation of conduct. A few examples follow.

*Material and substantial interference may be regulated.* Wearing black armbands to protest the war in Vietnam, as mentioned earlier, was found to be a protected mode of free expression in the *Tinker* (1969) case. In that case the Supreme Court held that the school, to justify prohibition of a particular expression of opinion, must be able to show that the regulation is caused by something more than "a mere desire to avoid discomfort and unpleasantness that always accompany an unpopular viewpoint." There must be a "showing that engaging in the forbidden conduct would 'materially and substantially interfere with the requirements of appropriate discipline in the operation of the school.'" The Court found insufficient evidence to show that wearing the armbands "materially or substantially" interfered with the appropriate discipline of the high school involved. Rather, the Court felt that the school officials had established the rule against armbands merely to avoid controversy. The Supreme Court commented favorably on words used by the court below which earlier had ruled for the students, namely that students do not leave their constitutional rights at the schoolhouse door.

Wearing buttons that read "One Man One Vote" and "SNCC" and that did not appear to hamper the regularly scheduled activities of a high school was deemed constitutionally protected and not prohibitable by a school regulation in *Burnside* v. *Byars* (1966).

However, locking doors, assaulting persons, or destroying institutional property usually have been found to constitute material and substantial interference with the normal operation of the institution.

*Clear and present danger may be regulated.* "Clear and present" danger is another, older test to determine whether a public educational institution may attempt to control individual speech or expression. Justice Holmes said, "The rules require that before an utterance can be penalized by government, it must, ordinarily, have occurred in such circumstances or have been of such a nature as to create a clear and present danger," such as shouting "fire" in a crowded theater. That would be an action bringing "substantial evils," and it would be within the power of government to prevent it (*Schenck* v. *United States*, 1919).

Intent is another factor added to the clear and present danger test by Justice Brandeis, who said, "No danger flowing from speech can be deemed clear and present, unless the incidence of the evil apprehended is so imminent that it may befall before there is opportunity for full discussion. If there be time to expose through discussion the falsehood and fallacies, to avert the evil by the processes of education, the remedy to be applied is more speech, not enforced silence" (*Whitney* v. *California*, 1927).

To sum up, Justice Black added, "What finally emerges from the 'clear and present danger' cases is a working principle that the substantive evil must be extremely serious and the degree of imminence extremely high before utterances can be punished" (*Bridges* v. *California*, 1941).

What is a "substantive evil" from which the state educational institution may protect itself? "Destruction or serious injury, political, economic or moral" are mentioned as exercises subject to restriction by Justice Brandeis (*Whitney*, 1927). Interference with "any lawful mission, process, or function of the institution" is another definition (*Buttny* v. *Smiley*, 1968). Again, each case has been decided on the basis of the strength of the particular evidence presented as to the substantive evil.

Examples of actions which have met the test for such "substantive evil," and therefore are subject to regulation and not protected by the First and Fourteenth Amendments, include participating in mass student demonstrations involving unlawful conduct such as the illegal blocking of a public highway and street and the destruction of school property (*Esteban*, 1968).

*Freedom of the student press: forecast rule.* The student press at public institutions is subject to restriction only where officials of the institution can "reasonably forecast substantial disruption or material interference" with school activities (*Tinker*, 1969). Mere apprehension about possible disturbance is not enough. Again, strong evidence must be presented to support an institution's use of the forecast rule to regulate the student press. The evidence must be of almost inevitable substantial disruption or material interference (*Scoville* v. *Board of Education of Joliet Township,* 1969).

*Unconstitutional restriction: rule prohibiting editorial criticism of governor or legislature.* A rule precluding editorial criticism of the governor or state legislature was held unreasonable, as follows: "State school officials cannot infringe on their students' right of free and unrestricted expression as guaranteed by the Constitution of the United States where the exercise of such right does not 'materially and substantially interfere with requirements of appropriate discipline in the operation of the school'" (*Dickey* v. *Alabama State Board of Education,* 1967).

*Unconstitutional restriction: application of state statute forbidding publicly mutilating or casting contempt on the American flag.* In another case, a student publication contained a photo of a burning American flag on its cover. A Maryland statute was cited which forbade publicly mutilating or casting contempt on the flag. The court found this statute unconstitutionally applied here because of a lack of necessary government interests. The court pointed out also that the institution's officials failed to provide evidence sufficient to show that the suppression of this photo was necessary for the maintenance or order and discipline in the school.

In this case, the court set forth what government interests are necessary for the state to restrict individual expression: (1) prevention of incitement of others to commit unlawful acts, (2) prevention of the utterance of words so inflammatory they provide physical retaliation, (3) protection of the sensibilities of others, and (4) assurance of proper respect for the national emblem (*Korn* v. *Elkin,* 1970).

*Permissible constitutional restriction of student press.* An example of permissible restriction of student press followed students' distributing of literature on campus urging students to stand up and fight and calling university officials "despots" and "problem children." These actions were termed by a court "an open exhortation to the students to engage in disorderly and destructive activities." The students had been given notice and hearing and then suspended, which the court upheld. Obviously, what specific words meet the definition of "fighting" words would be expected to change from time to time. The outcome of one of these cases surely would be contingent upon evidence of the current psychological force of the epithets or words used (*Norton* v. *Discipline Committee of East Tennessee State University,* 1969; *Chaplinsky* v. *New Hampshire,* 1942).

## Dress Codes

A dress code for students can be an emotional issue. Good advice would be to assess carefully the need for any dress code that goes beyond the standards of maintaining health, sanitation, and educational order. The courts are divided as to whether other limitations on dress and grooming at public institutions involve constitutional issues. Private institutions, of course, are not constrained by constitutional issues in most circumstances. One case involving hair length at a junior college is particularly instructive. In that case, the court distinguished between students of college age and those of elementary and secondary school age. The decision maintained that in the absence of a demonstration that unusual conditions exist, the regulation of college students' hair length or style is irrelevant to any legitimate college administrative interests. Any such regulation creates an arbitrary classification of college students and violates both the due process and equal protection provisions of the Fourteenth Amendment. The court went on to say that the "college campus is the line of demarcation where the weight of the student's maturity, as compared wtih the institution's role in his education, tips the scale in favor of the individual and marks the boundary of the area within which students' hirsute adornment becomes constitutionally related to the pursuit of educational activities" (*Lansdale* v. *Tyler Junior College,* 1972).

If an institution decides to develop a dress code, successful enforcement of it will depend on at least two things. First, it is important that the code be the result of a cooperative effort of students, parents, administrators, and faculty, so that the result is some sort of consensus. Second, reasonable enforcement rules with some form of due process should help to make the atmosphere of regulation as fair and non-arbitrary as possible.

## Religious Freedom

*Religion and public schools.* Religious activity in public schools is affected by the First Amendment of the U.S. Constitution and by similar provisions in state constitutions. The First Amendment prohibits the establishment of any religion by the government, and provides for the free exercise of religious beliefs.

At the elementary and secondary school level, a common complaint by parents of public school students has been the imposition by school officials of daily religious exercises, including reading from the Bible, recitation of the Lord's Prayer, or distribution of Gideon Bibles and other religious publications on school grounds. These practices somtimes result from state statutes as well as the policies of school boards.

At the higher education level, students at public institutions may seek recognition for student religious groups on the same basis as that sought by other student organizations. Courts generally have taken the position that students are exercising First Amendment rights through such organizations. Threfore, student religious groups usually must be recognized and funded equally with other student groups.

*Test for determining violations of First Amendment.* In 1971, the Supreme Court developed a three-part test for determining whether a challenged state statute violated religious freedom under the First Amendment. In this case, the Court said that a permissible statute would have to meet the following criteria: (1) The statute must have a secular, nonreligious legislative purpose. (2) It must have a "primary effect" that neither advances nor inhibits religion. (3) Its administration must avoid excessive government entanglement with religion, such as requiring substantial monitoring (*Lemon* v. *Kurtzman*, 1971).

*Distribution of Gideon Bibles held unconstitutional.* The matter of the distribution of Gideon Bibles had been handled specifically in an earlier case heard by the New Jersey Supreme Court in 1953. In that case, the court held that the distribution of Gideon Bibles to children in public schools was unconstitutional because it showed a preference by school authorities for one religion over another. The court found it was no defense to say that the Bibles were given only to children whose parents had signed a request slip for them (*Tudor* v. *Board of Education,* 1953).

*Bible readings and recitation of Lord's Prayer held unconstitutional.* The general rule about state statutes requiring religious exercises in public schools is well illustrated by a Supreme Court decision in 1963. In the *Abington* case, the Court held that such a statute was unconstitutional. These exercises consisted of reading verses from the Bible and recitation of the Lord's Prayer. The Court based its ruling on what it saw as a violation of the First Amendment's establishment clause. It rejected the defense's argument that morning devotionals had secular purposes such as "promotion of moral values," or that the Bible was used as a nonreligious moral inspiration or was a reference for teaching secular subjects. The Court held that if the "primary effect" of a challenged state statute is to advance or inhibit religion, then that statute must be deemed an unconstitutional violation of the First Amendment (*Abington Township School District* v. *Schempp,* 1963).

*Inculcation of Christian virtues held unconstitutional.* As recently as 1977 a Florida case concerning religion involved both a state statute and school board policy. The Florida statute in question had directed that public school officials "shall perform the following functions . . . [and] embrace every opportunity to inculcate by precept and example . . . the practice of every

Christian virtue." The Florida court found that such a statute violated the First Amendment's establishment clause, especially because of its mandatory language, "members *shall* perform." School board policy flowing from the statute encouraged daily Bible readings to public school students and permitted a religious group to distribute Gideon Bibles to students on school grounds. The court found these practices in clear violation of the First Amendment establishment and free exercise clauses (*Meltzer* v. *Board of Public Instruction of Orange City, Florida*, 1977).

## Athletics

Athletics at educational institutions is the focus of several legal concerns. Among the most pressing issues is the impact of civil rights laws on both academic and extracurricular athletic programs. These now must be set up in accordance with laws designed to bar discrimination on the basis of physical and mental handicaps, sex, and race, for example.

Another legal concern that has received much less publicity but that deserves close attention is the issue of whether a student has a constitutional property right, invoking due process, to participate in intercollegiate or interscholastic sports.

*Athletics and discrimination.* Handicapped persons are protected now by the recently issued regulations of the Rehabilitation Act of 1973. In effect, this act protects the civil rights of physically and mentally handicapped persons. The Act requires that such persons be "mainstreamed" into academic and other programs of educational institutions. That is, handicapped persons are not to be segregated into separate athletic classes or programs but are to be included in regular ones to the extent possible. Deadlines are set forth in the act indicating by what dates institutions are to accomplish the integration of handicapped persons by modifications in programs and in physical plant and facilities (see Appendix A).

Sex discrimination in sports is barred by Title IX of the Education Amendments of 1972, Appendix A, as well as by a number of state equal rights amendments. The goal of these laws is to provide equal opportunity for females and males to participate in sports activities. Questions have arisen over whether equal opportunity necessarily means equal funding and sexually integrated programs and teams. Title IX reads:

No person in the United States shall, on the basis of sex, be excluded from participation in, be denied the benefits of, or be subjected to discrimination under any educational program or activity receiving Federal financial assistance.

If an institution receives federal financial assistance, all parts of an athletic program are subject to the act, including those funded by student fees, gate receipts, alumni contributions, and so forth.

Institutions at the elementary school level must have complied with Title IX regulations by July 21, 1976. High schools and colleges must comply "as expeditiously as possible," but no later than July 21, 1978. In the meantime, they are to be making changes by use of transition plans.

The aim of Title IX is to require institutions to operate their athletic programs to provide equal opportunity to males and females to participate in the various athletic activities offered. The institution still determines what athletic programs it will provide; but under the Title IX regulations, whatever programs exist are to be available to both males and females. There can be separate male and female athletic departments at an institution, but student participation in the various sports is subject to the equal opportunity regulations implementing the act. Football, as a contact sport, would be exempt from any requirement that there be a coeducational team. Tennis, depending on the interest shown by females, may require funding for females to whatever extent it is funded for males. It could also operate as a coed sport, since it is not a contact sport.

Athletic scholarships, as mentioned earlier, must be awarded on a nondiscriminatory basis.

Sports requiring bodily contact and sports for which teams are selected by competition are exceptions to the nondiscriminatory rule. Among these sports are football, basketball, ice hockey, rugby, wrestling, and boxing. Institutions may offer separate or unitary programs in these sports. But institutions that choose to provide one program for both sexes should be aware that the Title IX regulations specify that if a unitary team does not give a real opportunity to females, because of their different range of ability, separate teams will be required. Under this regulation, many schools have set up separate basketball teams for males and females, for example.

Funding for such separate programs need not be mathematically equal but may reflect the amount of interest and participation shown by females. The test is whether the level of funding truly provides equal opportunity to participate, based upon a showing of interest by female students.

Some states have passed equal rights amendments that have an effect on athletic programs not federally funded that is similar to Title IX. To illustrate, a court struck down a bylaw of an association barring girls from interscholastic athletic competition with boys because it violated the state equal rights amendment. The association maintained that girls generally are weaker and more prone to injury. The court's opinion included the following statement:

If an individual is too weak or injury-prone, he or she may be excluded from competition on that basis. But a girl cannot be excluded solely because of her sex without regard to her relevant qualifications.

This case also determined that the association was involved in state action because its membership was largely public school teams funded by membership fees, public school funds, and fees collected at athletic events between public schools, which occurred within state-owned and state-supported facilities (*Commonwealth of Pennsylvania* v. *Pennsylvania Interscholastic Association*, 1975).

Similar state action (that is, children from public schools funded by public school funds playing on government-owned property) was found in *Fortin* v. *Darlington Little League, Inc.* (1955).

*Constitutional right to opportunity to participate in athletics.* Do students have a constitutional right to participate in athletics at a public institution? If so, who supplies the rules for due process, the institution or the National Collegiate Athletics Association (NCAA)? Courts have been asked to help clarify this situation, but their decisions have not been altogether consistent or helpful.

In one case, three basketball players had been accused of infractions of NCAA rules, but they were cleared of the charges after university due process hearings. The university refused to suspend the players. The NCAA thereupon imposed a probation on all the university's athletic teams because of the university's refusal to suspend.

The court held in this case that the opportunity to participate in intercollegiate basketball was a property right entitled to due process guarantees. Two reasons were given by the court for this decision: first, that such participation can lead in some situations to a very remunerative professional basketball career; and second, that intercollegiate competition is an important part of the student athlete's educational experience. Therefore, the lower court ordered the NCAA to lift its probation on the teams. Later, however, an appeals court reversed this decision without ruling on the matter of a constitutional right to participate in athletics (*Regents of University of Minnesota* v. *National Collegiate Athletics Association*, 1976).

A court decision that rejected the "constitutional right to participate" theory involves the University of Denver. There the NCAA believed the university had knowledge of a student's ineligibility but did not act on that fact in accordance with NCAA rules. The NCAA imposed sanctions, and the university and several students asked the court to enjoin or lift those sanctions.

The court held that the students' interest in participation in intercollegiate athletics did not reach the level of a constitutionally protected property right or liberty right sufficient to invoke due process guarantees. However, the court said that a hearing by NCAA was required before the university could be sanctioned on NCAA's claim that the university knew of a student's ineligibility (*Colorado Seminary [University of Denver]* v. *National Collegiate Athletic Association,* 1976).

Generally, courts have taken the view that a student has no right to a hearing on a question of eligibility, as in a case involving a student who accepted financial aid in excess of the amount allowed by the NCAA. "It is undisputed that the NCAA has the only authority over eligibility decisions and that its rules do not provide for a hearing" such as the student requested. A university is "compelled to follow NCAA's instruction to declare him ineligible or lose its own membership in the NCAA" (*Southern Methodist University* v. *Smith,* 1974).

The previously mentioned University of Denver case may imply that the NCAA may be required to afford the institution a hearing before terminating its membership, even if no hearing was required for the student.

### Governance

In Wisconsin, a state statute provided that students at each state institution of higher education shall have the right to organize themselves in the manner they determine and to select their representatives to participate in institutional governance. The Supreme Court of Wisconsin held that when that statute became effective the chancellor and the board of regents of the University of Wisconsin system lost authority to appoint student representatives to university committees. Students then became entitled to elect their own representatives to committees, and the student association had to be recognized as the organized representative of the students. (*Student Association of the University of Wisconsin-Milwaukee* v. *Baum,* 1976).

### Unauthorized Contracts Made by Students

A very common problem is that of the student who is unauthorized to do so but attempts to make a contract that is binding on the institution. As was mentioned earlier in Chapter 2, the unauthorized student is liable personally in such situations. The institution is bound only if it acquiesces to the contract later or ratifies it by accepting the benefits from it. If an unauthorized student signs a contract for laboratory equipment and the institution accepts and uses the equipment, the institution is liable. Student handbooks or other policy publications should delineate in detail what authority students have.

## Student Organizations

Student organizations such as homosexual organizations and student public interest research groups have been the subject of much litigation in recent years, particularly as to their right to be recognized and funded as are other student groups. Single-sex groups such as sororities, fraternities, Scouts, and Camp Fire groups have raised questions relating to the non-sex discrimination goals of Title IX. Religious worship as a student activity has been challenged when services were held by a religious group in a common area in a university dormitory. Student groups also must be concerned with how to accommodate physically and mentally handicapped students in their organizations.

There is emerging a certain *deja vu* as social fraternities and sororities once again appear at public institutions. Now, however, where "Greeks" are re-establishing organizations, the rules have changed to require nondiscriminatory operation of the groups.

*Gay liberation student groups.* Gay liberation student groups usually become involved in litigation when they seek to be recognized by an institution as a formal student organization in order to become eligible to use the institution's facilities or student fees for their business and social meetings. A number of institutions have attempted to refuse to recognize gay liberation groups. The reasons for such refusal are wide-ranging. Generally, the only successful refusals to recognize homosexual groups have been at private institutions.

"Protecting the campus environment from what the board has determined to be detrimental and anti-social influences" was the defense successfully given by Virginia Commonwealth University to a lower court in 1975 for its refusal to recognize a student homosexual group. Upon appeal to a higher court, however, that reason was deemed insufficient to overcome the First Amendment right of students to decide for themselves whether or not to join an organization. The university was ordered to recognize the homosexual organization (*Gay Alliance of Students* v. *Mathews*, 1976).

One temporarily successful refusal of formal recognition of a student homosexual group occurred in Missouri, where homosexual acts are illegal. It was premised on protecting students from an "association . . . likely to incite, promote and result in acts contrary and in violation of the sodomy statute of the State of Missouri." There the court discussed the problem of balancing the students' right to freedom of association against the legitimate interest of the university in maintaining order and decorum on campus. The court pointed out that an earlier case (*Healy* v. *James*, 1972) had enunciated the heavy burden of proof required here:

Certainly it is the law that the University, acting here as an instrument of the State, has no right to restrict speech or association "simply because it finds the views expressed to be abhorrent."

The court said that the First Amendment does not require recognition of a student organization that, as found from the evidence, is likely to promote illegal acts. The equal protection clause, said the court, was not meant to protect "a group presenting a clear and present danger of violation of the criminal laws of a state by comparing such a group with other groups who do not present that danger." This opinion has been overturned on the ground that mere membership in such a group need not lead inevitably to the commission of illegal acts (*Gay Lib* v. *University of Missouri*, 1977).

Attempts also have been made by universities to limit the officially recognized activities of student homosexual groups to nonsocial lectures, discussions, and business meetings. The response to such attempts by courts are illustrated by a case involving the University of New Hampshire. There the federal circuit court of appeals held that denying an officially recognized student group the use of university facilities for social functions violated the First Amendment. The court said the university could not treat various student organizations differentially (*University of New Hampshire* v. *April*, 1975).

*Student-funded group legal services (GLSs) and public interest research groups (PIRGs).* Legal services by and for students are a relatively new development in many institutions. These activities are quite separate from legal aid clinics that are part of the teaching program of a law school.

Two principal kinds of student legal service groups can be distinguished. The first is an organization which provides legal counseling to students, informing them of their rights and sometimes representing them in litigation. Examples of such a group's activities are help with landlord-tenant problems, traffic arrests, drug arrests, and complaints about consumer products.

The second is a group such as a public interest research group (PIRG) that targets a particular community or national issue, such as air pollution, and directs its energies toward informing and persuading the public and perhaps even litigating on the public's behalf. A third kind of group might be a combination of the first two.

Questions have been raised about whether student fees can be used to provide such services or litigate on behalf of issues or students, individually or in class actions. There appear to be no settled answers yet to these questions, as will be seen from recent cases.

Student-funded public interest research groups wishing to finance litigation as part of their activities have asserted First Amendment rights for protection. The Maryland Public Interest Research Group (MARYPIRG), an approved student organization at the University of Maryland, wanted to use funds appropriated by the student government to pay litigation expenses. The board of regents objected to this use of student fees. PIRG alleged that such objection abridged its right under the First Amendment to petition the government for redress of grievances. The board of regents argued that a state law would be violated if the funds were used in this way, but the court found no evidence that such a state law existed. The court then concluded that PIRG was entitled to an order enjoining the university from prohibiting or restricting the use by PIRG of student activity funds for litigation activities. The court said that litigation that MARYPIRG conducts to protect its interests as an organization or to enable it to gather information relating to public interest concerns affecting students at the campus was protected by the First Amendment (*Maryland Public Interest Research Group* v. *Elkins*, 1976). This ruling was reversed later by an appellate court which found that there was a compelling state interest sufficient to justify an exception to the First Amendment. The appellate court pointed out that MARYPIRG still would be able to litigate but would have to use non-state monies such as gifts and contributions to finance the litigation (*MARYPIRG* v. *Elkins*, 1977).

Several state attorneys general have given negative legal opinions on whether providing legal counseling and litigating services to students at a public university is a permissible use of public funds (Ohio, 1976) or of student fees (Connecticut, 1976). The negative opinions in these two instances are based respectively on arguments as follows: that a legal aid service cannot "be said to be reasonably incidental to the University's program of higher education," and that such legal advice "is so enmeshed with the private rights of the individual as not to be an activity for the benefit of the student body."

The possible use of student funds for litigation raises a number of thorny legal questions. For example, student fees may finance litigation against the institution itself, against persons and businesses in the community, or against various government officials. All that is clear now is that many more challenges will arise over permissible functions of student legal services groups before reliable guidelines are developed.

*Single-sex student organizations as affected by Title IX.* Institutions that receive federal financial assistance should be aware that single-sex student groups may be in violation of Title IX of the Education Amendments of 1972. Title IX requires that educational programs or activities receiving federal financial assistance shall be open to both females and males.

Exemptions have been provided for certain groups, such as social fraternities and sororities at the college level, which are exempt from taxation under IRS Section 501(a), Boy Scouts, Girl Scouts, Camp Fire Girls, YMCA,

YWCA, and certain other specifically designated voluntary youth organizations. Even these groups, however, are limited as to the kinds of activities they may conduct that exclude people of the other sex. For example, if any of these organizations conduct federally supported educational programs open to non-members, these programs must be operated in a nondiscriminatory manner. Father-son and mother-daughter activities are exempt, but if such activities are provided for students of one sex, "opportunities for reasonably comparable activities shall be provided for students of the other sex." Boys' State, Girls' State, Boys' Nation, and Girls' Nation conferences are exempt. Scholarships to postsecondary institutions won at beauty contests or similar competitions open only to one sex are exempt, provided other nondiscrimination federal laws are observed.

Honorary fraternities and sororities, formerly open only to males or females, are required now under Title IX to be open to both sexes. The reasoning behind this requirement is that membership in these honorary groups may give members of such groups special consideration when they apply for admission to institutions of higher education, for financial aid, or for other emoluments. Such membership also may serve as an additional qualification when applying for employment. Therefore, failing to be proposed for membership in these honorary groups because of sex could lead to one's not being considered for education or employment on an equal basis with those who are members of the eligible sex. In that regard, it is noteworthy that Title IX also requires that admissions officers, placement officers, and employers no longer take into consideration, or use as criteria, membership in honorary groups open only to one sex.

A number of public institutions have taken a middle position with regard to permitting national social sororities and fraternities and other national organizations to operate on their campuses. For example, some institutions have stipulated that all nationally affiliated student organizations, not just sororities and fraternities, must file a statement with the principal or campus president certifying that the organization does not discriminate regarding race, creed, national origin, sex, age, or disability. If the fraternity or sorority is affiliated with a national group, it too must meet the requirements of nondiscrimination. On the other hand, if it is merely a local social group, it may limit its membership to individuals of one sex. But it should be emphasized again that any such groups receiving federal funds for any activities come within the restrictions of Title IX.

*Required membership in student organizations.* "Students have a constitutionally protected right to not associate with any group, just as they enjoy a concomitant right to be associated with any group of their choice." So said the court in a case in which students were required to become members of the Associated Students of the University of Washington. The student plaintiffs charged that this student group did not represent their political viewpoints and that they should not be forced to be members of that group merely because a portion of the mandatory student fees was allocated to it. In this case, the court held that the students could not be compelled to be members of the association. While students may have to pay mandatory student fees to support student groups, they may not be required to become members of a particular student organization (*Good* v. *Associated Students of the University of Washington*, 1975).

*Student religious groups at higher education institutions.* Student groups that engage in religious activities at public higher education institutions claim a First Amendment right to freedom of religion as the basis for their protection, and rely as well upon the First Amendment establishment clause. A case arose out of a 1971 university directive which stipulated that "recognized [religious] groups may, upon proper registration, use space in the Student Center and other buildings for business meetings and social programs but not for worship services." A religious group violated this rule by holding worship services in a common area of a university dormitory provided for general student use. The university sought court enforcement of its rule. The students claimed the rule violated the First Amendment's establishment clause and right to freedom of religion. A lower court upheld the university rule, but a higher court struck it down. The higher court said that although the rule was "neutral," since it did not "advance" or "promote" religion, it placed a Constitutional burden on the free exercise of religion. Furthermore, the university showed no compelling state interest to justify the rule. The U.S. Supreme Court has been asked to review this case (*Keegan* v. *University of Delaware*, 1975).

### Dormitories

*Mandatory residence in dorms.* Institutions often require that certain students live in dormitories. There are several reasons for this requirement. One is an effort by an institution to provide a learning and living experience for the student which may help orient the student to academic study habits. Another quite different reason is to assure some level of net income from dormitory facilities to pay for the loans or bonds that financed the construction of such facilities, the dorms having been built in the first place to ensure adequate housing for students who wish to attend the institution.

Not all students are required to live in dorms. Often the requirement is applicable only to boarding school or undergraduate students relatively new to academic life, such as freshmen and sophomores. Even within this group, exceptions may be made for married students, students living in fraternity or sorority houses, students commuting from their parents' homes, students over a stated age, and veterans, among others.

Challenges to mandatory residence rules usually are unsuccessful. During the 1960s a general surge of independence began among college and university students. One manifestation of this was a reaction against mandatory residence requirements. The grounds used by students to mount a legal challenge to these rules at public schools included the constitutional rights of privacy or equal protection of law. These challenges have been unsuccessful in the great majority of cases.

At private schools, of course, if the terms of the contract provide that a student shall live in a dormitory, courts assume the student willingly accepted that requirement when he or she signed the contract of enrollment. This principle applies at private elementary and secondary schools as well.

A recent case at a public institution illustrates a prevailing view of the requirement that certain students live on campus. In this case, the court held that the state university's rule that all unmarried freshman and sophomore students (with stated exceptions) must live in the dorms does not deny these students their constitutional rights to equal protection of law or to privacy. The court found the regulation was directed toward a permissible state objective, which was reasonable rather than arbitrary. The court said that "the interest in living precisely where one chooses is not fundamental within our constitutional scheme." The student plaintiffs appealed this case to the U.S. Supreme Court, which denied their appeal (*Prostrollo* v. *University of South Dakota*, 1974).

*Prohibition against visitation in dorms by persons of the opposite sex.* Is the right to visitation by persons of the opposite sex protected by the U.S. Constitution or by an equal rights amendment to a state constitution? No, said the New Mexico Supreme Court in 1975.

The New Mexico case involved a regulation at New Mexico State University prohibiting persons of the opposite sex from visiting each other's rooms in residence halls. Students brought suit to prohibit members of the board of regents from enforcing the regulation on the grounds that it impinged upon the students' rights of free association and privacy; violated their right to enjoy life and seek happiness, as guaranteed by the state constitution; offended the equal rights amendment to the state constitution; and was arbitrary and unreasonable. The state supreme court affirmed the decision of the trial court, which dismissed the students' complaint, and said:

> Even assuming that the right of association is being infringed by the challenged regulation, such right, emanating from the First Amendment, is not absolute. Its exercise, as is the exercise of express First

Amendment rights, is subject to some regulation as to time and places. The power to control, manage and govern the University is vested in the Regents. An inherent part of that power is that of requiring students to adhere to generally accepted standards of conduct.

We are unwilling to hold that the Regents, who have the power and duty to enact and enforce reasonable rules and regulations for the conduct of the University, have infringed upon the plaintiffs' constitutionally protected rights. . . . We hold, as did the District Court, that the regulation is reasonable, serves legitimate educational purposes, and promotes the welfare of the students at the University (*Futrell* v. *Ahrens*, 1975).

*May a state university promulgate a rule forbidding children from living in dormitories set aside for married students?* Yes, according to a federal court of appeals. The State University of New York at Stony Brook had dormitory suites set aside for married students, but children were forbidden to live in the suites. The married students claimed this rule was unconstitutional and was not related to any college goal. A lower court agreed with the married students. However, a federal court of appeals reversed the lower court's decision, saying that "the right to housing is not a fundamental interest that would require the more stringent compelling state interest test" over the actual test used. That test was the "limited scrutiny standard," which requires that a statutory discrimination be set aside only if no set of facts can be adduced which reasonably may be conceived to justify it (*Bynes* v. *Toll*, 1975).

### Security

*Search and seizure.* In general, the rule governing searches and seizures can be briefly stated as follows:

1. Inspections for safety and health purposes by officials of the institution are permissible.
2. Searches and seizures involving drugs, stolen goods, or for other purposes by institutional officials without consent of the student are illegal, except in emergencies. Evidence so seized is admissible in an institution's disciplinary proceedings, although it is not usually admissible in governmental criminal proceedings.
3. Searches and seizures by police without a search warrant are illegal, except where a bona fide emergency exists; or where the search is incident to a lawful arrest; or where the search is with legitimate consent; or where the searcher is a private party and not the police. Again, evidence seized may not be used in criminal proceedings, but may be admitted in an institution's disciplinary proceedings.

Students generally rely upon the Fourth Amendment to the U.S. Constitution for protection against search and seizure of themselves or their property.

The Fourth Amendment provides that

The right of people to be secure in their persons, houses, papers, and effects, against unreasonable searches and seizures, shall not be violated, and no warrants shall issue, but upon probable cause. . . .

This Constitutional language has at least three kinds of protection within it: first, protection against searches and seizures of persons or property; second, protection against self-incrimination; and third, protection of one's right to privacy.

The Fourth Amendment provides significant protection for persons by placing a judge or magistrate between them and the police. Law enforcement officers are required to propose the search to a judge, who then decides— relying on standards of reasonableness, probable cause, and necessity— whether there is probable cause supporting the request for the proposed search (*Aguilar* v. *Texas*, 1964). But the police do not require a judge's approval for a search if the factual situation falls within one of the exceptions noted earlier, that is, if the police search is with legitimate consent (*Bumper* v. *North Carolina*, 1968), or it is incident to a lawful arrest (*United States* v. *Jeffers*, 1951), or an emergency exists (*McDonald* v. *United States*, 1951).

The balance to be struck in matters of search and seizure of students and their property is viewed generally to be between the student's constitutional right to be free from ureasonable searches and seizures and the institution's right to make reasonable rules and regulations to maintain order and discipline.

In the past, the greater weight usually rested with the institution. Today, a trend exists toward placing greater importance on students' rights. One factor which has added to this trend is the new significance given by courts to a person's right of privacy under the Fourth Amendment. Furthermore, the purpose for which the seized property will be used is also of significance—that is, whether the property will be used at a school disciplinary hearing or at a governmental criminal proceeding.

Courts have been asked many times to rule on the legality of searches of dormitory rooms. The searches have involved locating stolen property, searching for illegal drugs, or checking rooms for health hazards. In general, the rule is that a search must be reasonable to be constitutionally valid, as in the case of *Picha* v. *Wilgos* (1976). To test the reasonableness of the search, the court must balance the "need to search against the invasion which the search entails" (*Camara* v. *Municipal Court*, 1967). A quite recent court decision found that the need to search must be connected to the institution's functioning as an educational institution for the search to be considered reasonable (*Morale* v. *Grigel*, 1976).

In the *Morale* case, a room-to-room search of a men's dormitory was conducted by a head resident and an assistant, both state university employees, in a search for a stolen stereo. They testified that if a student was in his room, they asked permission to search. But if the student was not there, they opened his door with a passkey.

One particular student became an object of suspicion. He did not give formal permission for the search, but assumed that they had authority to search his room. The stolen property was not found there but, still believing this student to be guilty, they conducted further searches of the room. Marijuana seeds were found during one such search, and the seeds and a pipe were confiscated. A disciplinary hearing was held which led to the student's suspension from the university. The student maintained that the marijuana seized was the product of an illegal search, and that the evidence of his admission of ownership of the seeds should have been excluded from the college disciplinary hearing.

The court held that the search was indeed illegal, saying "the dormitory room is a student's home away from home and the Fourth Amendment by its very terms guarantees this." However, the court also held that the exclusionary rule, which prohibits the use of material found in the course of an illegal search in criminal proceedings, does not apply in college disciplinary proceedings. Therefore, the court found that the evidence produced by the illegal search was admissible in the disciplinary proceedings and that the student had been accorded due process.

It is also noteworthy that in the *Morale* case the court observed that administrative checks of students' rooms for health hazards are permissible in keeping with an institution's interest in maintaining its physical plant and the health of its students, as are searches in emergencies. However, the court said that searches for stolen goods serve no legitimate purpose of the university (*Morale*, 1976).

A search by state college officials was held illegal and resulting evidence not admissible in a disciplinary hearing. The college had regulations, stated as a blanket authorization in the dormitory room rental contract, permitting college officials to search dormitory rooms without search warrants. In a search of the rooms of five students, college officials found a substance alleged to be marijuana. The students, fearing a college disciplinary hearing, filed a civil rights suit in a federal court claiming violation of their Fourth Amendment rights and challenging the validity of the regulations and the search. The court found in favor of the students, and held that

- adult college students have the same interest in the privacy of their dorm rooms as any adult has in the privacy of his house, dwelling or lodging, for Fourth Amendment purposes.
- a blanket authorization in a student's contract for the rental of his dormitory room does not waive his Fourth Amendment rights.
- a college may not search dormitory rooms for contraband without probable cause and, unless there is an emergency, without a warrant.
- evidence seized in illegal searches may not be used in college disciplinary proceedings.

The judge said that a search warrant should have been sought by officials if they had, as they claim, "reasonable cause to believe" that students were violating college regulations or general laws (*Smyth* v. *Lubbers*, 1975).

An Arizona state court, on the other hand, held just the opposite in a case in which a student was convicted of possession of marijuana on the basis of the discovery and seizure of marijuana by student advisors making a routine room inspection. The court found no unlawful search had taken place, and that the student advisors were not "tainted with the degree of governmental authority which will invoke the Fourth Amendment." Moreover, these student advisors had given university and law enforcement officials entry to the student's room. The court took the position that seizure by these persons did not constitute a search because the marijuana and pipe were then out in plain sight. The court said that "the right of privacy protected by the Fourth Amendment does not include freedom from reasonable inspection of a school-operated dormitory by school officials" (*State* v. *Kappes*, 1976).

*Occupation of buildings.* Since the 1960s, there have been many instances of students using the occupation of buildings as a method of protesting institutional policies and decisions. Courts have been asked to rule on where the balance lies in situations in which a student's right to free expression clashes with an institution's right to maintain reasonable discipline in the conduct of the educational enterprise. Some cases brought to the courts have been tests of state statutes which were passed as a response to the violence and disruption resulting from occupations of buildings.

The New Mexico legislature passed a law providing that no person shall wilfully refuse or fail to leave a state university building upon the request of the university's chief administrative officer if that person is committing or threatening to commit a disruptive act. The state court of appeals held the statute valid, and the U.S. Supreme Court denied an appeal of that ruling.

The state court reasoned that there was "significant government interest in the control of campus disturbances" to warrant such legislation. The court also said that the language of the state statute provided reasonable time, place, and manner regulations. In instances of student expression via leaflets, speeches, and other demonstrations, the court upheld a regulation which permits free expression, even though it limits absolute freedom by regulating time, place, and manner. The New Mexico statute was found not to be unconstitutionally vague or overbroad on its face and not unconstitutional in delegating judicial power without adequate standards.

*Threats to life.* Institutions sometimes are faced with the most serious kind of security problem, that is, situations that pose a threat to life. Two recent cases involving death and severe injury of students come to mind immediately, namely the very serious incidents at Kent State and at Jackson State. Both cases are complicated by a dispute over the events that led up to the firing of weapons by government officials. In both incidents, the officials were able finally to allege successfully that they were fired upon or attacked by dangerous missiles thrown at them first, so that the shots they fired were in self defense. Therefore they asserted that their actions fell within the doctrine of qualified executive immunity as enunciated by the U.S. Supreme Court. The Jackson State case is known as *Burton* v. *Waller* (1974). It resulted in a verdict in favor of the government officials. However, the Kent State case, known as *Scheuer* v. *Rhodes* (1975), is being reheard. The original verdict was in favor of the officials. It will be some time before the outcome of the new trial is known.

In a different type of case, a California court was asked to decide a question involving confidential information in the possession of a university health service psychologist. A student under the care of the psychologist threatened to kill his former girlfriend, another student, as soon as she returned to the campus from a holiday. The psychologist believed the student patient was serious in his intent and referred the information to his superior, a university psychiatrist. The intended victim was not notified of the possible danger. The psychiatrist informed campus police, who apprehended the student. However, after questioning him briefly, the campus police released him. When his former girlfriend returned to campus, he killed her just as he had said he would.

The murder victim's parents sued the university, claiming that university officials should have informed them or the girl of the threats. The university responded that the doctor-patient relationship prevented the university from informing either the family or the girl. The university felt it had done its duty by having the student apprehended and questioned by the campus police. The court ruled that in a situation in which a doctor has a reasonable belief that a patient will carry out such a threat against a clearly identified individual, the normal confidential relationship between the doctor and patient becomes subservient to the greater public interest in protecting the life of the person in danger. In other words, a doctor who believes an identified person is in current danger has a duty to warn the person. This is one of the few known instances of a court decision not upholding the traditional confidentiality of the doctor-patient relationship (*Tarasoff* v. *University of California, Berkeley,* California Supreme Court, July 1, 1976).

## Discipline

As pointed out earlier, public institutions are required by the Constitution to provide due process when students are threatened with penalties such as suspensions and expulsions. Private institutions are not obligated to provide due process by the U.S. Constitution, but they may be required to do so by state statutes or their own written policies or handbooks. Private institutions may also choose to provide due process voluntarily for reasons of pedagogy or equity.

*Range of penalties.* Disciplinary penalties range from expulsion from the institution through suspensions, involuntary transfers, benching, study halls, and corporal punishment. The courts have recognized a difference in severity between penalties that remove a student from the educational setting entirely, such as expulsions or suspensions, and those that move a student to another part of the institution's environment, such as a study hall or special resource room. Furthermore, corporal punishment is treated by courts in a special fashion, as is the penalty of loss of federal financial aid by a student involved in violence against the institution.

*Penalty of suspensions of ten days or less requires due process.* In 1975, the Supreme Court set the following as minimal due process involving suspensions of ten days or less at public institutions: (1) The student must be given oral or written notice of the charges against him or her. (2) If the student denies the charges, an explanation of the evidence the authorities have must be given the student, as well as an opportunity to present his or her version of what happened. (3) Notice and hearing should precede suspension, except in emergencies involving danger to persons or property or disruption of the academic process, in which case the student may be removed immediately from school and a hearing follow within a reasonable time (*Goss* v. *Lopez,* 1975).

*Penalty of involuntary transfer requires due process.* One form of disciplinary sanction used by public institutions is the transfer of a student from one school to another. A recent case in Pennsylvania has held that a public school district's involuntary transfer of students from one school to another for disciplinary reasons involves significant property and liberty rights that cannot be denied without application of due process procedural safeguards. The court found that "disciplinary transfers bear a stigma of punishment . . . [and] any disruption of a primary or secondary education is a loss of educational benefits and opportunities. Realistically, many if not most students would consider a short suspension a less drastic form of punishment than an involuntary transfer" (*Evertt* v. *Marcase*, 1977).

The *Everett* case is instructive in that the parties to the suit agreed to a consent decree which would set forth minimum due process standards for a *Goss*-type hearing in situations involving lateral disciplinary transfers, as follows:

1. Pupils must be given some kind of notice and hearing.

2. Parents may bring to the hearing a representative of their choice who may be an attorney. However, there is no constitutional right to legal counsel which would permit indigent parents to obtain appointed counsel at public expense.

3. "The School Board shall have the right to designate the place and personnel to conduct the hearings, provided no principal or other person recommending a lateral transfer, nor anyone under their supervision, shall serve as a hearing officer." The court pointed out that the hearing officer could be a superior of the principal, for example someone from the school superintendent's office.

4. Due process in this situation shall consist of two steps. The first step is the informal hearing before the principal, who has the authority to order a lateral transfer. The second step, should such transfer be ordered, is a formal hearing before an appropriate hearing officer, such as a representative from the superintendent's office. The court found that due process does not require a third-step hearing or right of appeal.

5. "A transfer prior to final hearing, in the absence of an emergency situation, would appear to violate the due process prescribed in *Goss*-type suspensions." Accordingly, the court found a pupil has a right to continue attending a school pending final determination of the transfer.

*Penalty of prohibiting federal financial aid to students who forcibly disrupt institutions of higher education.* In 1975, Congress added a provision to the annual HEW appropriation which prohibits the payment of federal money to anyone "who has engaged in conduct on or after August 1, 1969 which involved the use of . . . force or the threat of force or the seizure of property under the control of an institution of higher education, to require or prevent the faculty, administrative officials, or students in such an institution from engaging in their duties or pursuing their studies at such institutions."

Section 407 of this legislation provides that deprivation of financial aid in such cases must be preceded by notice and an opportunity for a hearing. Administrators are advised to take care that appropriate notice and hearing procedures are in place at their institutions.

It is not enough that students are given a hearing before a college student conduct board for alleged misconduct. Students are entitled to notice that the matter of possible loss of financial aid is an issue, and the hearing itself must take place before an official body which has authority to terminate the financial aid.

A case in point involved students who occupied a college ROTC building and obstructed access to files and work areas by ROTC faculty and staff. Campus police removed the students. Hearings were held by the student conduct board, and each student was given disciplinary probation for one semester, as recommended by the institution's officials. The officials subsequently concluded that the students were no longer eligible for federal financial aid. However, the students alleged they had been deprived of the financial aid without the due process required by the congressional legislation. A three-judge federal court agreed, holding that a student conduct board which does not have authority to terminate such aid, and which held its hearing on student misconduct prior to notice that the aid might be terminated, is not a forum that meets due process requirements (*Corr* v. *Mattheis*, 1976).

## Placement Services for Students

Placement and career counseling have been affected substantially by equal opportunity and nondiscrimination laws. Successful court challenges have eliminated such practices as allowing recruiters to limit their interviews to males only or to whites only, or in other ways which violate Title VI, Title VII, Title IX, Executive Order No. 4, the Rehabilitation Act, or other relevant federal or state laws. A number of the federal statutes are discussed in Appendix A.

In *McDonald* v. *General Mills* (1974), a state college was ordered by a federal district court in California to be made a party to a sex discrimination suit brought by a female student against several business firms, because she utilized the college placement service in attempting to find a job. The graduate placement center had set up interviews and prepared the forms with "male/female" preferences. The suit was filed under Title VII of the 1964 Civil Rights Act, which prohibits unlawful employment practices by employers and employment agencies.

In *Kaplowitz* v. *University of Chicago* (1974), also under Title VII of the 1964 Civil Rights Act, a district court found that a law school's placement office falls within the statutory definition of "employment agency." In that case, the court held that the law school need not determine *beforehand* whether a recruiting law firm discriminates.

## RECOMMENDATIONS

The way in which an institution relates to its students is in itself a learning experience for students. Therefore, many institutions have used the daily operation of the institution as an opportunity to teach by setting exemplary behavior patterns. For example, the process of drawing up guidelines for responsible academic and student life behavior could involve participation by students, parents, faculty, and administrators, as well as other education officials. In this way, students may be exposed to the viewpoints of various constituencies within the educational institution. When regulations finally are adopted, the students will have had a chance to learn why each rule was formulated and why a certain sanction was set for its violation. They will also know what their rights are to due process, if appropriate. There is no question that an institution has the right to formulate rules in order that it may carry on its function according to certain standards and without substantial disruption.

### Academic Life of Students

A written academic code is essential. It should indicate what the institution expects with regard to student academic rights and responsibilities, including what constitutes unacceptable academic performance and behavior. It should state what penalties may be imposed when such behavior occurs, and what review procedures are available. It is also essential that the written document be disseminated to all students and other involved persons. The student code may cover requirements for class attendance, meeting course requirements, and plagiarism or cheating. A number of institutions have also written a similar document regarding faculty and administrators. The faculty code may provide, for instance, that faculty inform students of the grading criteria.

### Student Life

A student life code of behavior similar to the student academic code mentioned earlier should be developed. The differing legal rights of students at public and private institutions should be taken into account, particularly any constitutional rights. Much of what is suggested below applies principally to public institutions; private institutions may wish to follow along for educational rather than legal reasons.

*Free speech and press.* The student life code should contain rules about student publications, be they officially sponsored or "underground" publications. All student publications may be regulated as to the manner, method, time, and place of distribution. Effective supervision of official publications should include guidelines for students as to what may be considered coverage that would "materially and substantially disrupt the institution's educational activities." Guidelines for libel and obscenity may be included as well. If a publication is to be subjected to official review prior to official publication, very great care must be taken to set forth who shall be the reviewer, what time limits are set for review, and what appeal is possible from a decision not to permit publication of particular material. If prior restraint is not exercised and material is printed which is libelous, obscene, or causes material and substantial disruption of the intitution's activities, the students involved may be subject to institutional sanctions of various kinds. If the institution permits commercial advertising in its official publications, it should know in advance what its responsibility will be to accept political advertising.

Outside speakers may be regulated by requirements that the institution be notified in advance and that the speakers adhere to the time, place, and manner rules for such activities. If approval is to be required in advance, the institution must provide a process of immediate reveiw of any unfavorable decisions.

*Student religious activity.* Student religious groups are to be treated generally in the same fashion as other extracurricular student organizations. Students whose religious beliefs prevent them from taking part in patriotic activities such as saluting the flag should be excused from such observances. Public institutions may not permit prayers, Bible readings, or distribution of Bibles on their property during regular hours.

*Athletics.* Athletic programs probably would benefit from review and monitoring in order to be sure that students are not being discriminated against on the basis of handicap, sex, race, and the other proscribed classifications. Equal opportunity to participate, rather than precisely equal funding, appears to be a key element. Sex discrimination at the elementary school level should have ben eliminated by July 21, 1976. High schools and colleges have a deadline of July 21, 1978, for the elimination of sex discrimination in athletics.

*Governance.* Institutions should think carefully about students participating in institutional governance. It is important that once participation is permitted, the institution follow its own policies regarding it. Great advantage to students and the institution can result from student participation in institutional governance. However, if the institution deals halfheartedly and reluctantly with student governance committee members, the students may learn the opposite of what the institution hopes they might learn.

*Student organizations.* Written regulations regarding student organizations are suggested. They should set forth how an organization should seek official recognition, what its responsibilities are thereafter, and what sanctions may be levied if student organization regulations are violated. At public institutions, care must be taken that all student organizations are treated alike. At private institutions, equal treatment must be provided depending upon coverage of the institution by the various equal opportunity laws.

*Dormitory life.* Successful regulation of dorm life requires strong support of students. Therefore, student participation in developing the rules can be of enormous assistance in creating a consensus as to what kind of environment is to exist. Fair procedures for hearing complaints and for levying sanctions are requisite.

*Security.* A basic decision to be made by the institution is whether to set up an organization of peace officers or of police officers. The institution also needs to know what laws apply to it regarding searches and seizures, dangerous conduct, and ability to make arrests. It is imperative that students be aware in advance of how the institution's security system operates. Legal counsel is essential in setting up a security organization.

*Discipline.* As already emphasized, the institution has full rights to regulate its operation. How it chooses to do so is part of its students' educational experience. The optimum disciplinary system recognizes and balances both students' and institutional rights to the end that both groups have confidence that justice has been done to the extent possible. Fair play must be a part of such a process.

*Placement.* Persons in charge of placement and career counseling are advised to become familiar with equal opportunity and non-discrimination statutes as they relate to placement practices. In most situations, students should be given the opportunity to be interviewed by all recruiters.

# 5. Faculty and Administrators: Recruitment, Hiring, and Collective Bargaining

This chapter concentrates on the practices used in recruiting and hiring faculty and administrators, an area especially affected by new legal requirements. (Chapter 6 will consider legal matters that arise after an individual has been hired. These may involve educational issues such as academic freedom or employment issues such as promotion, tenure, or retirement.)

Probably the greatest number of complaints and lawsuits filed with administrative agencies and with courts have to do with allegations of discriminatory practices in recruiting, hiring, and subsequent treatment of faculty, administrators, and other staff. Rights to equal treatment arise from many sources, ranging from the Fourteenth Amendment of the Constitution, which requires equal protection and due process, through civil rights laws passed immediately after the Civil War, and up to contemporary civil rights acts and other statutes such as Title IX of the Educational Amendments of the Higher Education Act of 1972.

Violations of constitutional rights make up a large category of lawsuits filed by candidates for employment at educational institutions. The use of employment tests in various employment situations has led to a number of court decisions regarding their use. Other decisions affect how job descriptions are drawn up and how faculty and administrators are assessed as candidates for jobs.

Differences between employment conditions for administrators and faculty have taken on new significance. A desire for administrative professional standards regarding the rights and responsibilities of university administrators led to the founding of the American Association of University Administrators (AAUA) in 1970.

Administrators at elementary and secondary schools often have resorted to collective bargaining as one means of establishing their rights and responsibilities. The National Education Association (NEA) and the American Federation of Teachers (AFT) have worked to establish standards for this group. Faculty standards, of course, were the first to be established through the efforts of such organizations as the American Association of University Professors (AAUP), the NEA, and the AFT. Statements of the standards (or information on how to obtain copies) of all four of these groups—AAUA, AAUP, NEA, and AFT—appear in Appendix B. A new form of employment relationship for administrators is evolving; the old practice of "serving at the pleasure of" the employer appears to be undergoing gradual modification. This change should have a substantial impact on how administrators are recruited and hired.

Part-time employees have long been used by universities. For an equally long time, some would say, persons seeking part-time employment have used universities in similar fashion. The crucial variant today is a general concern that the status of part-time employees be clarified. Educational institutions will be challenged if they tend to use part-time status as a means of discriminating against minorities and women. On the other hand, legitimate use of part-time positions by universities must be protected.

Finally, it is essential that collective bargaining, or collective negotiations as it is sometimes called in educational circles, be examined, if only briefly, in order to fully understand the range of changes which have taken place in employment conditions at educational institutions. A number of organizations which were originated to formulate and protect professional standards have taken on the additional role of collective bargaining agents. The AAUP, NEA, and AFT are among these. However, the AAUA has adopted a policy against assuming such a role because its membership necessarily includes the whole spectrum of administrative personnel, including chief executive, academic, and business officers as well as all of their associates and assistants.

## IMPACT OF NONDISCRIMINATION AND OTHER STATUTES

### Job Descriptions

*Job descriptions should accurately state functions and qualifications.* A good general rule to follow, in meeting nondiscriminatory hiring requirements, is to try to ensure that all job candidates are judged in relationship to the job description rather than in the abstract (*Griggs v. Duke Power,* 1971).

It is imperative that the institution set forth in writing a description of the position, along with the minimal qualifications required to do the job. Care should be taken that qualifications for the position be clearly related to the functions to be performed, and not merely desirable in the abstract. For example, positions at entry level in teaching may not require that candidates for the position have a doctoral degree. To insist upon a doctoral degree for such a position may result in allegations by job candidates that such a qualification is merely a ruse to eliminate minorities or women as applicants for the position.

In addition, the job description should indicate whether the position is for a finite period of time, such as one year, or whether it has a possibility of continuing appointment or tenure. Salary should be given, of course, either in a specific amount or a salary range.

Nondiscrimination laws do not anticipate that unqualified job applicants are to be considered for positions. Instead, the laws stress the need for accurate assessment of what qualifications are valid for particular jobs. Then, qualified minorities and women, along with the other qualified candidates, are to be judged equally.

### Advertising: Affirmative Action

Advertising appropriately is crucial in meeting the good faith requirements of affirmative action plans. The way in which an institution advertises available job openings has become a matter of significant and special importance under equal employment opportunity laws. For example, Executive Order 11246 (1965), as amended by Executive Order 11375 (1967), requires that all educational institutions that receive federal funds pursue a program of affirmative action. They are to seek out qualified minorities and women as job candidates if such persons are underrepresented in their work force.

Institutions must show that they made a good faith effort to inform qualified minorities and women of available employment opportunities. One way to indicate that good faith efforts were made is to advertise job openings in newspapers and journals likely to be read by qualified minorities and women. Mimeographed notices to appropriate departments in other institutions where such persons are undergoing training also indicates good faith.

One basic purpose of affirmative action requirements is simply to increase the number of people who hear about job openings. In the past, it was not an uncommon practice for job openings to be filled with no advertising at all. A person at an institution seeking applicants would telephone a friend in a similar discipline at another institution and ask for the names of possible job candidates. This "old-boy network" still is useful. Affirmative action requires only that additional advertising be done so that news of job openings goes beyond traditional, restricted networks of communications.

### Interviewing: Nondiscriminatory Questions

A number of equal employment opportunity statutes require that interviewing be done in a nondiscriminatory fashion. All this means is that the same questions, and only those related to the candidate's qualifications, be asked of all candidates, whether they be male or female, black or white, and so on. More attention, therefore, needs to be paid to what questions are asked. Obviously, questions should be connected directly with the job description and the qualifications set forth in the advertisement for the job.

Interviewers have sometimes indicated concern about whether they will be able to construct nondiscriminatory questions. One suggestion which has been found helpful is that interviewers imagine that there is a solid screen between them and the job applicant, so that there is no way of knowing whether the applicant is male or female (assuming the voice is disguised) or black or white. In fact, symphony orchestras have conducted job interviews in just such a fashion, assuring that the evaluators could judge only the quality of the candidate's playing, without being influenced by knowing the musician's sex or race.

Pamphlets have been written for interviewers who wish to improve the quality of their interviewing techniques and questions by eliminating discriminatory practices. The key to nondiscriminatory interviewing appears to be, as always, an emphasis on the job description and the qualifications for the job. For example, questions regarding educational background, other employment experience, and references, all having to do with the particular job advertised, generally will be judged to be nondiscriminatory.

Discriminatory questions are those having to do with non-job-related matters. Marital status usually has no relation to a candidate's qualifications to do a particular job. Therefore, questions whether a person is married, has children, practices birth control, has made arrangements for children to be cared for when ill, or has spouse's permission to work all are likely to be judged to be non-job-related. The courts usually take the position that a married person applying for a job, even if children are involved, already has made arrangements for contingencies, and questions regarding these matters are inappropriate. In practice, it is seldom that a white male is ever asked whether he practices birth control. The foregoing assumptions are taken as a matter of course. It is this kind of equal treatment in interviewing which is the goal of equal employment opportunity laws.

## Hiring Practices

*Valid employment tests that have an adverse effect on minorities may be permitted if evidence shows there was no intent to discriminate.* Requirements that applicants for employment submit to tests of various kinds have been subject to court scrutiny in recent years. Thus far, the use of such tests in selecting faculty members does not seem to be widespread. Administrators and other staff personnel are more likely subjects of employment tests.

The Supreme Court set forth the general principle that hiring tests must have some proven validity in predicting ability to do the job being filled (*Griggs* v. *Duke Power Company*, 1971). However, in an extension of that decision, the Court recently found that a test which is validly job related, yet appears to have a disproportionate adverse effect upon a particular group, such as blacks, is constitutional unless an *intent* to discriminate is proved (*Washington* v. *Davis*, 1976).

The emphasis on intent to discriminate appeared in a decision involving police department recruiting procedures which included a written personnel test. The Supreme Corrt held that the constitution does not prevent the government from seeking, through a valid test, to upgrade the verbal skills and other communicative abilities of its employees. The test was found to be directly related to the requirements of the police training program, and the requirements themselves were determined to be correct for police work. The trial court also had found that the evidence showed that a positive relationship existed between the test and the training program, and that positive relationship was sufficient to validate the test. The blacks who filed the class action, said the Supreme Court, could not more ascribe their failure to pass the test to denial of equal protection than could the whites who also failed (*Washington* v. *Davis*, 1976).

*Meetings to discuss candidates should be appropriate as to attendees, time, and manner.* When meetings are held at which job candidates are discussed, several legal concerns arise. One is the matter of possible allegations of slander. There may be liability for placing a stigma or blot upon the reputation of the job candidate by improper meetings or discussion. Communications between the persons making personnel decisions should be limited to privileged situations—meetings that take place in appropriate settings and between appropriate parties.

Cases on privileged communications usually have required that comments be made in good faith and without malice *by* persons having an appropriate interest, right, or duty *to* persons having a similar interest, right, or duty. The meetings also should be held in an appropriate manner and at an appropriate time, for example a faculty personnel committee meeting where qualifications of candidates are being discussed that is attended only by authorized persons and carried out in a businesslike fashion (*Barr* v. *Matteo*, 1959).

*Sunshine laws.* Another concern is whether meetings involving personnel decisions are affected by recently enacted sunshine laws. Very few cases presently exist on the narrow issue of whether hiring decisions at public institutions must be made at open meetings. Most states specifically exempt personnel decisions from open meeting laws. Some states permit open personnel meetings at the request of the person being considered. Legal counsel should be sought by an institution where the question arises. Case law may have developed by then which sets guidelines to be followed.

*The decision to hire should be reached by putting each candidate through the same general process.* Any decision to hire should be the result of following all of the institution's regular hiring practices and procedures. For example, if there are policies or rules that candidates are to be interviewed by faculty committees, department heads, and deans as well as by the chief executive officer of the institution, it is imperative that these procedures be complied with in substantial form. Equal employment opportunity laws require that all candidates for positions be treated equally. For instance, an institution may have hired one candidate sight unseen over the telephone while insisting that another candidate travel to the institution, be interviewed by several groups of people, and perhaps present a colloquium. The second candidate may seek redress on two counts: first, that he or she was given significantly different treatment, and second, that the institution's own procedures were not being followed.

*Authority to hire should be clearly set forth.* The authority to hire, fire, transfer, and promote employees is given to specific individuals or bodies by statutes, policies of boards of trustees, or other similar documents. It should be clear that persons other than those specifically authorized to so act do not possess authority to offer employment to applicants for positions. In order that an agreement of employment be reached, the offer of employment must be made by a person or body with the authority to do so.

For instance, a job offer may be made by a department chairman who has no authority to make the offer. A job applicant may rely on that offer, sell his or her house, move to the new community, and find that no job exists. The result may be a lawsuit seeking various forms of actual and compensatory money damages from the institution or the individual administrator involved.

In a case illustrating an offer of employment from an unauthorized individual, the chairman of a department of a medical college offered employment to a physician to serve on the college's faculty. The college took the stance that it was not bound by such offer. The physician filed suit to recover damages for an alleged breach of his employment contract. The trial court found in favor of the physician, but the appeal court found in favor of the college. The appeal court held that the evidence indicated that the physician knew the department chairman at the college did not possess authority to employ individuals and that the chairman's offer of employment was not that of the college. Expert testimony was offered by the physician as to the customary hiring practices of schools of medicine, but the court refused to hear such testimony on the grounds that insufficient foundation had been laid for its admission (Personal Communication, 1976).

*Loyalty Oaths.* Several decades ago, many institutions established a requirement that applicants for employment sign a loyalty oath. The use of loyalty oaths was scrutinized by courts at various levels; some oaths were thrown out on constitutional grounds.

Loyalty oaths still exist and are still being challenged by applicants for employment. Today, however, the guidelines to determine whether a particular oath violates any First Amendment rights are much clearer.

A case in point involved a requirement at a public community college that applicants for employment take an oath to support and defend the state and the federal constitutions and to bear true faith and allegiance to them. This oath was challenged by an applicant for employment. Both the trial court and the appellate court held that the oath involved was not unconstitutional because it did not require the surrender of any First Amendment rights guaranteed by the federal constitution (*Chilton* v. *Contra Costa Community College District,* 1976).

*Irrebuttable presumptions not permitted: policy against hiring unwed parents or ex-convicts must permit rebuttal of past conduct.* Public educational institutions are subject to constitutional restraints with regard to irrebuttable presumptions of immorality. Thus, a public institution which has a regulation automatically disqualifying any unwed mother from employment violates the due process and equal protection clauses of the Constitution. In such a case the court said:

> Due process precludes a state from adopting an irrebutable presumption where a presumed fact does not necessarily follow from a proven one. Thus, unless present immorality necessarily follows from unwed parenthood, the rule must be held to violate due process. . . . By denying unwed parents a public hearing to which all other teachers charged with immorality are entitled the rule under attack denies equal protection of the law (*Andrews* v. *Drew Municipal School District,* 1975).

An employment policy that automatically rules out the employment of an exconvict is discriminatory. A railroad claimed that its policy against employing ex-convicts was related to its fear of cargo theft, railroad liability for the violent conduct of an employee, and the lack of moral character of persons convicted of crimes. The court said: "To deny jobs to such individuals because of some conduct which may be remote in time or does not significantly bear upon the particular job requirements is an unnecessarily harsh and unjust burden." The court thought that such factors might be pertinent in making individual hiring decisions. No justification existed, however, for making such a practice an absolute hiring policy which precludes the presentation of evidence as to the applicant's behavior and experience since his or her release from prison (*Green* v. *Missouri Pacific Railroad Company,* 1975).

## Mutual Understanding of Terms of Employment

Mutual understanding of the terms of the employment contract is a key to good personnel management. It is essential that the employer and the job applicant, at the time of hiring, are clear in their own minds about all conditions of employment. Litigation arises in situations where one party believes the agreement to contain matters which the other party disagrees are part of the mutual understanding. For example, an individual may be hired under a one-year agreement with language referring to annual renewal. It is imperative that both parties be clear about whether their agreement is for a finite period of time or contains expectations of continued employment. Evidence produced at trials in such situations has resulted in courts' finding that faculty members have acquired de facto tenure, as in *Perry* v. *Sindermann* (1972).

Any contract of employment between the institution and its faculty, administrators, or other staff should be reduced to writing and appropriately executed by the parties. Certainly, the contract should contain, at minimum, the following: the term or length of employment (a beginning and an ending date), a job title, and financial remuneration.

The parties should have agreed in advance also on such matters as a clear job description, job qualifications, regular evaluation, a process of review, date of notification of action regarding renewal or continuance, a written statement when leaving the insitution regarding job performance and circumstances regarding departure, assistance offered by the institution in case of termination due to retrenchment, and appropriate due process procedures. The understanding regarding such matters should be in writing—in a publication such as a faculty or administrator's handbook, in policies of the board of trustees, or in a statute, if not in the contract of employment itself.

Care should be taken also not to give the impression that a job candidate is being offered perquisites beyond the normal salary and fringe benefits for the job. For example, a newly hired faculty member is sometimes given the false impression that he or she has been promised special laboratory space, secretarial aid, graduate assistants, or similar benefits. Of course, if special perquisites are part of the offer of employment, they should be reduced to writing, as well.

## Part-Time Employees

*Part-time employees are actively seeking recognition and more equitable remuneration.* Educational institutions traditionally have employed persons in part-time jobs, both teaching and nonteaching. Persons who fill part-time jobs recently have become more aware of the importance of their role in the general scheme of operating an educational institution. A number of part-time employees are actively seeking to secure greater recognition of their value to the institution and thereby improve their condition of employment.

Distinctions are now being made, for example, between permanent part-timers and temporary part-timers; that is, between those who are hired semester after semester to teach a course or administer a mini-program and those hired for a brief period of time on a one-time basis.

Among the more obvious conditions of employment which part-time employees have sought to improve are salaries and fringe benefits such as vacation pay, sick leave, and seniority. Many institutions voluntarily have reviewed the relationship and provided improved conditions, while other institutions find themselves subject to federal or state laws which set forth conditions of employment for part-time employees (see Equal Pay Act, Appendix A).

In addition to salary, part-time faculty members have been concerned with the traditional practice of being denied tenure-earning status. Historically, there are few precedents on which part-time faculty may rely as standards for their treatment regarding tenure. Thus, tenure possibilities for part-time faculty members usually depend upon the existence of statutory provisions or collective bargaining provisions to bring about change.

To illustrate, two female physicians at a university medical center attempted to use Title VII (CRA) as a vehicle to protest their non-tenure earning status. They claimed discrimination on the basis of sex in setting up employment conditions for doctors hired for part-time work. The district director of the Equal Employment Opportunity Commission, who heard the case, pointed out that the employees were part-time employees by choice. He said the conditions of employment for all persons in the part-time category were uniform. The fact that all or most of the part-time doctors were female was found to be merely incidental. Full-time status was open to all, and the medical center had a number of full-time female doctors on its staff (*Holmes & Lansley*, 1976).

## ADMINISTRATORS AND FACULTY: EMPLOYMENT TERMS COMPARED

Traditionally, administrators at educational institutions have served "at the pleasure of" the employing body. Typical of the employment contingencies faced by such administrators are involuntary pay cuts, transfers, and arbitrary dismissals.

Faculty, on the other hand, have for many years been protected by the two important concepts of academic freedom and tenure. The purpose of these concepts was to protect faculty members' freedom of inquiry in the classroom and in scholarly research (see Appendix B, 1940 "Statement of Principles on Academic Freedom and Tenure," American Association of University Professors and Association of American Colleges). Untenured faculty, however, began to feel the need for protection against arbitrary loss of employment. Consequently, they developed a receptivity to various forms of protection of economic security. Employment contracts for untenured faculty was one such form of protection. Usually these contracts were negotiated individually. Ultimately, some of the individual contractual relationships led to a desire for collective negotiations, and unionization of faculty at many educational institutions began to grow.

Meanwhile, administrators, excluded from the protection afforded by academic freedom, tenure, and contracts, soon saw the advantages of the economic security provided to faculty by contracts and collective negotiations. Contractual protection for administrators took hold. It exists today more at the elementary and secondary levels than at the level of higher education, but the trend toward all administrators serving in a more protected employment relationship than "at will" appears to be growing.

### Professional Standards for Administrators

The administrator's employment relationship with the institution/employer is changing. A major force for change was the realization that human resources required the same or greater degree of management care as did material resources such as funding, physical plant, equipment, and supplies. Poor management of human resources costs money, time, and prestige. New administrators must be recruited, trained, supervised, evaluated, and given time to acquire experience. The trend appears to be shifting toward a more careful assessment of job descriptions, evaluation of candidates more carefully before hiring, and even use of a probationary period of employment to permit both employer and employee time to make a better informed decision regarding employment for a definite period of time. The formerly unquestioned tradition of administrators' serving at the pleasure of the employer appears to be evolving into a more rational, businesslike, and predictable pattern. Many cost-conscious governing boards have come to believe that from-the-hip hiring and firing of administrative personnel is a luxury no longer to be afforded. Indeed, the time may be approaching when one of the criteria for evaluating an administrator is his or her ability to recruit and hire good personnel and thus cut down on the costs of avoidable turnover.

Change in the employment relationship appeared first in elementary and secondary schools where contracts for administrators are more common than not. In higher education, chief executive officers began to be given contracts a few years ago. These often require reevaluation after three or five years. The founding of the American Association of University Administrators in 1970 and its adoption of "Professional Standards for Administrators in Higher Education" in 1975 was another sign of the pressures for change. More recently, a number of prestigious institutions, private and public, large and small, have been circulating questionnaires seeking information about model contracts for administrators. They ask specifically about basic conditions of employment such as length of a contract, continuing appointments, wages, evaluation procedures, and requirements for notice prior to termination. Fringe benefits, vacation benefits, holidays, medical benefits, and retirement plans also are asked about.

The AAUA's professional standards also have been helpful to institutions wishing to upgrade the quality of their administrative personnel by attracting administrators whose skills make them highly marketable and who tend to accept positions at institutions with high administrative standards. AAUA standards for employment include, among other things, a written statement of employment covering conditions such as wages, fringe benefits, term of office, process of review, notice of renewal or continuation, and responsibilities of the position. Other specific standards for administrators may be found in Appendix B.

Questions still arise over who shall participate in the selection of persons to serve as administrators, and whether administrators should be eligible for tenure or some form of continuing employment. Confusion often is created when an administrator also has a faculty appointment, although he or she may not actually teach students. How is such a person to be evaluated for promotion or tenure? When a faculty member who agrees to serve in an administrative role later returns to faculty status, does the time spent as an administrator count as a bonus or a penalty in the resumed faculty role?

The answers to many of the employment questions regarding administrators are found in basic contract law. In the case of public institutions, constitutional rights of individuals carry weight as well.

Resort to collective negotiations by administrators of elementary and secondary schools has provided solutions to many of the employment problems of administrators. Reliance on the AAUA "Professional Standards" as protection for administrators' rights at higher education institutions also is increasing.

## Contracts of Employment for Administrators

*Involuntary pay cuts may be experienced by administrators who are unprotected by contracts.* Administrators who serve "at the pleasure of" and who have no contractual or other protection may be required to accept involuntary pay cuts. For exmaple, in September, 1976, the Boston School Committee voted to hold the current year's school costs down. In order to implement that decision, the committee directed the superintendent of schools to reduce the next year's expenditures by about $15 million, beginning with a 10-percent across-the-board pay cut for central office administrators. Since most Boston school administrators and teachers were covered by collective bargaining contracts, only about twenty top-level employees, including the superintendent, the associate superintendents, and the superintendent's administrative assistants, would suffer from the proposed 10-percent cut (*Boston Globe*, September 14, 1976, p. 1).

*Reductions of administrators' appointments from twelve months to ten months have occurred.* Some institutions recently have accomplished cost-cutting through a reduction in the term of some administrators' contracts. The administrators affected usually have been those whose jobs have been redefined in such a way that their tasks can be accomplished in ten months and do not require the physical presence of the administrator for a full twelve months. The change in employment conditions is accomplished involuntarily and without legal recourse at institutions where administrators serve at the pleasure of their employer. Where AAUA professional standards are observed or where an individual or collective bargaining contract exists, the change usually has to be voluntary and with prior notice. As current contracts expire, the changed conditions may take effect with the new contract. "Grandfather clauses" sometimes are used to preserve the twelve-month status for employees with prior service, while new employees are hired only under the new ten-month term.

*Transfers of administrators may not require due process.* Transfers of administrators at public institutions at the end of a term contract usually do not require due process, unless a willful or a malicious purpose is proved. A case in point involved an assistant to the president of a public college. When the assistant's contract in that post ran out, the college did not renew him in that position; instead, they transferred him to another post. The court found no demotion involved and no evidence to establish malice or willfulness. It therefore concluded that the failure of the board to renew his contract as assistant to the pesident had not violated his due process or other constitutional rights (*Roberson* v. *District of Columbia Board of Higher Education*, 1976).

### Tenure or Continuing Appointments for Administrators

*Tenure or continuing appointment for higher education administrators seldom is found.* The purpose of tenure, according to the 1940 "Statement of Principles on Academic Freedom and Tenure" of the American Association of University Professors, is to protect faculty members' freedom of inquiry in the classroom and in scholarly research. Generally, the concept of tenure or continuing appointment has not been deemed appropriate as a protection for higher education administrators, and has seldom been found. However, in view of the various roles of many administrators, it is no longer altogether clear that administrators ought not to be afforded some sort of protection as they carry out their administrative tasks. Scholarly research is carried on by some administrators, and certainly there ought to be protection afforded administrators as they pursue such research. The concept of "administrator freedom" as a parallel, perhaps, to academic freedom needs to be explored and considered. At present, however, courts generally have not extended the concept of academic freedom to cover administrators. In response to such refusals by courts, as well as in response to a need for economic security, term contracts and continuing appointments have been developed in recent years as mechanisms to permit administrators to function in a more stable managerial environment.

Contemporary management values also have affected a change in attitude toward the employment of administrators. That is, administrators today often are viewed as human resources in which the educational institution has invested time and money. Therefore, the institution has become more interested in careful and judicious use of these resources. More attention is therefore being given to developing better selection criteria, methods of evaluation, and career development opportunities for administrators. Consequently, a more reliable set of human potential indicators may emerge on which to rest decisions to promote, transfer, or dismiss administrators.

Another consequence of viewing administrators as valuable resources is the tendency toward including in the evaluation of an upper-level administrator a query about how well he or she develops subordinates. Too much turnover can be very costly to an institution. The following cases are typical of those having to do with tenure status of higher education administrators.

A director of a federal research project being conducted at a private university sought tenure or severance pay when the government terminated its arrangement with the university. The court held that the director's employment was at will so long as government funding was available. Therefore he was entitled neither to tenure nor to severance pay (*Goodman* v. *New York University*, 1975).

The position of departmental chairpersons is a confusing one. Often, the faculty views the chairperson as its advocate to the administration; but the administration views chairpersons as its representative to the faculty. Usually, the chairperson is a faculty member selected by the administration after consultation with other faculty members in the department. Does a faculty member's tenure protect the appointment as chairperson?

In Washington State, the departmental chairpersons in a state college learned that chairpersonships had been abolished in an administrative reorganization. They sued the college district, asking for a clarification of their status. They claimed their appointments as chairpersons were tenured faculty appointments. They pointed out that tenured faculty appointments could be terminated only according to statutory procedures and regulations, which had not been followed here. The court held that the administrative chairperson-ships were not protected by tenure. The court referred to the 1940 AAUP "Statement of Principles on Academic Freedom and Tenure," which empha-sized that the purpose of tenure is to protect the faculty members in the classroom and in scholarly research. The court felt that such purposes would not be served by extending tenure to department heads. The court also said that administrative considerations militate against such an extension (*Barnes* v. *Washington State Community College District No. 20*, 1975).

### Dismissals of Administrators

*Dismissal of administrators may involve breach of contract or violation of constitutional rights.* A contract at a private institution creates rights for an administrator such as the right to damages for breach of contract. At a public institution, contitutional rights exist in addition to contractual rights.

*Dismissal where no contract exists requires no reasons or due process.* If an administrator at a public or private institution has no contract, he or she usually may be terminated without reasons having to be given or due process observed (*Beale* v. *Knoxville College*, 1973; *Thomas* v. *Kirkwood Communi-ty College*, 1971). This is the common situation that exists when an adminis-trator serves "at will" or "at the pleasure of" the hiring body.

*Dismissal from public institution where contract exists requires due process.* A contract at a public institution creates a property right, and due process is required if an administrator is to be terminated during the term of the con-tract.

The president of a public junior college was terminated for conduct which probaby constituted just cause. However, the dismissal occurred during the term of the president's employment contract, and without a hearing. In this case, the court of appeals held that the administrator's Fourteenth Amendment due process rights were violated by the college board's failure to afford him a hearing. The administrator was entitled to recover damages against the board. The case then was sent back to the trial court for a deter-mination of the amount of damages to be assessed. Damages were to be based upon the particular mental distress, humiliation, or other injury to the plain-tiff, as well as upon the general injury inherent in the nature of the wrong.

The fact that just cause probably was involved in this dismissal was brought to the attention of the trial court. It agreed that justice would not be served, and the plaintiff would be given a windfall at the expense of the tax-payers, if the court found him entitled to the same damages that would be recoverable if the contract had been terminated without just cause. The trial court pointed out, however, that another court, in *Zimmerer* v. *Spencer*

(1973), had adopted the opposite approach to the issue of just cause. The *Zimmerer* decision rested on the theory that the wrong done was not the termination of employment for whatever cause; it was the deprivation of procedural due process right to notice and hearing. Nevertheless, this court disagreed with the *Zimmerer* reasoning, and assessed damages ameliorated by the factor of probable just cause for the dismissal (*Hostrop* v. *Board of Junior College District No. 515*, 1975).

*Dismissal involving stigma by public institution requires due process.* Dismissal procedures at a public institution which include attacks upon the reputation and future career opportunities of an individual may involve a deprivatin of the person's liberty interest, and due process is required.

For example, a counselor and registrar of a state university was denied tenure. He was dismissed under circumstances which included "accusations which would call his reputation into the gravest doubt." The court found that the individual was denied a liberty interest requiring due process under these circumstances (*Francis* v. *Ota*, 1973).

In another instance, a California appeals court said that if the college rules so provide, a chairman may be removed without a hearing. But, if the method of removal damages the person's reputation and career, a liberty interest is involved and due process is required. A hearing should be held giving the person an opportunity to rebut the evidence that damaged his or her reputation and career (*Zumwalt* v. *Trustees of the California State Colleges*, 1973).

*Personal Liability of individual board members is possible in similar cases since Wood decision.* It should be noted that these cases were decided before *Wood* v. *Strickland* (1975). If they had been decided after *Wood*, the additional issue of personal liability of the individual board members who terminated these contracts probably also would have had to be determined. This matter is considered further in Chapter 2.

*Dismissal in cases of dual appointments as administrator and faculty member.* Sometimes an administrator has a dual appointment, for example as president of the institution and as professor on the faculty. The appointment as president may be "at the pleasure of," while the appointment as professor may be with tenure. If such a president is dismissed as president, he or she is not entitled to due process, having been employed in that capacity "at will." Presumably the person returns to faculty status (*Powell* v. *Board of Education of City of New York*, 1971).

*Dismissals from auxiliary private corporations at public institutions do not require due process.* Some administrative employees may not be entitled to due process because they are employees of an auxiliary private corporation rather than of the public educational institution itself. To illustrate, a former manager of a student bookstore, operated by a nonprofit auxiliary corporation of a state university, challenged his dismissal. He claimed he was a university employee and thus entitled to protection from dismissal without good cause and a hearing. The court found that the bookstore manager was not an employee of the college or of any governmental agency. Rather, he was the employee of a private corporation. He was not protected as were employees of the university (*Wanee v. Board of Directors of the Associated Students of California State University, Chico,* 1976).

*Reasons given for dismissals from private and public institution often are found to be inaccurate.* Administrators at private and public institutions often complain that when reasons are given for their dismissal, the reasons are inaccurate. The most common problem is giving incompetence as a reason for dismissal when in fact the dismissal has resulted from an incompatibility of personal style or characteristics between the terminated administrator and his or her supervisor. The AAUA receives many requests for assistance in having the record correctly state the reason for dismissal.

This is not to say, of course, that administrators are never incompetent. Rather, it is to emphasize that dismissed administrators are entitled to have their professional competence accurately described. They should be able to seek new employment from the strongest possible position.

Incompatibility of styles, if properly documented in periodic, reasonable evaluations of job performance, may be recognized as a legitimate reason for termination under the "Pickering exception" (*Pickering v. Board of Education,* 1968). It refers to the fact that public employees have the right to publicly criticize their superiors with one exception: they are not free to publicly criticize superiors with whom their work relationship is so intimate that such criticism necessarily would undermine it.

### Financial Exigency

*Financial exigency may be a reason to terminate employment contracts of administrators.* Financial exigency has been found by courts to be a legitimate reason for termination of employment contracts between administrators and educational institutions. The institution, of course, generally bears the burden of proof that it is suffering bona fide economic distress requiring cuts in its budget.

A leading case on the necessity of showing bona fide financial exigency as the cause of termination of employment contracts of personnel at an educational institution involved the discharge of a number of tenured faculty members. All remaining instructors were placed on one-year contracts. The court in that case found that the dismissals and one-year contracts were not caused by bona fide financial exigency. Rather, they were caused by the proved intention of the president of the college to eliminate tenure (*AAUP* v. *Bloomfield College*, 1975).

Administrative personnel, as well, have found that their contracts of employment may be terminated by financial exigency. A California appellate court held that evidence supported the trial court's finding that the dismissal of the employee was due to a budget cut in *Amluxen* v. *Regents of the University of California* (1975).

### Administrators' Research Activities

Many administrators who do not serve also in faculty roles have become interested in doing research, and questions have been raised whether they should engage in research activity. A number of institutions have benefited substantially by the findings of research conducted on administrative issues, the prestige lent to the institution by having such research originate there, and the funding received to carry out the research projects. The development of research as an accepted area of work for administrators carries with it the need for the institution to develop policies and procedures to handle such research. Related issues of seminal importance include academic freedom, sabbaticals, and use of graduate assistants.

## COLLECTIVE BARGAINING

Collective bargaining is divided into three parts: (1) organizing the employees, (2) negotiating a contract, and (3) administering the contract. Then, when the contract expires, the whole process starts all over again.

It is important to remember that employees bargain collectively because they have chosen to do so. They can change their minds later. As a contract reaches its expiration date, employees may decide to vote on whether they want to continue to be represented by the present bargaining agent or switch to a different one. Or they may decide they want to stop bargaining collectively altogether, and return to bargaining individually. Employees also can change their minds while a contract is in force. They may vote to decertify the bargaining agent. Thus, when a contract expires, the parties do not begin automatically at step two, to negotiate a renewal of the contract. There must first be an assurance that the employees still wish to bargain collectively and be represented by the same bargaining agent.

The National Labor Relations Act (NLRA) provides the basic legal framework for collective bargaining at private educational institutions. Public Employee Labor Relations Acts (PELRAs) have been passed in many states, and public institutions in those states are covered by them rather than by the

NLRA. Some states do not permit public educational employees to bargain collectively.

Aside from the legal guidelines and restraints upon the parties, the climate of a collective bargaining relationship between employer and employees is whatever they choose to make it. It may be combative; the parties may argue and fight over every nuance of every condition of employment. Or it may be cooperative; the parties may have an overall understanding under which they recognize a common goal of promoting education. They may try, in as cooperative a fashion as possible, to settle amicably the conditions of employment. In the former instance, the primary emphasis is on a struggle between the parties for power and authority. In the second instance, the goal of providing quality education appears to give the parties a common meeting ground on which they attempt to work out mutually agreeable conditions of employment. Most employer-employee relationships at educational institutions fall somewhere between the two extremes.

Finally, a word about terminology. Collective bargaining is often called collective negotiations when it takes place in an educational setting, and a union representing educators often is called an association. This language resulted largely from an expectation that there would be substantial differences between unionized educators and other kinds of unionized workers. It was thought that teachers would be unwilling to strike and use other similar actions in order to press their claims. Experience has shown that educators do strike, even when it is prohibited by law. Collective bargaining in educational settings has turned out to be not all that different from collective bargaining in other settings.

## Jurisdiction of National Labor Relations Board and State Public Employee Labor Relations Acts

*Jurisdiction of National Labor Relations Board (NLRB) extends over private institutions.* Organizing of employees of educational institutions increased substantially in the late 1960s. By 1970, the National Labor Relations Board successfully asserted its jurisdiction over private educational institutions on the basis that such institutions had substantial impact on interstate commerce (*Cornell University*, 1970).

The NLRB then enunciated a rule that it included in its jurisdiction all private institutions having "gross annual revenue from all sources (excluding only contributions which, because of limitation by the grantor, are not available for use for operating expenses) of not less than one million dollars" (35 *Fed. Reg.* 18370).

A number of questions have been raised over the years regarding the NLRB's jurisdiction over private institutions of education and their employees. As recently as 1975, an appellate court was asked again to review the jurisdiction of the NLRB. In that case, the court said:

It is not an abuse of the discretion of the board to reappraise its position in light of developments in society, as long as its new construction is consistent with the language and tenor of the Act. . . . We are unable to convince ourselves that all faculties of all private, non-profit institutions of higher learning in the nation are so situated as to fall outside the ranks of the "employees" under the act (*NLRB* v. *Wentworth Institute and Wentworth College of Technology*, 1975).

*NLRB jurisdiction over secondary Catholic schools denied.* Using public monies to fund church-related schools and higher education institutions is discussed in Chapter 7. A guiding principle in that situation is just how sectarian an effect the teaching and operation of the particular institution is likely to have on students. For instance, public monies have been permitted at higher education church-related institutions, but sometimes not at elementary and secondary schools. A similar issue arose when the NLRB sought to assert jurisdiction over employees at secondary church-related schools in Chicago. The court held that the NLRB's assertion of jurisdiction over secondary schools operated by the Roman Catholic church violated the First Amendment principle of separation of church and state. The court found that the bishop operated these schools for the purpose of carrying out the teaching mission of the Catholic church. The fact that a secular education also was provided did not detract from the fact that the religious mission was the only reason for the school's existence. Thus, the court appeared to be saying that if secondary church-related schools are too sectarian to receive government aid, it follows that they are too sectarian to be regulated by government agencies like the NLRB. This case raises matters that undoubtedly will be before the courts again (*Catholic Bishop of Chicago* v. *NLRB*, 1977).

*An initial determination must be made regarding whether an institution is covered by federal or state labor law.* The NLRB often is asked to rule on whether an educational institution is a private institution or a public institution. Private institutions fall within the jurisdiction of the NLRB, but public institutions fall within the jurisdiction of state Public Employee Labor Relations Acts (PELRAs), where they exist.

The National Labor Relations Board has no jurisdiction over "any state or political subdivision thereof." The NLRB, in determining whether an institution is private or public, generally uses the two-pronged test of amount of state financial assistance and amount of state regulation.

The NLRB ruled, for instance, that the University of Vermont, with its

State Agricultural College, together form a private institution of higher education, not a public institution. Therefore, it falls within the jurisdiction of the NLRB. The board found that although the college received 25 percent of its total revenue from the state, it in fact is completely independent of the state in administration, personnel policies, accounting procedures, and other essential areas. A report of the NLRB decision appeared in *The Chronicle of Higher Education* on April 12, 1976.

*Agency shop for public employees held constitutional.* Agency shops are permitted in some states, including Minnesota, Michigan, and New York. That is, the employer and union may negotiate a clause in the agreement which provides that every employee in the certified bargaining unit has a right not to join the union. But in that case, the employee is required to pay a service charge (equal to regular union dues) to the union. This charge covers the cost of handling grievances of nonunion employees in the unit, whom the union is bound by law to represent in like manner as union members.

By contrast, a union shop clause requires all employees in the unit to become members of the union after a specified date. A closed shop clause, now legal in only a very few industries, including the construction industry, requires prospective employees to be union members. This system remains in industries where employers find it essential to the operation of their businesses to be able to call a union hiring hall and pick up skilled employees on short notice.

The agency shop was recently challenged in court by Detroit teachers who asked that the agency shop clause be declared invalid under the Constitution as a deprivation of freedom of association protected by the First and Fourteenth Amendments. The case ultimately went to the Supreme Court, which held that the Michigan agency shop law was constitutional for all the same reasons that the National Labor Relations Act was held constitutional. The Court, however, held that as in the case of the NLRA, compulsory dues for political purposes are illegal, so agency fee payers and union dues payers have a right to know how fees and dues are spent by the union in order to be able to rest assured that none are being used for political purposes (*Abood* v. *Detroit Board of Education*, 1977).

### The Organizing Campaign

Contrary to common belief, most organizing campaigns originate not because a union is looking for new employees to organize, but because dissatisfied employees are seeking a union that will listen to their problems and indicate a willingness to represent them. Thus, when union organizers appear on a school or college campus, administrators and faculty with managerial duties and responsibilities well may ask themselves, "What has gone wrong?"

Collective bargaining usually does not appear out of thin air. It is generally a response to inadequate, inappropriate, or incompetent negotiation of conditions of employment with employees on an individual basis. It is a harsh truth that employees who are relatively satisfied with their conditions of employment are not likely to be interested in switching from a system of individual negotiation to one of collective negotiation.

The two most common complaints nonunion employees appear to have are lack of job security and lack of an adequate grievance procedure. Wages and other benefits usually are next in line.

*Various organizations may seek to be recognized as the bargaining agent at an institution.* In most instances today, the organization seeking to be recognized as the bargaining agent of employees at an educational institution is directly or indirectly affiliated with a larger national or state organization. Among national organizations representing teachers, for example, are the National Education Association, the American Federation of Teachers, and the American Association of University Professors. (The American Association of University Administrators has a policy against serving as a bargaining agent.) A large organization representing clerical workers is the Civil Service Employees Association. Nonteaching professional employees may be accepted as members of one of these organizations, or they may join a smaller organization made up of their own kind, such as school superintendents.

Some organizations, however, are much smaller. They may comprise employees at only one school or campus and be totally unaffiliated with any other organization.

Theoretically, any group of employees can form an organization and seek to be recognized as a bargaining agent. The major restriction is against having any financial or other support from the employer. It is this latter requirement which has prevented a number of faculty senates from being recognized as bargaining agents. Most senates are financed or otherwise accommodated or supported by their institutions. Generally, then, it is assumed there would be an insurmountable conflict of interest were a faculty senate to attempt to bargain with the institution by which it is supported. Most decisions on this particular matter have found that there was too much institutional control over the faculty senate in order for it to qualify as a union.

*An appropriate bargaining unit must be determined.* A crucial question to be answered at the outset of collective bargaining is what constitutes an appropriate bargaining unit in any particular situation. A unit may be single or multiple-employer, or single or multiple-employee craft. For instance, a bargaining unit may be composed of a single educational institution, or it may include the employees of an entire citywide or statewide system. It may be composed only of individuals having one skill, such as teaching, or it may include those having different skills, such as a unit combining teaching and nonteaching professionals. If the parties cannot voluntarily agree on an appropriate unit, the question will be determined by a hearing officer of the NLRB or state PELRA.

Public elementary school employees and secondary school employees may be in separate units or in the same unit within a single school district.

Higher education public employees often are in statewide units, such as that approved by the Minnesota Public Employment Relations Board and later affirmed by judicial review. The court agreed that a statewide unit, including faculty members at all state colleges, was the appropriate unit. The reason given was that the state board serves as the "appointing authority" for all state college system faculty members (*Minnesota State Colleges Board* v. *Public Employment Relations Board*, 1975).

Private school and college employees usually are in a unit consisting only of their own institution, similar to the single-employer unit in the industrial sphere. One private institution may find itself dealing with several unions, since its teachers, clerks, and security forces may be represented by different unions. This is roughly analogous to craft unions, as compared to industrial unions in the private industrial sector.

Church-related institutions have special unit problems. For example, a church-related educational institution raised the question whether priests and religious personnel should be included in a collective bargaining unit along with the lay personnel (*Niagara University and Niagara University Lay Teachers Association*, 1976).

The final determination was made on the basis of who owned the institution. It was found that the priests and religious personnel at Niagara University were not necessarily members of the order that owned the institution. They were not, then, members of the employer group. They were permitted to be included in the bargaining unit.

On the other hand, religious personnel at Seton Hall in New Jersey were found to be members of the order which owned the institution. They were, in effect, part of the employer group. They were not included in the Seton Hall bargaining unit (*Seton Hall College*, 1973).

*Students generally are not eligible to be in a bargaining unit.* Student interns and graduate assistants usually are not considered employees for the purposes of collective bargaining.

Students who serve an educational institution in a student/employee relationship often ask that they be considered primarily employees rather than students. This would permit them to bargain collectively with the educational institution about their financial remuneration and other conditions.

This issue has been raised most often by graduate assistants and clinical interns. The decisions affecting both private and public institutions have been relatively consistent in finding that both of these groups of students are primarily students, not employees. The institutions therefore generally are not required to bargain collectively with graduate assistants or clinical interns, although they may choose to do so voluntarily, assuming there is no statutory prohibition.

The rationale behind the decisions that students are not employees usually is that these students are performing the work they do as part of their course of instruction. The "stipend" students receive is a living allowance, not compensation for service rendered. Such a decision was reached in the public sphere in *Philadelphia Association of Interns and Residents v. Albert Einstein Medical Center* (1976), and in the private sector in *Cedars-Sinai Medical Center* (1976).

Exceptions to the general rule do exist, however. For example, Rutgers University was ordered to negotiate with its faculty union on hours, compensation, and working conditions of teaching assistants and graduate assistants (*State of New Jersey: before the Public Relations Employment Commission,* 1976).

Another exception to the general finding that graduate assistants and interns are students and not employees arose in a case involving a student enrolled in the University of Washington for work on his doctoral thesis. The student was employed by the university as a predoctoral lecturer in two quarters of 1970 and two quarters of 1971. When his employment was terminated, he filed an application for unemployment insurance benefits. The student's right to unemployment insurance benefits depended upon his being declared an employee rather than a student. The court found that the student was an employee. The decision was based primarily upon the court's interpretation of a state statute (RCW 50.44.040) which provides that "the term 'employment' shall not include services performed . . . by a student in the employ of a school, college or university, if such services are performed by a student who is enrolled, and is regularly attending classes at such school, college, or university. . . ." The evidence convinced the court that this particular student was enrolled but was not "regularly attending classes." His thesis requirements mandated merely that he consult with the faculty committee which was overseeing his doctoral program (*Warmington v. The Employment Security Department of the State of Washington,* 1975).

The weight of the decisions, however, in both the private and the public sector tend to support the premise that students serving as graduate assistants or as clinical interns are primarily students, not employees, for purposes of collective bargaining.

*Students' stipends are "wages" under IRS decisions.* Determinations by the Internal Revenue Service and by tax courts, as mentioned in Chapter 3, confuse the issue further by finding that the stipends of students such as medical interns or postdoctoral graduate assistants, who have completed their degrees and graduated, are deemed to be wages for services rendered. These stipends must be included in gross income for federal income tax purposes.

Thus, one government agency (NLRB) views new medical doctors serving their hospital internships as students, not employees. Another agency (IRS) views these same individuals as employees rather than students. This is an example of the confusion that still exists in trying to sort out basic issues in collective bargaining in its presently immature stage of development in academic settings.

*Certain organizing tactics may be improper.* The goal of federal and state rules regarding unfair organizing tactics prior to elections is to permit employees to make up their own minds, without restraint or coercion by either the employer or the union. Examples of forbidden conduct are surveillance by an employer or a promise of waiver of initiation fees by a union. A great variety of cases arise over what constitutes fair and proper communication with employees prior to an election.

For instance, a union seeking to organize employees at the University of Northern Iowa filed improper practice charges against the state and the university on the grounds that denial of campus mail privileges interfered with the union's organizational rights. The charges were dismissed. The National Labor Relations Board held that the law did not require that a union be given every possible means, or the most convenient means, of reaching the minds of individual workers and communicating with them (*University of Northern Iowa Federation of Teachers—Local 1894, American Federation of Teachers, AFL-CIO, Complainant and Robert D. Ray, Governor, etc.,* 1976).

A major precedent was overturned by the NLRB in 1977 when it ruled that elections no longer will be set aside on the basis of misleading campaign statements. The board declared that it will not probe into the truth or falsity of campaign statements, but will intervene only when a party engages in such deceptive campaign practices as using forged documents which render the voter unable to recognize the propaganda for what it is. Thus, the board will not be concerned with misrepresentation, but with the deceptive manner in which it was made (*Shopping Kart Food Market, Inc.,* 1977).

### Negotiating the Agreement

*Student input into bargaining.* A number of states, including Maine, Montana, and Oregon, have passed legislation providing for some form of student participation in collective bargaining negotiations between faculty unions and institutions. Student representatives may be permitted to be present at the bargaining sessions; they may be allowed to make comments, or to be available for consultation.

In Maine, for example, students participate in bargaining between faculty representatives of the state university system and the trustees. A three-person student team represents student concerns relating to faculty bargaining. The board of trustees has the power to appoint students to the team. The trustees are required to meet with students when the union presents its initial proposal and again prior to the execution of a written agreement between the two parties (*NACUBO College University and Business Officer,* July 1976, Vol. 10, no. 1).

*Good faith bargaining.* After an institution/employer has voluntarily recognized an employee bargaining agent, or after a bargaining agent has been elected and certified by the appropriate federal or state agency, the negotiation of a collective bargaining agreement begins. Most bargaining statutes require that the parties bargain in good faith. The obligation to bargain in good faith usually is defined by courts as meaning that the employer and the bargaining agent must meet and confer. Good faith bargaining does not compel either party to make concessions or to yield any position fairly maintained. It does require the parties to bargain with an open mind and a sincere intention to reach an agreement (*Lipow* v. *Regents of the University of California,* 1975).

When asked to decide whether a party has been bargaining in good faith, courts appear to rely heavily upon evidence of the subjective intention of the party to reach an agreement, as shown by its bargaining behavior. Evidence of bad faith bargaining has included a refusal by the employer to meet with union representatives. Refusal to discuss mandatory subjects of bargaining, such as a grievance procedure, is also evidence of bad faith, as is the bypassing of union representatives to discuss proposed contract terms directly with employees.

*Scope of the negotiations: mandatory and permissive subjects.* Subjects to be negotiated are divided into two general classifications: mandatory and permissive. Mandatory subjects of negotiation are those which the parties are required by law to negotiate at the request of either party. Permissive subjects are those which the parties may negotiate if they voluntarily choose to do so. Employers generally take the view that it is to their advantage to bargain over as few subjects as possible, whereas bargaining agents tend to wish to include as many subjects as possible in the negotiations. Since the parties are under a legal duty to bargain in good faith, many disputes arise over exactly what subjects must be included in the negotiations. A party who refuses to bargain over a mandatory subject usually will be found in violation of law.

Mandatory subjects of negotiation usually include wages, hours, and similar terms and conditions of employment which do not fall clearly into the category of management prerogatives or are illegal. Having said that, however, the task remains of deciding whether a particular demand falls within or outside the basic mandate that parties must bargain over wages, hours, and other terms and conditions of employment.

Wages and hours clearly include a mandate to discuss payment for overtime work. For instance, if a faculty member's normal work year is the usual academic year, the union is entitled to seek an agreement regarding method of compensation for work done during a summer session. An institution/employer that refuses to discuss such an issue would not be bargaining in good faith.

Insurance benefits and plans also are mandatory subjects of bargaining. Employers must bargain as well on how employees are to be selected for layoff. If an institution proves bona fide financial exigency, it may not have to bargain over which department it will eliminate, but must bargain over the effects of the elimination.

*Collegiality as a mandatory subject for collective bargaining is an unresolved issue.* The concept of collegiality as it exists in educational institutions may be one characteristic which makes collective bargaining in educational institutions different from collective bargaining in the usual business or industrial setting. Collegiality is the practice whereby the person or governing body having the power to make decisions does so only after consulting with and considering the recommendations of colleagues. In earlier times, collegiality included the authority of one colleague to nullify the decisions of another. Today, collegiality exists most often in higher educational institutions, but may be found also in some secondary and elementary schools.

Collegial practices which employment labor relations boards have been asked to examine and issue determinations upon include the following: faculty participation in the selection of deans; faculty representation on a board of trustees; faculty participation in developing a statement of criteria for the selection of administrators; participation in the selection of the president or other executive officer; participation in the evaluation of administrators; and the reverse of such practices, such as participation of administrators in the selection and evaluation of faculty members.

The allegation that a conflict of interest is inherent in such practices also is made frequently. The concept of dual loyalty, in which responsibilities are owed both to the institution and to the faculty, which collects and evaluates applications for employment, causes a great deal of judgmental anguish to an employment labor relations board asked to rule on these practices. As might be expected, the board decisions regarding these practices are conflicting.

Collegiality also includes the practice in the academic world of persons moving back and forth quite freely and easily between what might be termed the "management" and "labor" sides of the enterprise. For example, it is a normal practice for faculty members to serve in administrative roles such as personnel committee member, department chairperson, academic or business dean, and president and vice-president of institutions. Later, having spent a predetermined or self-determined period of time in that role, the individual may move back to a regular faculty position and resume the responsibilities of teaching and research. Likewise, administrators who were hired initially to carry out management tasks sometimes move to a teaching or research role. They may or may not move back into a post involving administrative duties. This particular kind of moving about within the educational enterprise, serving in positions which could be considered "management" and then back to "labor" or vice-versa, is relatively rare in most business or industrial organizations.

Confusion and disputes over collegiality, therefore, are to be expected when federal or state employment labor relations boards are asked to determine whether the issue of collegiality is one which is a mandatory or a permissive subject of collective bargaining. There are few precedents to follow.

The basic question to be resolved is whether such practices are terms and conditions of employment within the meaning of the labor relations statute or whether they are managerial rights and prerogatives.

*Examples of collegial practices found not to be mandatory subjects of bargaining.* Decisions which found collegial practices *not* to be mandatory subjects of negotiations are illustrated by the following examples:

A faculty union took the position that the following four practices were mandatory subjects of negotiation: inclusion in the contract of the AAUP's 1966 Statement on Campus Government; faculty participation in the selection of deans; faculty representation on the board of trustees; and a statement of criteria for the selection of administrators. The NLRB found that these contract proposals were not mandatory subjects of bargaining. They were viewed by the National Labor Relations Board as concerning primarily managerial rights and prerogatives and not terms and conditions of employment within the meaning of Section 8(d) of the National Labor Relations Act. The decision went on to say that a mandatory subject of bargaining might be a contract proposal aimed at securing for unit employees the opportunity for promotion into managerial positions. The board found this was distinguishable from the actual selection of supervisory and administrative personnel. The decision also mentioned conflict of interest as a reason to view these proposals as nonmandatory. It pointed out that "there might be mixed loyalties of those selected, with obligations running not only to the institution but also to the faculty to which they would be indebted for the appointment, and to which, in the case of Deans, they would be subject to evaluation in order to retain their positions" (*St. John's Chapter of the American Association of University Professors*, 1975).

The general counsel of the National Labor Relations Board, in his quarterly report published June 20, 1975, by the Bureau of National Affairs, Inc., said that colleges and universities are *not* required to bargain over the issue of "collegiality." His report said in part:

Membership by a bargaining unit employee on the Board of Trustees would create a conflict of interest between his status as a trustee and an employee, particularly as the Board of Trustees has responsibility in all affairs of the university, including those of utmost significance to the bargaining unit, such as promotion, conferral of tenure, removal and suspension. Likewise, a conflict of interest could arise from the participation of unit employees in the selection of the president and deans who owe primary responsibility to the employer. Faculty participation in the evaluation of deans would make the dean dependent upon the faculty for retention of their positions.

A case decided by New York's PERB held that all union demands that would place control of educational and administrative policy decisions in the hands of the faculty were *not* mandatory subjects of negotiation (*Orange County Community College Faculty Association* v. *Orange County Community College and County of Orange*, 1976).

*Collegial practices found to be mandatory subjects for bargaining.* Collegial practices *were* found to be required subjects for negotiations by the New Jersey Public Employment Relations Commission in a case involving contract negotiations between the faculty union and Rutgers University. The commission concluded generally that, subject to the state labor relations act's mandate, "there is no reason the systems of collegiality and collective negotiations may not function harmoniously." The commission found the following to be required subjects for negotiation: procedures to be followed in the selection of departmental chairpersons; scope of tenure; aspects of affirmative action plans relating to or having impact upon terms and conditions of employment; and hours, compensation, and working conditions of teaching assistants and graduate assistants (*State of New Jersey: Before the Public Employment Relations Commission*, 1976).

*Permissive subjects for collective negotiations: academic freedom, reduction of work year.* A school board refused to approve reading assignments of *A*

*Clockwork Orange* and *The Exorcist*. The collective bargaining agreement provided that the school board agreed to respect the professional views of teachers regarding instructional material but specifically stated that the board had final authority over such material. If there were a conflict between the board and teachers as to the assignment of specific reading material, the agreement provided that the teachers would accept the directions of their employer. Some legal commentators have viewed this case as saying that the Constitutional protection of the First and Fourteenth Amendments may be bargained away. It is probably too early to make such a statement, but this case and others like it bear watching (*Cary* v. *Board of Education of the Adams-Arapahoe School District*, 1977).

The New Jersey Public Employment Relations Commission determined that the decision of a board of education to reduce the work year of school principals from twelve to ten months is not a required subject for collective negotiations, but merely a permissive subject (*Fair Lawn Board of Education*, 1975).

## Administering the Agreement

*Copies of the agreement should be given to all employees and managers.* Federal and most state labor laws require that members of the bargaining unit receive copies of the signed agreement. Managers, as well, obviously should have copies of the agreement.

*The agreement should be explained.* It is very helpful to all persons who will be using the contract to have some sort of informal or formal orientation to it. Some institutions provide a short series of meetings for management personnel at which the various provisions of the agreement are explained and questions answered. A discussion of matters not covered by the agreement is also worthwhile. Employees and managers may need to be reminded that the educational institution is an organization having many diverse activities, not all of which concern terms and conditions of employment. Thus, numerous activities, practices, and procedures will not be affected by a collective negotiation agreement.

Bargaining agents, too, have found it beneficial to provide similar orientation. Before voting on the contract, members of the bargaining unit will have had an opportunity to ask questions of particular concern to them. After the contract is signed, it is useful to provide information about the background of some of the provisions as well as their contemplated implementation.

*The grievance procedure is a major provision in an agreement.* The grievance procedure often is as important to employees as financial issues. Sometimes the principal reason employees have decided to bargain collectively is to achieve a regularized grievance procedure.

Special importance should be paid to an explanation of the grievance procedure in order that all persons dealing with the contract understand how the system operates and which matters are "grievable." Timeliness is often important in filing a grievance, and deadlines are of special importance.

*Wages.* Contract provisions regarding only the possibility of a wage increase often form the basis for a dispute between the parties. The parties may not be clear in their own minds about the meaning of the wage increase provision.

Wage increase provisions are of two basic types. One type provides automatically for a specific wage increase at a specific time. The other provides that annually or at a certain time the parties will discuss the possibility of a wage increase. The latter arrangement is merely a right to talk about a wage increase, not a right to have a wage increase.

A case in point involved a request for an interpretation of such a clause at a state college. The non-teaching employees' union alleged that the contract provision granted them the right to a wage increase. The Higher Education Personnel Board alleged that the clause merely said that a pay increase could be granted, but did not require that it be granted (*Washington State Employees Association Petitioner*, 1975).

A wage reopener clause may provide that, annually or on a set date, the parties will negotiate regarding a wage increase for employees in the bargaining unit. A question may arise as to who has the authority to bind the employer to grant a wage increase. Unless otherwise stipulated in the agreement, the authority to grant such a wage increase on behalf of the employer rests with whatever person or body has the official and legal authority to represent the employer. Usually, of course, the empoyer will be represented by the same person or body during the wage reopener bargaining sessions as during the negotiation of the agreement. Confusion has resulted when, for example, the party or body negotiating the annual wage increase appears to have such authority, but is not the same person or body that represented the employer in the original negotiation of the agreement.

In one case involving a public community college, a wage increase was negotiated under a collective bargaining agreement by the school district board. The state supreme court held that since the wage increase had been negotiated by the school district board sitting as such, and not in its capacity as the governing board of the college, the settlement was not binding upon the college (*Busboom* v. *Southeast Nebraska Technical Community College*, 1975).

*Payroll deductions may include check-off of union dues.* Payroll deductions for union dues, sometimes referred to as the check-off system, may be negotiated with the employer. If it becomes a part of the collective bargaining agreement, the institution/employer is bound to adhere to its agreement to deduct union dues during the life of the agreement.

If the deduction of such dues has not been negotiated formally and agreed to by the institution but is carried out on a voluntary basis by the institution, it may be discontinued by the institution.

*Rival union representatives are permitted to be at an institution.* Only the recognized legal bargaining agent of the employees in a bargaining unit may represent those employees in dealings with the employer institutions. However, representatives of other labor unions may have a right to be at an institution for other legitimate purposes if they do not claim that they represent the employees in the bargaining unit.

One institution granted use of its facilities to an unregistered student organization for the purpose of conducting a meeting. A rival union planned to appear and express its views to students about a strike at the clinical campus of the institution. The recognized union protested. It charged that providing such facilities to a rival union would constitute a violation of the collective bargining agreement between the state and the union. The state court held that a collective bargaining agreement did not prevent the university from permitting such a meeting to take place on campus (*Civil Service Employees Association* v. *State University at Stony Brook*, 1974).

*An institution may transfer employees from one bargaining unit to another unless prohibited by the contract.* The language of the collective bargaining agreement controls an institution's right to transfer employees. This is particularly true when that transfer moves employees from one bargaining unit to another. Unless such transfers are specifically prohibited by the bargaining agreement, an employer is free to transfer a worker out of the bargaining unit (1) if the employer bargains in good faith about the transfer and (2) if the employer is not motivated by antiunion animus (*University of Chicago* v. *National Labor Relations Board*, 1975).

*Unsettled disputes usually are resolved by arbitration.* Many collective bargaining agreements have as part of their dispute-settling machinery a provision for submitting unsolved grievances to an impartial arbitrator. The arbitrator's findings and award may be only recommendatory to the parties, rather like a "white paper." Most arbitration provisions, however, are for the purpose of settling the disputed issue once and for all, and thus contain language indicating that the arbitrator's findings and award shall be final and binding upon the parties. In this latter case, the arbitrator's award, should it not be abided by, may be enforced through resort to the judicial process.

Generally, an arbitrator's award is not subject to judicial review for errors of fact or law. The award may be reviewed only with regard to the arbitrator's staying within the scope of his or her authority to interpret the language of the agreement.

*Strikes and lockouts usually are barred by the agreement.* Most collective bargaining agreements outlaw strikes. The parties to the agreement usually set up a system of settling disputes through a grievance procedure that provides for review at various steps and levels. It often concludes with binding arbitration. The contract usually contains prohibitions against strikes by the employees and lockouts by the employer.

While a contract may prohibit strikes during the term of the agreement, the prohibitions do not apply after the expiration of the agreement. It is in these situations—unsuccessful negotiations when no contract is in effect—that most strikes occur.

A strike is normally a weapon of last resort by employees. In most cases, striking employees are subject to dismissal and replacement by the employer. Rehiring of fired strikers is sometimes arranged as part of the overall settlement of a strike. However, unless an employer voluntarily agrees to take back such fired strikers, they have no rights to the jobs they left.

In the public sector, many states have legislation that makes strikes by public employees illegal. Penalties such as loss of tenure, loss of job, or payment of fines may be imposed upon the individual employees, as well as upon the union representing them. In such situations courts have authority to issue injunctions ordering the employees back to work. Failure to obey such injunctions may place persons in contempt of court and subject to imprisonment. In spite of such statutes however, strikes do occur in the public sector. In recent years it has become not at all uncommon for teachers and staff members at educational institutions to resort to strikes and picket lines in order to bring pressure to bear upon negotiations for a new or renewed contract. They and their union leaders sometimes have been jailed. When the strike finally is over, and an agreement has been reached, the effects linger on. Speculation exists, for instance, about how such activities are viewed by students. There appears to be little data collected as yet on such matters.

## RECOMMENDATIONS

### Impact of Nondiscrimination and Other Statutes

Possible liability of the institution and individual educators exists for noncompliance with laws such as Title VII of the Civil Rights Act, Title IX of the 1972 Educational Amendments, the Equal Pay Act, and the Rehabilitation Act. The statutes set forth in Appendix A should be read carefully with one's own practices in mind. State laws may apply also.

## Mutual Agreement on Employment Terms

Carefully written employment agreements which accurately set forth the mutual understanding of employee and employer should prevent most lawsuits regarding conditions of employment. Foreseeing unusual circumstances, such as financial exigency or elimination of mandatory retirement, is to be encouraged in every possible way.

## Part-Time Employees

Use of part-time employees can be of great value to any organization. Equitable treatment and fair practices are statutory requirements in many instances.

## Administrators and Faculty: Employment Terms Compared

Contracts for administrators at higher education institutions appear to be the coming norm, as is already the case at elementary and secondary schools. Advance planning for this transition should include the gathering of information on professional standards for administrators and on contracts already in effect. Emphasis should be on improving the institution's recruiting and hiring procedures so that greater care is taken to evaluate candidates prior to hiring. Minimal contract terms should be in writing and should include information about salary, fringe benefits, term of office, process of review, notice of renewal or continuance, and responsibilities of the position.

## Administration as a Profession

Educational administrators are educators as well as managers. Administrative actions are exemplars to students. They directly affect the "value education" students receive at the institution simply by being there. Therefore, for educational and for managerial reasons, high professional standards of administration should be adopted and upheld by educational institutions. The bottom-line in educational organizations is education.

## Collective Bargaining

The institution's experience in dealing collectively with its employees will be affected enormously by its attitude toward this particular method of setting terms and conditions of empoyment. Expert legal advice is essential whatever basic stance the institution chooses to take.

# 6. Treatment of Faculty and Administrators: Academic and Employment Issues

## ACADEMIC ISSUES

### Academic Freedom

Academic freedom has been described as the freedom to inquire, to teach, and to learn. Freedom of inquiry has included the concept of following research wherever it leads. Freedom to teach includes not only teaching a particular subject according to one's own professional decision, but also includes the freedom to discuss in the classroom all kinds of views on a topic whether they are popular or not. Connected to the freedom to inquire and to teach is the student's freedom to learn. An early Supreme Court decision held that a state cannot decide arbitrarily "to contract available knowledge" and, in effect, withhold knowledge from students (*Meyer* v. *Nebraska*, 1923). Academic freedom is not an absolute freedom, of course. Like other free-doms, it can be restrained through proper and reasonable means. Supreme Court decisions cannot be said to have recognized academic freedom as a constitutional right, but courts do tend in most cases to recognize and protect the concept of academic freedom by using various legal theories.

The 1923 *Meyer* decision contained language that came very close to finding that academic freedom was a constitutional right. In that case a teacher at a private school had been tried for violating a state criminal statute which forbade the teaching of foreign languages in the first eight grades of any school. This parochial school teacher was found guilty and sentenced to jail for teaching children the German language. The Court found that teaching is a liberty interest protected by the Fourteenth Amendment, and that it can be restrained only through the proper and reasonable exercise of the state's police power. Part of the Court's opinion said that the teacher had the right to agree to teach the German language, and the parents had the right to engage him so to instruct their children as part of their liberty under the Fourteenth Amendment.

In 1957, the Supreme Court heard a case arising from a state statute authorizing the state attorney general to investigate subversive activities. A state university teacher was questioned by the attorney general about his political affiliations and also about the content of his classroom lectures. The Court held that the state could not interfere, without compelling reasons, in the four essentials of academic freedom: that is, who shall teach, what shall be taught, how it shall be taught, and who shall be admitted to study (*Sweezy* v. *New Hampshire*).

In 1968, the Supreme Court dealt with a state law prohibiting consideration of the theory of evolution in public schools. The Court struck down the law on the grounds that it was enacted for religious reasons and conflicted with the First Amendment prohibition against governmental establishment of religion (*Epperson* v. *Arkansas*).

Contemporary legal problems regarding academic freedom include some enormously complex questions about research. Local governments, for example, have attempted to regulate experiments done at universities or other educational institutions located within their political boundaries. Of special concern are those involving recombinant DNA and nuclear energy. Professionals in these two areas of research disagree with one another as to the amount of possible danger their research may cause to the general population. A number of professional societies have taken cognizance of the serious issue raised, namely how to balance academic freedom with public interest in safety. They are attempting to provide some guidelines for researchers in these areas.

Academic freedom to teach usually has been defined in this country as how a particular subject is taught, rather than whether the subject should be taught at all. In other countries, freedom to teach sometimes has included the teacher's right to decide which subject he or she is going to teach. Here, our accrediting processes have supported the right of states to decide, in general, what basic subjects ought to be taught. This is based on the notion that the state has a compelling interest in its citizens' being able to read, to write, to understand mathematics, and to know about the history of the country and how the government operates. Aside from these basic subjects, however, most states permit local schools, colleges, and universities to determine for themselves what other topics shall be included in their curriculum. Disagreements over curriculum still do arise. For example, a federal district judge in New Jersey recently held that transcendental meditation could not be taught with federal funds in four public school districts where it had been offered. After examining a chant being used and finding references to "the Lord" in it, he held that the teaching of TM in school was "religious in nature," and ordered it stopped as a violation of the First Amendment (*New York Times*, November 6, 1977, p. 28).

## Free Speech

*Free speech of faculty and administrators at public institutions is protected.* In general, faculty and administrators at public institutions may exercise their rights of free speech and other First Amendment rights under the same principles as do students—that is, the form of such expression must not disrupt the operation of the educational process (*Tinker* v. *Des Moines Independent Community School District,* 1969). Educators also should make known whether they are expressing personal opinions or speaking officially for the institution.

Restraints upon the exercise of free speech, association, and press rights, guaranteed by the federal and various state constitutions, often have been subjected to court scrutiny and sometimes have been found to be unlawful.

*Free speech was found unlawfully restrained by police surveillance.* Covert police surveillance in the classroom was challenged by a professor at the University of California at Los Angeles, who brought a taxpayer's suit against the chief of the Los Angeles Police Department. Undercover police agents were attending classes and participating in other activities on the university campus. The suit alleged that it was illegal to spend public money to finance covert intelligence-gathering activity at the university. The court agreed and ordered the surveillance stopped. The decision held that such surveillance, lacking any compelling state interest that could not be served by less intensive means, poses unlawful restraint upon the exercise of free speech and association rights guaranteed by the federal and state constitution (*White* v. *Davis,* 1975).

The Federal Bureau of Investigation also has engaged in counterintelligence activity against college faculty and administrators. In a letter to the American Association of University Professors, Attorney General Edward H. Levi gave his assurance that the Department of Justice and the FBI would no longer engage in such activities (*The Chronicle of Higher Education,* April 21, 1975).

## Dress and Grooming Codes

*Dress and grooming codes at public institutions generally are impermissible.* Grooming regulations affecting faculty and administrators as well as students have been challenged over the years. A number of cases have held that grooming regulations are constitutionally impermissible. This is true especially in the case of adults. However, there are notable exceptions.

The same comments may be made about adult dress codes as were made in Chapter 4 about student dress codes. The initial question is whether there is a need for such a code. If so, what is the purpose of the code? Codes that set standards relating to health or educational order usually are sustained by courts. Private institutions have a fairly free hand in determining what their employees shall wear or how they shall be groomed. It is in public institutions that most questions of constitutionality arise. Faculty and administrators often maintain that they have a constitutional right to free expression, which includes how they dress and look. Academic freedom, too, is raised as support for this viewpoint.

The courts have struggled with the matter of dress codes for adults at public institutions for a number of years. There still does not appear to be a clear-cut answer. Illustrative of this situation is a case involving a teachers' dress code in an East Hartford public high school. The dress code required male teachers to wear a shirt, tie, and sports jacket. A teacher of English and filmmaking asked permission to wear a turtleneck sweater with his sports jacket instead of a shirt and tie. He was granted the variance for the film-making class but not for the English class. He sued, claiming a constitutional right of free expression. The appellate court at first agreed with him that his Fourteenth Amendment liberty interest and his First Amendment interest had been violated. However, the appellate judges then decided to rehear the case en banc, and vacated the three-judge decision. They held that a public school board may impose reasonable regulations governing the appearance of the teachers it employs (*East Hartford Education Association* v. *Board of Education of the Town of East Hartford*, 1977).

On the other hand, another case in point involved a member of the faculty of a public junior college who charged that his civil rights were violated by a regulation against the wearing of beards. He sought a permanent injunction against the enforcement of the regulation and reinstatement to his job. (He had been fired because he refused to abide by the regulation.) Both the trial court and the appellate court held in favor of the faculty member; the appellate court said that such a discharge was constitutionally impermissible under the Fourteenth Amendment.

A second issue in this case involved the awarding of back pay to the faculty member. The college alleged that because it was a public institution, the Eleventh Amendment precluded the award of back pay. The court held that under state law, junior college districts are primarily local institutions created by local authority and supported by local revenue. Therefore the Eleventh Amendment is not applicable. The court said that the Eleventh Amendment restricts federal jurisdiction only in those cases in which the state is the real party in interest (*Hander* v. *San Jacinto Junior College*, 1975). Even where the state is the real party in interest, it will be liable for payment of back pay if Congress has passed a statute making it possible (*Fitzpatrick* v. *Bitzer*, 1976). Title VII (CRA) has such a statutory provision for payment of back pay by a state, for example.

Adult dress codes at public educational institutions have not yet been considered by the Supreme Court to this author's knowledge. However, a case involving a student dress code was denied a Supreme Court review. This left standing a decision which drew a distinction between dress regulations at elementary and secondary schools and those at the college level (see Chapter 4; see also *Lansdale* v. *Tyler Junior College,* 1972). The matter of the constitutional rights that may be involved is basically unsettled.

It should go almost without saying that adult dress codes ought to be drawn up with the cooperation of the persons who will be affected by the codes. Such participation may help to ensure relative peace in enforcement based upon a mutual agreement on the purpose of the code.

One final note is necessary on the question of "undress." There was a case several years ago in which a high school teacher was fired because he appeared nude in a feature story and centerfold of *Playgirl* magazine. Eventually the teacher was rehired on the ground that his decision to commercialize his beauty, although poor judgment, was not fatal to his employment relationship or to the educational climate in his school.

## EMPLOYMENT ISSUES

### Impact of Nondiscrimination Laws on Employment

The most casual observer of discriminatory employment practices in this country cannot fail to be struck by how such discrimination is affected by the overall availability of jobs. To take a classic example, discrimination in employment disappears almost completely in wartime. When there is much work to be done and relatively few people around to do it, employers somehow switch off discrimination. Instead, they judge job applicants on the basis of present or potential ability to do the job. Characteristics such as handicaps, race, and sex are put aside. Qualified applicants are hired and the jobs are done, often better and faster than ever before. However, when the job market shrinks back to normal or worse, the discrimination switch flips to "on" again. With extraordinary speed, the handicapped, minorities, and women once again find themselves judged by standards other than their ability to do a job.

A commentator on the contemporary scene, Russell Baker, wrote recently and trenchantly that this country "obviously does not provide enough jobs and schools," and in its attempt to be as egalitarian a society as possible, "it is developing a system under which duty in the have-not division can be rotated from generation to generation" (*New York Times Magazine,* July 24, 1977, p. 4). White males today argue that they are being pushed aside as a result of the way nondiscrimination laws are affecting employment opportunities.

Laws requiring nondiscriminatory employment practices include, for example, civil rights statutes from the post-Civil War era to Title VII of the 1964 Civil Rights Act. They also include more specific laws such as the Rehabilitation Act of 1973, Title IX of the Education Amendments of 1972, and the Age Discrimination in Employment Act of 1967.

Affirmative action to assist in the elimination of discrimination in employment is required by one presidential executive order and by two congressional laws. Affirmative action requires an employer to review his or her present labor force to see if certain groups are underutilized. If so, good faith efforts must be made to seek out, hire, and promote qualified applicants. An affirmative action plan, setting forth goals and timetable, must be developed. The executive order is 11246, as amended by 11375. The laws are the Rehabilitation Act of 1973 and its newly effective regulations, and the Vietnam Era Veteran's Readjustment Act of 1974, still awaiting regulations. All of these nondiscriminatory laws and orders are described in Appendix A.

Alleged discriminatory employment practices form the basis of an enormous number of lawsuits and complaints filed with governmental administrative agencies against employers. Many institutions have suffered great losses in time, money, and prestige in responding to such allegations. It is no wonder that they are beginning to add to their criteria for evaluating educators the ability to function in a manner that will prevent unnecessary law suits and complaints to administrative agencies.

### Nontenured Status

*Nontenured status offers protection only to the extent agreed to by the parties.* There appears to be much myth and folklore regarding the legal status of nontenured persons. The unvarnished truth, in simplest terms, is this. Unless evidence of statutory, contractual, or constitutional rights can be produced to the contrary, most nontenured employment relationships carry with them

- no expectancy of further employment
- no right to notice of non-reappointment
- no right to a hearing
- no right to reasons for non-reappointment

Two basic facts must be kept in mind regarding the nontenured condition of academic employment. First, it is viewed generally as a probationary period of employment, since the ultimate condition of academic employment is a tenured one. Second, the legal relationship between employer and employee during a probationary period is governed by whatever the parties have agreed to, plus the usual statutory and constitutional rights that exist.

Thus, nontenured employment relationships may run the gamut from an unwritten agreement that the employee is serving at the pleasure of the employer, to situations involving written term contracts providing for timely notice of non-reappointment. Nontenured administrative employees often are employed under the first set of conditions, while nontenured faculty employees generally are hired under the latter conditions.

Courts assume that the parties to nontenured working arrangements are adults who understand and have consented to whatever their working agreement provides. This includes length of employment, salary, job description, requirement for giving notice, reasons for non-reappointment, and so forth.

*Nontenured persons in public institutions have constitutional rights.* Nontenured persons in public institutions have a constitutional right to due process under the Fourteenth Amendment. They cannot be deprived by governmental action of life, liberty, or property without due process of law. However, it must be emphasized that a nontenured person must produce evidence that a liberty or property right exists before due process can be sought.

Due process includes both substantive and procedural rights. For example, a nontenured person has a substantive constitutional right to free speech under the First Amendment. If evidence proves that a nonrenewal or termination resulted from exercising the right to free speech, such dismissal has been held unconstitutional (*Pickering* v. *Board of Education,* 1968).

Procedural due process rights of nontenured persons are illustrated by the following cases:

A property interest would be in jeopardy, and due process required, when evidence has established that the parties mutually understood that there was an expectancy of further employment (*Perry* v. *Sindermann,* 1972).

A liberty interest would be in jeopardy, and due process required, when evidence shows that a charge has been made that may place a stigma on a person's good name and reputation so as to foreclose future employment opportunities or seriously damage his or her standing in the community (*Board of Regents* v. *Roth,* 1972).

To illustrate further, a nontenured faculty member at a public institution was not entitled to a pre-termination hearing before his employment was terminated either under state law or due process principles, in the absence of allegations that (1) the decision was made in retaliation for his exercise of the right of free speech; (2) his eligibility for other employment had been foreclosed; (3) he was entitled to continuous employment; or (4) his termination was maliciously or vindictively inspired (*Setty* v. *Minnesota State College Board,* 1975).

Thus, unless a constitutionally protected property or liberty interest is at stake, a public employer is not required to provide notice and hearing or a statement of reasons for non-reappointment. In situations where a non-tenured person alleges that there was an expectancy of further employment or that nonrenewal was due to a constitutionally impermissible reason, the person has the burden of proving such allegations at the hearing provided by the employer.

## Promotions

*Promotion decisions usually are left to academic experts.* Courts traditionally are reluctant to substitute their judgment for the judgment of those whom they recognize as educational experts, such as administrators and faculty members.

A typical case illustrating this situation is that of a university faculty member whose application for promotion was supported by all the full professors in his department and the chairman of his department. It was not approved by the college dean or the university president. The court in that case said:

> Performance evaluation and like considerations relating to professors' promotions and salary increases involve judgmental decisions which are, at best, difficult and, in the Court's opinion, are best left to those entrusted to make the same, i.e., college administrators (*Goolsby* v. *Regents of the University System of Georgia*, 1976).

Quite a different situation would exist if an institution had not followed its own rules in considering the promotion. Similarly, if an institution acted arbitrarily or maliciously, a court very probably would be willing to intervene.

## Tenure

Tenure, basically, is a contract of continuing employment between an individual and an institution. It may be acquired in at least three ways. The first is by formal granting procedures, resulting in contractual tenure. The second is by the informal conduct of the institution which is relied upon by the faculty person, resulting in de facto tenure. The third way is by the operation of a statute, which, for example, may provide that upon completion of three years of satisfactory service, tenure is acquired.

*Contractual tenure.* Contractual tenure is the result of a series of formal reviewing procedures. These usually begin with a review of the candidate's academic and scholarly competence by peers in a specific discipline. For example, the qualifications of a candidate for tenure in a chemistry department would be reviewed initially by a committee of peers from the chemistry department. Later steps in the reviewing process may include reviews and recommendations by the academic dean and the chief executive officer of the institution, such as the president. Authority to award tenure often resides with the highest level governing body, such as a board of regents or board of trustees.

Institutional rules usually require a stated period of years of satisfactory probationary service before tenure can be awarded.

There is a dual rationale for granting contractual tenure. On one hand there is the evaluation of the performance and qualifications of the individual. On the other hand there is the evaluation of the need of the institution for the services of the individual. For example, a department tenure review committee may find that an individual meets its standard for acquiring tenure. However, the administration may note that four of the five departmental faculty positions are held already by tenured persons. The decision, then, may be against awarding tenure. The institution may fear it will not be able to function and grow properly if all positions in a department are held by tenured persons. Thus, even though an individual is qualified, tenure may be denied on grounds that the institution's needs would be adversely affected.

*Authority to confer contractual tenure rests with one specified group or person.* Contractual tenure may be granted only by the person or body having specific power to do so. Such authority is set forth in documents or statutes under which the institution operates. Usually, the authority to award tenure at a university rests with the highest governing body, such as the board of trustees. All other decisions in the course of the review process are recommendatory in nature.

A court was asked to resolve a typical "lack of authority" dispute in which the pesident of a university informed a nontenured member of the faculty in writing that the board of visitors had continued him "without term." Later, a new president was appointed. He told the faculty member he would not be renewed. The professor asked the court to prevent his being terminated without a hearing. The court dismissed the professor's suit on the grounds that the former president's letter to the professor was not binding because "Only the board may elect an individual to the faculty and only the board may confer the equivalent of tenure by electing a faculty member without term" (*Sullivan* v. *Dykstra*, 1976).

*Delegation of authority to confer tenure is limited to negative decisions.* Trustees may delegate to the president of a state institution the authority to make negative decisions in tenure cases. They cannot delegate their power to award tenure (*Abramson* v. *Board of Regents, University of Hawaii*, 1976).

*Tenure is not conferred by rehiring beyond probationary period.* Occasionally, when tenure has not been granted and the faculty member has been notified of that fact, an additional year's appointment will be offered to the faculty member. Such additional term may be at the request of the nonrenewed faculty member or it may be the result of the need of the institution. The question arises whether such rehiring beyond the expiration of the probationary period has the effect of automatically granting some kind of tenure. The courts generally have said no.

A case in point involved an associate professor who was specifically denied tenure before the expiration of the probationary period, but was rehired for an extra year. The court found there was no provision in the faculty manual that prohibited a faculty member from being employed without tenure beyond the expiration of his probationary period. The court concluded that the rehiring did not confer tenure when the professor had been notified properly of denial of tenure (*Kilcoyne* v. *Morgan,* 1975).

*Tenure by default, due to lack of timely notice, generally is not possible.* Timely notice of nonrenewal or denial of tenure is required by most institutional policies or state statutes. When proper notice is not given, a claim may be made by the faculty member that tenure has been conferred by default. However, courts have tended to find that the awarding of tenure can be the result only of an intentional act, not of mere negligence. When proper notice is not given, courts may find that the teacher has been damaged. Some sort of redress may be made, perhaps by an additional period of employment, or by payment of money damages in the amount of one or two years' salary. Tenure, though, generally is found not to have been conferred.

An assistant professor alleged, for example, that he had acquired a contractual right to tenure due to the administration's failure to give him notice of termination. The university asserted that the trustees alone were authorized to award tenure. It alleged that a default by the administration could not result in the award of tenure. The state trial court agreed with the university (*Gorman* v. *University of Miami,* 1975).

Procedures of tenure review have been challenged. A former university professor claimed that the procedure by which he had been denied tenure violated due process. He had been excluded from the initial faculty committee meeting where his tenure was discussed. The court held this did not violate due process. The court also said that the committee could consider evidence beyond that which it had before it at the meeting (*Stebbins* v. *Weaver,* 1975).

*De facto tenure may result from rules and understandings fostered by an institution's officials.* The best known of the de facto tenure cases arose at a junior college. The college's official faculty guide had for many years contained the following provision:

Teacher Tenure: Odessa College has no tenure system. The administration of the College wishes the faculty member to feel that he has permanent tenure so long as his teaching services are satisfactory and as long as he displays a cooperative attitude toward his co-workers and his superiors, and as long as he is happy in his work.

The state system also had guidelines indicating that a person employed in the system as a teacher for seven years or more had some form of job tenure. A teacher was employed in the state system for ten years, the last four as a junior college professor under a series of one-year written agreements. He was then fired without a hearing. The Supreme Court held that he had acquired de facto tenure. This created a property interest which required that he be given a hearing and reasons why he was being fired (*Perry* v. *Sindermann*, 1972).

*Statutory tenure.* Under state statutes, tenure may be acquired upon completion of a stated number of years' satisfactory probationary service. After such tenure is acquired, due process is required in order to terminate employment.

Statutory tenure is found most often in elementary and secondary school systems. Junior colleges also sometimes rely on statutory tenure. Higher education institutions usually operate contractual tenure systems.

*The scope of tenure may be systemwide or limited to one institution.* A tenured teacher sometimes asserts that tenure has been granted in an entire institutional system rather than within one unit of the system. To support such an assertion, evidence would have to show that systemwide tenure clearly was intended by statutory or other policies.

A teacher unsuccessfully claimed he had been granted permanent tenure in the entire University of Nevada system, not merely in the division of the system known as the Desert Research Institute. The court said, "A fair reading of the record demonstrates that there is substantial evidence to support the decision of the trial court that Winterberg did not receive Systemwide tenure, but only that within the division of the DRI" (*Winterberg* v. *the University of Nevada System*, 1975).

*An institution is very rarely ordered to grant tenure.* It is rare indeed for a court to order an educational institution to grant tenure. In a recent test case, the New York State Commissioner of Human Rights found that a professor had been denied tenure because of her sex. The New York Court of Appeals then was asked to determine whether the commissioner could order the institution to grant tenure to the professor. The court found that the commissioner did have the power to order tenure, but should exercise it only in the most extraordinary situations. The court held that in this case the record showed "no circumstances of sufficient gravity to justify the imposition of tenure." The court said the commissioner should fashion appropriate remedies, short of the imposition of tenure, to redress the conceded discrimination and effectuate the purposes of the Human Rights Law. Appropriate remedies might include rehiring for a limited period of time, money damages, and assistance in seeking new employment (*New York Institute of Technology* v. *State Division of Human Rights,* 1976).

### Termination

*Termination of tenure requires adequate cause and, at public institutions, appropriate constitutional safeguards.* Once tenure is acquired, a contract of continuing employment exists. It generally can be terminated by the institution only upon showing adequate cause and, at public institutions, appropriate constitutional safeguards. The definition of adequate or just cause may be determined by reference to professional standards or documents such as collective bargaining agreements. For example, the 1940 "Statement of Academic Freedom and Tenure" of the American Association of University Professors and Association of American Colleges (see Appendix B) is such a set of professional standards. If adopted or otherwise accepted by the institution the definition of adequate cause for termination of tenured persons would include professional incompetency, moral turpitude, bona fide financial exigency, and discontinuance or curtailment of a program or course of study. Interpretations of these terms also may be set forth. The 1940 statement defines moral turpitude, for instance, as involving cases of "behavior that would evoke condemnation by the academic community generally" rather than behavior that would affront the moral sensibilities of persons in the particular community. If an institution wishes to define standards of moral behavior, for example between teacher and student, it should do so clearly in documented form such as a faculty handbook so that there is a mutual understanding of the standard. Appropriate review of any charges of deviations from the standard would be advised as well.

*Public institutions must provide due process.* Impermissible causes for termination at public institutions include the exercise of First Amendment rights such as expressing political views or freedom of the press (*Endress* v. *Brookdale Community College,* 1976).

Procedural due process generally is required at public institutions in situations involving termination of a contract of tenure. Notice must be given of the reasons why tenure is to be terminated, and a hearing must be held where the tenured person has an opportunity to rebut the evidence offered as the cause of termination (see *Chase* v. *Board of Trustees of Nebraska State*

*Colleges*, 1975).

An impartial decision maker is part of a fair hearing process. Occasionally, the body that terminates an individual turns out to be the same body designated to serve as an impartial decision maker in a hearing to review the original decision to terminate. Courts have held that if no evidence of bias or lack of honesty or integrity is shown, the same body may serve in both capacities. Such a sequence of events was recently reviewed favorably by the Supreme Court. A school board had the duty to negotiate a collective bargaining agreement with its teachers. It also had the power to hire and fire the teachers. When the teachers struck, the school board fired some of them, as permitted by Illinois law. The teachers alleged that the school board was not an impartial decision maker and that, therefore, the teachers had been deprived of due process. The Supreme Court held that the teachers

> failed to demonstrate that the decision to terminate their employent was infected by the sort of bias that we have held to disqualify other decisionmakers as a matter of federal due process. A showing that the Board was "involved" in the events preceding this decision, in light of the important interest in leaving the Board the power [to hire and fire and run the school system] given by the state legislature, is not enough to overcome the presumption of honesty and integrity in policymakers with decisionmaking power (*Hortonville Joint School District No. 1* v. *Hortonville Education Association*, 1976).

*Homosexuality has been held grounds for dismissal.* A public high school teacher was dismissed on the basis of his avowed homosexuality; the fact of his homosexuality had been discovered after he had been teaching for thirteen years. Evidence indicated that his teaching performance had been excellent, and there was no evidence showing that he had engaged in sodomy or other illegal acts. The State of Washington Supreme Court found that the teacher was properly dismissed from his teaching position. It ruled that his avowed sexual preference constituted "immorality" and impaired his teaching efficiency and injured his school (*Gaylord* v. *Tacoma School District No. 10*, 1977). This decision was allowed to stand by the U.S. Supreme Court (October 3, 1977). Compare *Gaylord* with *Aumiller*, page 34.

*Dismissal for criticizing a superior at a public institution may be unconstitutional.* The employment relationship between teachers and the state, and between administrators and the state, creates an area of special concern regarding the right to free speech. A question arises about the right of a public employee, such as an administrator or faculty member, to exercise the right of free speech by criticizing a superior. Three cases come to mind with regard to court decisions on this question.

The first case involved a high school teacher who was discharged for writing a letter to a newspaper criticizing the way the school board and the school superintendent had handled recent bond issues. The Supreme Court held in that case that the board's action violated the teacher's right of free speech. However, the court also adopted a new balancing test in this case. The test weighs the employee's interest in free speech against the harm likely to result to the state's interest in promoting efficient peformance of its employees. Crucial to the balance struck is the hierarchical proximity of the criticizing employee to the body or person criticized. The court felt that when the working relationship between the parties was very personal and intimate, such criticism would seriously undermine the working relationship between them. Then the balance would be shifted toward the state and away from First Amendment protection for the employees. The criticism would result in dismissal. The court felt that to be protected such statements of criticism (1) must be of public importance, and (2) must not cause a disruptive impact between the employee and a proximate supervisor (*Pickering* v. *Board of Education*, 1968).

The second case involved an associate professor at a university who was discharged for criticizing the acting chairman of her department at a faculty meeting. The court found in this case that the employee's statements were not protected under the *Pickering* test. The statements did not rise to the level of public importance, and did have a disruptive impact. The court felt that an attack on the integrity of the chairman in a faculty meeting would have a serious effect, interfering with a harmonious relationship between the employee and her superiors and coworkers. Thus, the court found that the employee's statements were not protected by the First Amendment. They could permissibly form a part of the basis for her discharge (*Roseman* v. *Indiana University*, 1976).

The third case involved an administrator who was an assistant district attorney. He served as the Philadelphia district attorney's immediate deputy in administrative and policymaking matters. He was discharged for publicly disputing his superior's integrity in handling criminal matters. The court found he was not entitled to First Amendment protection for a speech that seriously undermined his employment relationship with his superior and aroused public controversy. The court found in this case that this public administrator's speech failed the *Pickering* test: although the speech was of public import, it did cause a public uproar, which thoroughly curtailed the employee's usefulness to his superior (*Sprague* v. *Fitzpatrick*, 1976).

*Summary of the "Pickering rule."* When a public employee wishes to criticize his employer, three essential elements are involved in determining whether such speech is protected by the First Amendment, according to the *Pickering* rule: (1) the hierarchical proximity of the employee and the superior; (2) the public import of the statement; and (3) a nondisruptive impact on the working relationship between the employee and the superior.

### Financial Exigency

*Termination of tenured staff due to financial exigency.* Financial distress of the institution as a permissible reason for terminating tenured staff has been tested extensively in the courts (*Lumpert* v. *University of Dubuque,* 1977; *Sokolowsky* v. *Antioch College,* 1975). Questions arise such as how to substantiate and prove bona fide the institution's claim of financial exigency. What criteria will be used to determine specifically which units of the institution and which individuals in those units will be terminated?

*Proving bona fide financial exigency is essential.* The Bloomfield College case, mentioned in the last chapter, is illustrative of the kind of evidence required to support a claim of bona fide financial exigency.

In that case the college attempted to terminate tenured faculty members because of the institution's financial problems. Evidence was presented that the trustees had decided not to sell a golf course owned by the college. The teachers alleged that this decision was evidence that the financial distress was not bona fide. The court found that the decision was within the business judgment of the trustees and did not make illegitimate the financial exigency of the college.

This case is particularly interesting because while the court found that the evidence supported the college's claim of financial exigency, the court also found that financial exigency was not the bona fide reason for termination. Rather, the judge said that the financial exigency was merely an excuse to facilitate elimination of tenure as a whole at the college. The judge pointed to numerous statements in the record and various internal memoranda which indicated a "hostility to the basic concept of tenure." Thus, the court found that the financial distress was real, but was not the true reason for terminating the tenured professors (*American Association of University Professors, Bloomfield Chapter* v. *Bloomfield College,* 1975). The teachers were ordered reinstated.

*Procedure to be used to determine which individuals shall be terminated.* Once the decision has been made as to which units are to be decreased, the next step is to identify individuals who will be recommended for dismissal. The identification procedure may be set forth in the institution's own regulations, in a state statute, or in a collective bargaining contract. Professional standards of teachers or administrators may apply. The recommendations for specific dismissals then would be forwarded to the person or body having the official authority to hire and fire, such as a board of regents or board of trustees.

On this issue, a court has ruled that "where lack of funds necessitated releasing a sizeable number of the faculty, certainly it was peculiarly within the province of the school administration to determine which teachers should be released, and which retained" (*Levitt v. Board of Trustees of Nebraska State Colleges,* 1974).

The issue still remains of who has the right to present evidence to the administration during the time it is deciding which teachers shall be released. A collective bargaining agreement, a statute, or the institution's own rules may require that the administration consult either with representatives of persons whose jobs are in jeopardy or with the individuals themselves prior to making recommendations.

*Attempt to terminate tenured professor for financial exigency without due process was ineffective.* Two germane issues were raised by a case involving a tenured teacher at a state college. First, if a collective bargaining grievance procedure is used by the terminated teacher, does he thereby waive his other contractual or constitutional rights to due process? Second, if a hearing is provided, what will be discussed?

In the case in point, the legislature reduced the college budget. The college dismissed a tenured history teacher without a hearing. Evidence presented at the trial indicated that the teacher had a right to a hearing prior to termination for financial exigency. This right was proclaimed in the faculty handbook and in the collective bargaining agreement. The college claimed, however, that it had the right to terminate for financial exigency. Once it exercised that right, a teacher's tenure ceased to exist. Thus, there remained no grounds on which to seek redress from a court. The terminated teacher sued for damages. He lost in the lower court, but won in the upper state court.

The court found that a tenured professor, who began the grievance procedure under a collective bargaining agreement, did not thereby waive his contractual rights nor his constitutional rights to due process. This was because the college's own rules had become part of his contractual relationship with the college. His total contractual relationship included both the provisions in the faculty handbook and those in the collective bargaining agreement.

The court agreed with the college board of trustees that it possessed the final authority to decide which individuals would be terminated. But, the court ruled, the college must provide a hearing to tenured teachers in order that the teacher may present reasons why he or she should be retained and some other individual retrenched.

The court held that the contract termination here was ineffective. The teacher was entitled to damages based upon the amount of his salary for the last effective year of his contract, less the amount he earned (or with reasonable diligence could have earned from other employment) during the contract renewal period (*Brady* v. *Board of Trustees of Nebraska State Colleges*, 1976).

*Relocating and retraining employees affected by retrenchment.* Assisting employees to relocate is necessary only to the extent the law or mutual agreement requires. Professional standards, too, may be relied on. The 1975 AAUA "Professional Standards for Administrators in Higher Education" provides that "an administrator has the right, in cases of termination of employment due to a reallocation of resources, to be assisted actively by the institution in seeking new employment" (see Appendix B). Another set of standards relied upon in such cases is the 1968 "Recommended Institutional Regulations on Academic Freedom and Tenure" propounded by the AAUP (*AAUP Bulletin*, vol. 54, p. 448). These standards provide that the institution will attempt to place faculty members in other suitable positions if their own program or department is to be abandoned.

At one institution, a question arose as to whether a faculty person had to be involved in such a search for another suitable position. The court said no. The evidence showed that the institution had undertaken "a detailed review" of all other suitable programs and positions before it sent a termination notice to the tenured faculty person (*Browzin* v. *Catholic University of America*, 1976).

Unless there is a mutual agreement between the parties regarding retraining of retrenched persons, the courts have not indicated any responsibility of institutions to do so. However, a number of educational institutions that view their faculty, administrators, and other staff as valuable human resources have begun to explore the possibility of providing opportunities for retraining persons who wish to voluntarily participate in such programs. Statutes may provide an opportunity for retraining, as well.

*Right of terminated tenured person to reemployment.* Collective bargaining agreements or statutes may require that tenured persons who were terminated be given priority when the financial emergency is past and hiring of faculty is possible again.

Retrenched persons also may claim a right to be considered for reemployment as jobs open in other programs or departments. It is possible that an individual's basic disciplinary training and experience may make it feasible for him or her to be placed in any number of departments or roles.

### Seniority Rights

Rules regarding seniority rights are especially important during periods of layoffs of employees for financial or other reasons. Some seniority systems permit an employer to keep on the payroll persons having special skills even though they have less seniority than other employees.

An example of how such a concept operates at an academic institution is found in a situation that arose in a state university in California. There an employee who possessed special skills was kept on the payroll when another employee having more seniority was terminated. A court found this rule not to be either arbitrary or capricious and said:

> The evidence shows that a minimum of one year, and perhaps longer, would be required to retrain appellant to perform the duties of the two employees who were retained under this provision. Thus, appellant's contention that respondent is obligated by the layoff policy to retrain senior employees is without merit.

It should be noted that this case also contained an allegation by the terminated employee that he had a right to be retrained by the university. The court ruled that without specific agreement by the university regarding such an obligation, the responsibility to retrain employees about to be terminated does not exist (*Smith* v. *Regents of University of California*, 1976).

### Resignations

When an employee of an educational institution wishes to resign his or her position, notice of the intended resignation should be sent to the person or body authorized to accept it. Generally, the appropriate person or body is the person or body who has the authority to hire, fire, promote, and discharge employees. In an institution of higher education, for example, the board of trustees usually has such authority. By statute, a board of trustees may be empowered to delegate authority to hire, fire, promote, and discharge employees to another person or body, such as the president of the institution. A similar pattern of authority often exists at elementary school and secondary school levels, where a school board sometimes has original authority but is empowered to delegate all or part of that authority to others.

The question of who had authority to accept a resignation arose at a community college in the state of New York. There a faculty member sent a letter of resignation to the college president, who accepted the resignation. The faculty member later changed her mind and sought reemployment at the college through an action filed in a state court. The case was ultimately decided by the appellate division of the state supreme court. It held that the evidence indicated that the community college president had been delegated the authority to hire, fire, promote, and discharge employees, and that incidental to that authority he had the authority to accept resignations as well. The appellate court also held that the faculty member had been advised of his acceptance of her resignation in clear language. The resignation having been sent to and accepted by an authorized party, it was too late for the faculty member to ask that it be withdrawn (*Carroll* v. *Onondaga Community College*, 1976).

## Remedies for Wrongful Discipline or Termination

*Remedies for wrongful discipline or termination in violation of constitutional or other federal statutory rights at public institutions.* The Civil Rights Act of 1871, 42 U.S.C. Sec. 1983, forms the legal basis for redress when teachers at public institutions allege that they were disciplined or terminated in violation of their constitutional or other federal statutory rights. As already noted, that act permits persons to bring actions against public officials for deprivation of civil rights. Personal liability of public officials is a possibility which was discussed in Chapter 2.

Specific legal remedies permitted include relief in the form of actual, compensatory, and punitive money damages. Equitable relief is permitted also in the form of injunctions and declaratory judgments. Reinstatement may be possible in some cases.

To illustrate, a case arose in which a number of teachers had to be released because of a budget crisis (*Boyle* v. *Renton School District*, 1972). A state court found that the process used to dismiss them deprived them of procedural due process rights under both state law and the federal constitution. The court set aside the nonrenewals. In determining damages, the court first awarded damages for injury to reputations, careers, and status in the teaching profession, because subjective criteria had been applied in selecting teachers to be terminated. Second, the court awarded damages for the frustration, anxiety, and mental suffering caused by nonrenewal. Third, the court compensated teachers for specific losses, such as these:

- loss of salary due to not finding another teaching position;
- differential in salary between old and new jobs;
- costs associated with seeking new employment, such as résumés, postage, additional courses, photocopying, newspaper subscriptions, long distance telephone calls, mileage, and transcripts;
- loss of state retirement benefits;
- cost of replacing medical insurance;
- cost of medical expenses incurred between old and new medical insurance coverage;
- cost of selling a house to move to new locality;
- moving expenses;
- extra costs of driving to new, more distant school system.

In some situations, attorneys' fees may also be awarded. In certain circumstances, for example those regarding free speech and race, reinstatement is a possibility. Suits based upon the Civil Rights Act generally are filed in federal court, but may be filed in state courts.

*Remedies for breach of contract at private institutions.* The employment relationships at private institutions are contractual in nature. The basic remedy, therefore, is a suit for breach of contract.

Generally, damages would be sought for injury to one's career and for mental suffering. Compensation would be asked for loss of income and relevant incidental costs similar to those indicated above.

## Retirement

*Mandatory retirement age.* Federal legislation has been proposed, and may be enacted, to eliminate the requirement that persons retire at a certain age. A number of education associations have asked that teachers be exempt from any new law of this kind, because allowing people to stay on the job longer would depress employment opportunities for young educators and would also foster debilitation of the enterprise—teaching, research, and administration.

The present retirement systems have generated a great deal of litigation. Some cases have been based on allegations of denial of equal protection of the laws. Other cases have claimed violation of the Federal Age Discrimination in Employment Act (ADEA), Title VII (CRA), or Title IX of the Education Amendments. Several examples follow. Also, a number of states have human rights laws which prohibit discrimination in employment based upon age (forty to sixty-five), race, creed, color, national origin, and sex.

*Equal protection found not violated by two different retirement ages.* A community college board of trustees adopted a mandatory retirement age of sixty-five. In the same state, the state universities and colleges had a mandatory retirement age of sixty-seven. The teachers' union alleged that the community college teachers were being denied equal protection of the laws. It asked the court to require the community college board to retain certified teachers until the age of sixty-seven and thereafter, unless it was determined that the teacher was physically or mentally incapable of carrying out his or her teaching duties. The court held that the community college teachers were not denied equal protection either by the adoption of a mandatory retirement age of sixty-five or by the fact that they were required to retire at sixty-five while teachers at the state universities and colleges were permitted to continue to teach until age sixty-seven (*American Federation of Teachers College Guild, Local 1521* v. *Los Angeles Community College District Board of Trustees*, 1976).

The U.S. Navy for some time has permitted female officers to remain in service longer than males prior to mandatory retirement. This was upheld by the Supreme Court as a constitutionally permissible classification aimed at reducing "disparity in economic conditions between men and women caused by the long history of discrimination against women" (*Schlesinger* v. *Ballard*, 1975).

*Remedies for violations of the Age Discrimination in Employment Act: damages for pain and suffering under ADEA.* One of the earliest legal challenges to mandatory retirement arose under the Age Discrimination in Employment Act of 1967. A person who was involuntarily retired not only suffered money damage, but went into a decline and died. His widow filed suit. In that case, a lower court held that the act "essentially establishes a new statutory tort" (civil wrong). It ruled that the ADEA permitted a court to award damages for pain and suffering, in addition to damages for loss of income. However, a state appeal court reversed the lower court. It held that the act created no new tort. The appeal court pointed out that the act's enforcement provision, 29 U.S.C. Sec. 626(b), does not mention any money damages other than "amounts" measured by "unpaid minimum wages or unpaid overtime compensation" and "liquidated damages." The court went on to say, "If the employer's conduct has been such as to merit punitive treatment, then the employer is to be penalized by doubling the damages awarded. To allow psychic distress awards in addition would in a very real sense thwart the limitations Congress thought advisable to impose." Accordingly, the state appellate court concluded that involuntary retirees may seek redress including unpaid wages or overtime compensation and liquidated damages, but not damages for pain and suffering (*Rogers* v. *Exxon Research and Engineering Company*, 1977).

On the other hand, pain and suffering were allowed by a federal court in another case, decided after the *Rogers* case. That court found that the ADEA does authorize a court to award damages for physical and mental suffering, contrary to the reasoning in *Rogers*. Thus, there is conflict between jurisdictions as to whether the ADEA permits damages for pain and suffering in addition to other damages (*Bertrand* v. *Orkin Exterminating Co.*, 1977).

*Bona fide retirement plans are permissible under ADEA.* It is unlawful to discharge an individual because of age. However, there is no statutory provision prohibiting involuntary bona fide retirement on a pension. Therefore, an employer's involuntary retirement of a sixty-four-year-old employee did not violate the ADEA. A retirement plan is permitted that gives an employer the option to involuntarily retire employees between the ages of sixty and sixty-five and provides an adequate pension.

In reversing the lower court's finding that all involuntary retirement of employees before age sixty-five is unlawful, the appellate court said:

> The primary purpose of the Act is to prevent age discrimination in hiring and discharging workers. . . . There is, however, a clear, measurable difference between outright discharge and retirement, a distinction that cannot be overlooked in analyzing the Act. While discharging without compensation is obviously undesirable, retirement on an adequate pension is generally regarded with favor. Careful examination of the legislative history demonstrates that, while cognizant of the disruptive effect retirement may have on individuals, Congress continues to regard retirement plans favorably and chose therefore to legislate only with respect to discharge.

Thus the court found that a bona fide employee benefit plan giving an employer the option to involuntarily retire employees before age sixty-five is permissible under the act (*Zinger* v. *Blanchette*, 1977).

*Sex discrimination in amount of contributions paid into retirement plans, eligibility for benefits, and amount of benefits paid out.* Most claims that retirement plans discriminate against females concern plans that require females to pay higher premiums or receive lower benefits than males. The major trouble spots are at the points of pay-in and pay-out. The problems arise because present actuarial statistics indicate that, in general, females have a longer life expectancy than men. This is viewed as a temporary state of affairs; it is expected that as soon as females achieve full rights to stressful jobs, their life expectancy will more closely resemble that of men. In the meantime, courts and administrative agencies are asked to sort out the immediate inequities.

For example, a case arose involving an employee pension plan that required females to make higher contributions than men because of their longer life expectancy. A federal court ruled that the women were victims of unlawful discrimination under the provisions of Title VII of the Civil Rights Act of 1964, as amended. The court said:

> To require every individual woman to contribute more than her male counterpart because women, on the average, live longer than men, is just the kind of abstract generalizations applied to individual women because of their being women, which Title VII was designed to abolish (*Manhart* v. *City of Los Angeles Department of Water and Power*, 1976).

This case may be reviewed by the Supreme Court.

Two other cases had to do with elibigility of widows and widowers for social security benefits. Widows did not have to prove dependency before collecting survivors' benefits; however, widowers did. A widower filed suit and ultimately won. The Supreme Court held the relevant section of the Social Security Act unconstitutional. There was some discussion about whether the discrimination was against the deceased wife by providing less protection to families of females than males, or whether it was against the surviving widower (*Califano* v. *Goldfarb*, 1977).

Earlier the Supreme Court had found unconstitutional a social security provision that permitted insurance benefits to widows with children in their care, but denied them to widowers in that circumstance (*Weinberger* v. *Wiesenfeld*, 1975). In both cases, it was a male rather than a female who successfully proved sex discrimination.

The amount of social security benefits paid out was the subject of another Supreme Court decision. The Court upheld a provision providing a different formula for computing the amount of old age insurance benefits for women, which results in higher payments to them. The Supreme Court's ruling was based upon the fact that the statute "operated directly to compensate women for past economic discrimination," which was judged permissible (*Califano* v. *Webster*, 1977).

A similar situation regarding equality of benefits paid out arose in Indiana. There, before 1972, equal benefits were paid to females and males. A mortality table that ignored the sex of annuitants was used. After 1972, a revised table, taking sex into account was used. The result was that retired female teachers received less per month than retired male teachers. An Indiana court ruled that the use of separate actuarial tables for females and males in computing retirement benefits for teachers violated the equal protection guarantees of the U.S. and Indiana constitutions (*Reilly* v. *Robertson*, 1977).

### Pregnancy: Childbearing and Child Rearing

At present, employers covered by Title VII of the Civil Rights Act are not required to provide disability coverage for pregnant employees (*General Electric* v. *Gilbert*, 1977). Federal legislation has been introduced to require such coverage. It has not been passed as of this writing. However, it is a violation of Title VII for an employer to deny employees returning from pregnancy leave their accumulated seniority (*Nashville Gas Company* v. *Satty*, 1977).

However, most institutions covered by Title IX of the 1972 Education Amendments and which provide temporary disability benefits for employees must cover pregnancy; so ruled the HEW office for Civil Rights after the *Gilbert* decision. There is an exception which must be noted. In Romeo,

Michigan, a pregnant guidance counselor who was denied sick pay sued under Title IX. A federal court ruled that HEW had no authority under Title IX to regulate employment practices. The *Romeo* decision affects only that court's jurisdiction in Michigan. HEW apparently intends to appeal the decision as going against congressional intent (*Romeo Community Schools* v. *HEW*, 1977).

In the meantime, Title IX still applies to educational employees outside the district court's jurisdiction. Section 86.57(c) of the Title IX regulations states:

> Pregnancy is a temporary disability. A recipient shall treat pregnancy and recovery therefrom and any temporary disability resulting therefrom as any other temporary disability for all job related purposes, including commencement, duration, and extensions of leave, payment of disability income, accrual of seniority and any other benefit or service, and reinstatement, and under any fringe benefit offered to employees by virtue of employment.

State human rights laws also may provide that covered private institutions treat pregnant employees in the same manner as other employees disabled by a nonoccupational illness or injury.

Time off for fathers for the purpose of child rearing has also been made a benefit under some employer-employee relationships. Such time off may be at the time of the birth of a new baby, or at a time when a parent is needed at home to care for a child.

### Wages

*State institutions are not covered by the federal Fair Labor Standards Act (FLSA).* The minimum wage and maximum hours requirements of the Fair Labor Standards Act does not apply to employer-employee relationships when the employer is a state or one of a state's poltical subdivisions.

The legal challenge to the 1974 FLSA amendment, which had extended the act's minimum wage and maximum hours provisions to almost all employees of the states and their poltical subdivisions, was heard ultimately by the Supreme Court. It held that in attempting to displace the states' own ability to structure employer-employee relationships in areas of traditional governmental functions, Comgress acted outside the authority granted to it by the commerce clause of the Constitution. Thus, the federal minimum wage and maximum hour statutes do not apply to most public institutions of higher education (*National League of Cities* v. *Usery*, 1976).

The FLSA has been found to apply to school districts and to some junior or community colleges on the grounds that they are local institutions and no state interest is involved.

Private schools are covered by the Federal Fair Labor Standards Act.

*Equal Pay Act of 1963.* In contrast to the above ruling, a later case found that public and private institutions of education are subject to the provisions of the Equal Pay Act, which requires equal pay for equal work (*Usery* v. *Bettendorf Community School District*, 1976).

Interestingly enough, the earliest cases at educational institutions claiming violation of this act were filed by female custodians. They claimed that the cleaning work they did was equal to that done by males, and they asked for equal pay. The decisions in these cases were based on evidence presented which did or did not sustain the institution's claim that there were two categories of custodial work, heavy and light.

The other major cases have to do with allegations by female educators that the work they do equals that of males as to skill, effort, and responsibility and is performed under similar working conditions. Their claim is that they receive less pay for such work than do males. Quite a number of these claims have been settled out of court. A number of others have required judicial intervention for successful redress. Some were legitimately disproved. For instance, if a Ph.D. was required for a particular level of pay, and all other persons at that level had Ph.D.'s, then a female without a Ph.D. would be unsuccessful in a claim that she was being denied equal pay. These cases involve an enormous amount of documentation and proof regarding equal skill, effort, responsibility, and similar working conditions.

*Authority to deny salary increase to faculty member.* The attorney general of the state of Oklahoma was asked by a state senator: "Can a faculty member of an institution of higher education be denied a salary increase for the reason that such faculty member does not donate money to the institution employing such faculty member?" In opinion no. 76-32 (September 28, 1976), the attorney general replied that a decision on a salary increase must be related to job performance, qualifications, skills, or educational achievements of the facuty member, and not in an unreasonable or arbitrary manner as would be the case if the salary increase were denied for the reason that the faculty member did not donate money to a particular fund at the institution.

*Furloughs without pay.* Financial exigency, which permits the curtailment of academic programs and services with its concomitant layoff of personnel, also may provide a basis for scheduling payless furloughs for employees.

The Board of Higher Education of the city of New York, reacting to the city's financial distress, adopted a resolution scheduling payless furloughs for members of the instructional staff of the City University of New York. It hoped to save approximately $32 million. The union representing the instructional staff at CUNY filed a suit challenging the authority of the board to take such action. The state court found that the Board of Higher Education had authority—granted to it by Education Law, Section 6206, subdivision 2— to schedule payless furloughs for the faculty and staff (*Professional Staff Congress, CUNY* v. *Board of Higher Education of the City of New York*, 1976).

## Taxation of Income

Faculty members and administrators routinely come in contact with two principal kinds of decisions dealing with their annual federal income tax returns. A number of questions arise regarding what must be included in gross income. Another set of issues has to do with what expenses may be deducted from gross income.

*What must be included in gross income.* Included in total gross income must be the value of unsolicited books sent as samples by publishers and accepted by the administrator or faculty member (*Haverly* v. *United States Court of Appeals for the Seventh Circuit*, 1975). The taxpayer in this case was an educator who had received unsolicited sample textbooks from publishers and then donated them to the school library.

Whether tuition remissions and scholarships granted to the children of employees could be excluded when figuring total amount of gross income was a serious question raised recently by the Internal Revenue Service. In fact, the Treasury Department had issued proposed regulations which would result in such items being included in gross income for tax purposes. Fortunately, these proposed regulations have been dropped.

Another item that must be included in total gross income is the amount of money received as reimbursement for lunches eaten during non-overnight trips away from one's normal duty area. Such reimbursement constitutes wages subject to income tax withholding under S.3401(1) of the Internal Revenue Code (*Central Illinois Public Service Company* v. *United States*, 1976).

*Expenses that may be deducted from gross income.* An income tax deduction may be allowed for expenses of education (including travel, meals, and lodging) undertaken to maintain and improve present professional skills (Treasury Department Regulation 1.162-5; *Coughlin* v. *Commissioner*, 1953).

Costs incurred while training for a new profession, however, cannot be deducted from gross income. For example, a person having a bachelor's degree and employed as a social worker cannot deduct the costs of studying for a Ph.D. degree in order to secure new and permanent employment to a university faculty (*Davis* v. *Commissioner,* 1976).

A person who works at a college far from where his or her family is living cannot deduct the cost of living nearer (*Liang* v. *Commissioner,* 1975).

*New IRS test for office at home.* The new IRS rules will affect many educators who in the past deducted the expenses of maintaining an office at home. The 1976 IRS regulations, Section 601, provide that to be eligible for deduction from gross income, such expenses must be the result of using the home office on a regular basis as the principal place of business of the taxpayer. Also, the business use of an office at home must be for "the convenience of the employer."

*Deduction of expenses of attending foreign conventions.* Section 102 of the 1976 Tax Reform Act limits to two per year the number of foreign professional meetings which may be used as deductions. If fewer than half the days of a trip were spent on professional activities, the deduction is reduced. Also, the deduction can be no more than the equivalent of the daily allowance permitted federal employees in that part of the world. As of this writing, Canada and Mexico are considered foreign countries, which is a change from former IRS interpretations.

## RECOMMENDATIONS

### Academic Issues

Academic matters are, after all, the heart of the educational enterprise. It is very worthwhile to spend time and care critiquing academic policies and review procedures to ensure that they reflect the institution's mission and high professional standards. Faculty, administrators, and students should understand clearly their academic responsibilities in such procedural matters as meeting classes, holding finals, reporting grades, and handling academic dishonesty. Substantive matters such as the quality of teaching or research can be handled by peer judgment. It is important that some sort of review process to handle adverse decisions be in place. Courts tend to prefer that academic decisions be made and reviewed by academics. However, if academics refuse to follow their own procedures, or make decisions maliciously, capriciously, or arbitrarily, courts have intervened.

### Employment Issues

Most lawsuits against educators and institutions concern employment matters, and discrimination claims against institutions are the most numerous of all. Personal liability is possible for officials at public institutions who are found to have violated constitutional rights. Such rights may arise out of employment contracts which involve liberty (reputation) or property (job) interests. Preventive measures must be taken, as suggested in this chapter and in Chapter 2, to avoid exposure to claims. A number of institutions have begun to include in criteria for evaluation of their officials the incidence of unnecessary lawsuits and legal costs.

Involuntary retirement and termination are two other matters of special concern, particularly when they result from financial exigency or discontinuance of programs. A number of institutions are experimenting with alternatives such as early retirement, retraining in a related field, part-time or reduced employment commensurate with the individual's age and status, or opportunities for employment in some other part of the institution or system.

# 7. Funding and Facilities

This chapter deals with several of the more pressing current legal problems that arise in the general areas of financing educational institutions and maintaining and operating their physical plant and facilities.

## FUNDING

The kinds of legal questions that arise concerning funding may relate to the use of public tax monies for a school or university. They may evolve around issues such as whether a particuar educational institution is public or private. If it is private, is public tax money being used to support church-related activities? Legal questions also may concern exemption from taxation. Should income produced by activities at the educational institution be taxed as unrelated business income? Are certain gifts made to an institution subject to taxation?

### Sources of Funds

Three principal sources of funds for private and public educational institutions are (1) public tax monies, (2) private gifts, and (3) student fees and tuitions.

Public educational institutions, of course, are funded primarily by public taxes. Public elementary and secondary schools usually charge their students no tuition, although there may be nominal fees for some extracurricular equipment or services. Public higher educational institutions routinely expect that a share of their financial burden will be paid by students. In addition, public educational institutions at all levels receive private gifts in various forms to assist them with their educational endeavors. For example, special video or athletic equipment may be donated by private persons to public schools. Or, in the case of colleges and universities, private persons may donate large sums of money to public institutions to be used for specialized purposes, such as medical education or rehabilitation of handicapped persons. Private educational institutions, on the other hand, depend largely for their financial support on private sources, such as student fees, tuition, and private gifts. Many private schools and colleges, however, do receive public funds for student transportation or textbooks or for building funds.

Educational institutions are assisted in other ways as well; they save money by being tax exempt. The taxes from which educational institutions are excused may be income taxes, property taxes, or gift taxes.

*Unequal funding of public institutions.* There have been legal challenges to systems used by states to finance public school which base per pupil expenditures in a school district on the wealth of the district. Such plans largely rely on local property taxes collected within the district.

A case brought under the equal protection provisions of the Fourteenth Amendment of the U.S. Constitution found such a financing system constitutional. The Supreme Court held that education is not a fundamental interest because it is not guaranteed or protected by the *federal* constitution. Therefore, the classification based upon wealth was not suspect. It passed the test of "rational relationship" to the state's interest (*San Antonio School District v. Rodriguez*, 1973).

The opposite result was reached by the California Supreme Court, which held that the equal protection clause of the state constitution was violated by a financing system based upon the wealth of a particular school district. It found that education was a fundamental interest under the *state* constitution. Therefore, the court employed a "strict and searching scrutiny" test, and found the classification based on wealth unnecessary to achieve any compelling state interest. In effect, the California Supreme Court said that the state's public school financing system invidiously discriminated against the poor because it made the quality of a child's education a function of the wealth of the child's parents, neighbors, and school district. California's system of public school financing, based primarily on local real property taxes, resulting in wide disparities in per pupil expenditures, was found to violate the state, but not the federal, constitution (*Serrano v. Priest*, 1976).

*Student volunteer programs.* Private institutions have been in the vanguard of recognizing the potential human resources available to them in the form of student volunteers to perform various services. Student volunteers rotating on cleaning crews, for instance, have saved one private institution at least $40,000 per year in cleaning bills. Annually, senior volunteers clean out a small pond on the institution's premises. Volunteers also repair and repaint fences, insulate and shingle buildings, and repair and enlarge theatrical equipment. The possibilities are virtually unlimited.

Similar projects could be initiated at public institutions. The major legal concern would be that students at public institutions freely consent to participate in such programs. At private institutions, participation could be assured by indicating in the institution's bulletin that it is expected of students.

*Contracts with foreign government.* A number of institutions, particularly higher education institutions, have sought to improve their financial status by contracting with foreign governments for services of various kinds. These may include enrollment of foreign students, consulting by faculty, or research studies and projects.

The 1976 Education Amendments, Section 182, requires nondiscriminatory contracts by higher education institutions, as follows:

> Institutions of higher education receiving federal financial assistance may not use such financial assistance whether directly or indirectly to undertake any study or project or fulfill the terms of any contract containing an express or implied provision that any person or persons of a particular race, religion, sex or national origin be barred from performing such study, project, or contract except no institution shall be barred from conducting objective studies or projects concerning the nature, effects, or prevention of discrimination, or have its curriculum restricted on the subject of discrimination, against any such person.

This provision resulted from private contracts between institutions and Arab countries that barred Jews from employment under those contracts. The amendment forbids discrimination in employment under domestic contracts and those originating overseas.

*Federal taxation of unrelated business income.* Private and public educational institutions generally are tax exempt. In the case of public educational institutions, it was thought ridiculous to supply public tax money with one hand, and then take away with the other hand part of that same tax money in the form of income tax. In the case of private educationsl institutions, public policy that supports education as a benefit to society in general is used as the rationale for permitting tax-exempt status for traditional private schools, as well as permitting receipt of some public monies.

However, some activities carried on by private and public educational institutions which are tax exempt have been called to the attention of Congress by businesses and other taxpaying organizations. These businesses supply the same services and must compete in the general marketplace with the tax-exempt organizations on what the taxpaying organizations believe is an unfair basis.

For example, there probably would be little challenge to the sale of textbooks in an institution's bookstore. Textbooks are clearly related to the educational function of the institution. But a school store that sells clothing, phonograph records, or stereo equipment may find itself challenged in court by local businesses that sell similar items and must pay taxes on their business income. The local business people very likely would take the position that the sale of clothing, phonograph records, and stereo equipment by the institution is not a function related to the educational purposes of the institution. Indeed, there have been numerous such challenges made. The resultant rulings by the Internal Revenue Service may appear at first glance to be not entirely consistent.

The IRS does try as much as possible to judge complaints about school business activities against certain standards adopted to handle such complaints. An unrelated trade or business which produces unrelated business income, and therefore is taxable, has been defined by IRS as one not related substantially to the institution's exempt purposes. Thus, the original example of a school store which sells textbooks would meet the test of being substantially related to the institution's exempt purpose.

Another test used by IRS is whether the trade or business activity is regularly carried on. A business venture such as a rock concert, held once a year in order to raise funds for some school-related activity, may not meet the test of promoting an educational function of the school. It may be acceptable to IRS, however, because it is not a business activity that is regularly carried on. Therefore as a matter of public policy it is not a continuing threat to the commercial taxpaying local businesses that may offer similar entertainment services.

These two tests—first, that the business activity be somehow educationally related, or second, that it not be regularly carried on to the detriment of commercial taxpaying businesses—are quite simple to state. They are tremendously difficult and complex to interpret and to implement, even when all parties concerned are acting in absolute good faith.

Historically, the case which caused the greatest concern and resulted in a change of attitude toward a much stricter scrutiny of business income generated by educational institutions was the case involving New York University and the Mueller Spaghetti and Macaroni Company. In briefest terms, the spaghetti company was given as a gift to New York University, which then operated the business. It took the position that the profits of the company were tax exempt because the company was being operated by the university, which qualified as a charitable institution. Thus, a charity was operating a commercial business, but was paying no taxes on the profits of the business. Competing spaghetti and macaroni companies pointed out that the savings in taxes permitted the Mueller company to have a competitive pricing advantage when compared to competitors whose profits were taxable. Other flagrant cases at the time involved educational institutions' acquiring an investment property on credit and then not being liable for the usual taxes. Congress was forced by abuses such as these to legislate rather severely in the area of unrelated business income of tax-exempt organizations.

Several other points need to be emphasized. It is not enough that the revenues from a business activity benefit the school's educational function; the business itself must be educationally related. That is, were an institution to operate a pizza parlor on its premises after school hours, and turn over all revenues to the institution for the purchase of new textbooks, a clear violation would exist. The fact that the revenues are being used for an educational purpose does not overcome the fact that an after-hours pizza business is not an educationally related function of the institution.

It is not uncommon for an institution's facilities or staff to be used for a combination of related and unrelated business activities. In such a case, the expenses must be appropriately allocated between the related and unrelated uses.

It is often the case that an educational institution will be carrying on several different unrelated business activities. IRS regulations provide, fortunately, that all gross unrelated income may be aggregated, as may all unrelated deductions. The unrelated losses may offset the unrelated profits. Thus, after all unrelated business income or losses are accumulated, there will be either a total loss or a total gain in unrelated business income.

Some income of educational institutions may be debt-financed. If the debt-financed property is related to the educational functioning of the institution, such as borrowing money to build a dormitory, the income produced by the dormitory is not considered unrelated business income. However, if the debt-financed property is, for example, a commercially rented building, such as an apartment house or a commercial store or warehouse, the income from such property is considered unrelated business income, and it is taxable.

Not considered unrelated business income are the following three kinds of income. First, ordinary investment income—such as dividends, interest, annuities, royalties, capital gains, and specially defined rents from real or personal property—is excluded from unrelated business income. Second, a trade or business carried on primarily for the convenience of students, faculty, staff, or patients, for instance running a cafeteria or a textbook store, would not be considered unrelated business income. Third, most research income received from research conducted under a government grant or similar entity would not be considered unrelated business income.

All three of the above simply defined varieties of educationally related businesses may be operated in a fashion which could include non-educationally related business income. To take the same kinds of income in the same order, let us discuss possibilities in which unrelated business income may exist in each of the three categories.

First, with regard to ordinary business investments, it is possible that some real or pesonal property may provide rent which must be included in unrelated business income.

Secondly, as to businesses run for the convenience of persons at the educational institution, selling textbooks in a book store is quite permissible, but selling stereo equipment may not be. Likewise, maintaining a cafeteria or similar food service for persons at the institution may be quite permissible; but running a gourmet restaurant may not be.

Third, receiving income to carry on research to extend the limits of current knowledge or to discover new knowledge is quite permissible. However, receiving monies from commercial drug companies to create or test new products that will be part of the drug company's regular commercial operation would necessarily fall into the category of unrelated business income.

Other activities common at educational institutions cause concern. The more questionable activities include the following.

Athletics at educational institutions sometimes produces revenues through gate receipts or radio or television broadcasts. The general rule has been that gate receipts for regular season games at educational institutions are considered educationally related income rather than unrelated business income. Complications have arisen when, in some instances, radio and television commercial stations have broadcast athletic events. Very substantial revenues have been received from the radio or TV station by the educational institution, and IRS has been considering taking a new position with regard to the situation. The new IRS stance would be based upon the fact that the income is not received directly from a TV or radio station run and operated by the university as a learning experience for students. It is received from commercially operated TV and radio stations, which serve as conduits of revenue between the consuming listener or viewer and the university.

The 1976 Copyright Reform Act also may affect such events. A fee may have to be paid to the copyright owner of music performed at educational events where admission fees are charged.

The matter of special athletic events, such as postseason games, is a confusing one at the present time. Again, IRS ultimately may make a distinction depending on whether special postseason games are broadcast over university owned and operated radio and TV stations or commercially owned and operated radio and TV stations.

Advertisements that produce income for student newspapers have generally been determined to be educationally related revenues, because student newspapers are being run and operated by the school for the training and education of the students, who write and produce the newspaper themselves.

Alumni publications are a different matter. Usually the difference hinges on the fact that students do not operate them. Alumni publications often are written and maintained by professionals hired by the university. The alumni publications, then, are not a truly educationally related function of the institution. Revenues generated by such alumni publications well may be considered unrelated business income.

Alumni organizations also may run travel operations. Tours have become a popular means of generating enthusiasm among alumni for continued interest in and support for the educational institution. IRS rulings generally hinge upon the purpose of the tour rather than upon the size of the tour group. If the tour has a clear educational purpose, either producing academic credit or being operated in good faith as part of a credit-free continuing education operation, the revenues produced usually will be considered educationally related income. Commercial travel agents, however, have taken a strong stand against alumni tours that are purely for the entertainment and recreation of alumni. Commercial agents point out that to permit revenues from such tours to be tax exempt would constitute unfair competition against them.

A computer owned and used by an educational institution, may not be fully utilized every minute of the day by the institution, and it is not uncommon for such extra computer time to be made available to outside organizations. If the institution's computer clearly is used the majority of the time by the institution, if it is not commercially advertised for use by commercial operations, and if charges for computer time merely cover operating expenses, IRS usually takes the position that revenues thus accumulated are educationally related. On the other hand, if a large amount of the computer time is offered to outside nonexempt business or commercial organizations and a fairly substantial time charge is made, the revenues produced may be classified as unrelated business income and be taxable.

Educational institutions, having become very cost conscious over recent years, have tried to develop methods to keep their overhead operating costs as low as possible. One of the more common methods is to try to use all of the physical plant and other resources of the institution as fully as possible all year round. Many institutions operate on a semester-by-semester basis, and may ordinarily be closed or operating at a very low level during the summer or between semesters. It has been thought wise to try to generate interest by various groups and organizations in using the universities' buildings, classrooms, dormitories, sports facilities, laboratories, and even academic and administrative staff during ordinary "down time." Questions arise, then, whether the income produced during this time is educationally related or unrelated business income. The usual tests have been used by IRS to try to answer questions in this general area. For example, if the groups using the facilities are themselves tax-exempt organizations, or their activities are educationally related (as, for example, a professional organization that rents space and reimburses salary for academic and administrative personnel to provide continuing education courses for its members), the revenues produced will usually be considered educationally related. On the other hand, if an institution rents its facilities to a person who is using the facilities to run a weight-reducing endeavor for paying members of the general public, the income so produced probably would be considered unrelated business income. Somewhere between these two extremes are the rentals of facilities to professional athletics teams, which often desire practice facilities prior to their regular commercial season games. Such commercial athletic groups probably should be considered the producers of unrelated business income by the educational institution.

Some institutions now are fortunate enough to have on their grounds facilities that combine meeting room space with hotel and dining accommodations. These facilities are for holding conferences on academic subjects or for accommodating visits to the institutions by prospective students and their parents or by parents and friends of presently enrolled students or faculty. The question of whether the revenues produced by these conference centers or campus inns is tax exempt is being scrutinized by IRS. Obviously, most institutions hope to continue to consider these revenues to be educationally related income.

Health services or cooperative teaching hospitals generally are considered to generate non–business related income, if their purpose is to provide a health service for the convenience of students or to provide teaching experience for students.

Theaters which are owned and operated by the university and its non-professional enrolled students also usually generate revenue considered to be educationally related and therefore not taxable as business income.

In the examples given, it is clear to see what the tests are. The trade or business to be considered educationally based and not included in unrelated business income must be a part of the educational function of the institution. It must not be carried on in a regular ongoing fashion in competition with commercial taxpaying businesses that offer similar services. To recapitulate, excluded from unrelated business income would be routine convenience services such as a textbook store, a cafeteria, a student health service, rent from non-debt financed property, state receipts from regular sports activities, inome from basic research projects, and similar activities. On the other hand, included in unrelated business income would be rents from debt-financed property investments which are unrelated to the educational function of the institution, advertising in alumni publications operated in typical commercial fashion, income from applied research projects, income from alumni tours run for entertainment and recreational purposes only, computer services offered to the general public in substantial fashion and for substantial charges, and similar commercial-like business ventures.

Careful mention should be made of the fact that there is no prohibition against an educational institution carrying on commercial-like business services—they simply must be willing to compete with other commercial operations. They must pay appropriate and requisite taxes on the operation of their businesses and the revenues accumulated therefrom.

It is strongly recommended that educators who intend to engage in any of the more unusual activities already discussed, or who contemplate becoming involved in lending securities or writing options, take full and prior advantage of consultation with their legal advisors. In some instances, legislation or an IRS ruling may be quite clear and unequivocable. Legal advice will prevent any unnecessary retroactive assessment of tax on what turns out to be unrelated business income. Likewise, advice from the institution's legal counsel may result in going ahead with a project even though it will produce unrelated business income. Advantages may accrue to the institution which will more than offset any amount of taxes payable on the unrelated business income.

### Public Aid to Church-Related Institutions

*Constitutional barriers.* Public aid to church-related educational institutions has consistently generated a large number of lawsuits. The basis for these lawsuits usually is the so-called establishment clause of the First Amendment of the U.S. Constitution, which prohibits the establishment or advancement of religion by government. It reads:

> Congress shall make no law respecting the establishment of religion, or prohibiting the free exercise thereof; or abridging the freedom of speech, or of the press; or the right of the people peaceably to assemble and to petition the Government for a redress of grievances.

The Supreme Court has interpreted the First Amendment to mean that the government may not establish, assist, or diminish any religion. In other words, the government is to remain apart from all religious activities.

The proscriptions in state constitutions against establishment of religions often are set forth in language even more restrictive and specific than that in the U.S. Constitution. The New York State Constitution, for example, provides:

> Neither the state nor any subdivision thereof shall use its property or credit or any public money, or authorize or permit either to be used,

directly or indirectly, in aid or maintenance, other than for examination or inspection, of any school or institution of learning wholly or
in part under the control or direction of any religious denomination,
or in which any denominational tenet or doctrine is taught.

Nevertheless, the U.S. Supreme Court most often has been the final
arbiter as to what kind of public aid may be offered to students who attend
church-run schools without violating the U.S. or a state constitution.

*Reasoning of the Supreme Court.* First, the Supreme Court has evolved a
three-prong test (purpose, effect, and entanglement) for determining whether
a challenged statute violates the First Amendment, as follows:

1. The statute must have a secular legislative purpose; that is, the aid
must be directed to students' education and health, not inculcation of religion.

2. It must have a "primary effect" that neither advances nor inhibits religion; that is, the student's education rather than the school must benefit
primarily.

3. Its administration must avoid excessive government entanglement
with religions; that is, the secular and religious activities of the institution
must be easily separated so that excessive surveillance of the use of the aid is
not required. Such excessive surveillance would involve impermissible church-
state entanglement (*Lemon* v. *Kurtzman,* 1971).

Second, the Court also has taken into account whether the financial aid
assisted the students themselves (which the Constitution permits, according
to the Court), or whether the financial aid in fact benefitted the school. The
Court has said the latter is not permitted by the Constitution (*Everson* v.
*Board of Education,* 1947; *Board of Education* v. *Allen,* 1968; *Meek* v.
*Pittenger,* 1975).

Third, the Court has been influenced by whether services paid for with
public funds are generated and administered by public officials or by church-
related officials.

Fourth, it appears to matter whether the services are offered off or on
the premises of the parochial institution.

Fifth, the Supreme Court has distinguished elementary and secondary
schools from higher education institutions. The Court believes that a college's
secular program may be independent of its religious program to a degree not
possible in elementary and secondary schools. At the college level, evidence
may show that the emphasis is on academic freedom and generally accepted
professional standards for teaching academic courses and administering the
institution. At the elementary and secondary levels, the emphasis, by contrast, may be on dissemination of a particular religious doctrine. Academic

courses necessarily then are permeated by sectarian concepts (*Tilton* v. *Richardson*, 1971).

*Specific Supreme Court rulings: elementary and secondary school cases.* In attempting to determine whether the use of public tax monies for certain specific purposes in aiding church-related schools violates the First Amendment, the Supreme Court has been asked to rule on many proposed specific uses. In each specific instance, the Court in effect has been asked to decide whether using public tax monies for the proposed specific purpose breaches the "wall of separation between church and state," as the issue was stated by Thomas Jefferson.

In 1947, the Supreme Court held that tax money constitutionally could be spent to transport children to parochial schools. Bus transportation was compared to peripheral services like police and fire protection (*Everson* v. *Board of Education*, 1947).

In 1971, a Rhode Island act which provided salary supplements to nonpublic elementary school teachers of secular subjects was found unconstitutional. Similarly, a Pennsylvania statute was ruled unconstitutional which allowed the state to directly reimburse nonpublic schools for actual expenditures for teachers' salaries, textbooks, and instructional material relating to secular subjects. These statutes were held unconstitutional because the cumulative impact of the entire relationship involved excessive entanglement between government and religion. It was too difficult to monitor the aid to see that it went to secular rather than religious functions (*Lemon* v. *Kurtzman*, 1971).

Specific plans for funding of buildings and tuition also were found unconstitutional earlier. The case involved a tuition reimbursement program whereby New York gave low-income parents who sent their children to nonpublic schools a direct and unrestricted cash grant of $50 to $100 per child, but paid not more than 50 percent of the tuition. The state's justification was that aid flowed to parents rather than to church-related schools. However, the evidence convinced the Court that no endeavor was made to guarantee separation between religious and secular educational functions, and to ensure that the state aid supported only the latter, as bus transportation in *Everson*. The Court found that this grant program served to establish religion and was unconstitutional. Also involved was an unconstitutional scheme to fund buildings. A plan to loan textbooks to pupils was ruled constitutional (*Committee for Public Education* v. *Nyquist*, 1973).

In 1975 the Supreme Court held constitutional part of a Pennsylvania state statute permitting the loan of standard public school textbooks to nonpublic school students. This, the Court said, did not violate the establishment clause of the First Amendment. However, the Court held unconstitutional those parts of the statute permitting the loan of other instructional material and equipment to such schools. It also found impermissible the providing of secular "auxiliary services" such as remedial accelerated instruction, guidance counseling, and testing, speech, and hearing services. These services were provided by publicly paid personnel, but they were held on the premises of the parochial school. In such circumstances the Court felt that there may be a failure to separate secular from religious instruction. Thus certain sections of the statute were held uncontitutional on entanglement grounds. It was believed that continual surveillance on the premises would be required (*Meek* v. *Pittenger*, 1975).

In June 1977 in *Wolman* v. *Walter*, the Supreme Court handed down its most recent ruling on public aid to church-related institutions. The case involved an Ohio law which provided for the furnishing of state aid to private institutions over a two-year period. The Court once again relied upon its earlier three-prong test, as in *Lemon*, for assessing the constitutionality of aid to students in parochial schools: that is, the aid must have a secular or nonreligious purpose, its primary effect must not be to advance or inhibit religion, and there must not be excessive church-state entanglement. The Court also considered whether the aid went direcly to students or to the schools themselves. State aid for the following specific purposes was held constitutional:

1. Textbooks and textbook supplements, such as nonconsumable manuals and workbooks.

2. Standardized academic testing services in secular subjects if the contents of the tests are controlled by and the tests are administered by public school employees.

3. Diagnostic tests such as standard speech, hearing and some forms of psychological diagnostic testing services, if provided to both public and nonpublic school students, and if the persons giving the tests are public school employees. (The test may be given in the parochial school, but any treatment required would have to be done away from the school.) Diagnostic tests were found permissible because the Court believed that the pressure on a public health diagnostician to allow intrusion of sectarian views is greatly reduced. Such may not be the case between a teacher and his or her pupil, and between a guidance counselor and his or her client-pupil. Earlier cases have established that the provision of health services to all school children, public and nonpublic, does not have the primary effect of aiding religion. For example, in *Lemon* the court said:

> Our decisions from *Everson* to *Allen* have permitted the states to provide church-related schools with secular, neutral, or nonideological services, facilities, or materials. Bus transportation, school lunches,

public health services, and secular textbooks supplied in common to all students were not thought to offend the Establishment Clause.

4. Therapeutic services (as distinguished from diagnostic tests), which may include remedial reading and speech therapy or psychological guidance in specialized cases, were found constitutionally permissible. Again, they must be provided by public employees at a neutral site off the premises of the parochial school (even mobile units). The Court felt that these conditions would provide less chance of the church environment overwhelming the public employee.

Specifically prohibited by the Court's June 1977 *Wolman* decision, however, are loaning state equipment such as projectors, record players, wall maps and globes, tape recorders, science kits, and weather forecasting charts to students or to their parents. The Court said that such equipment is stored on nonpublic school premises or distributed by the nonpublic school. It is really a loan to the school and not to the student or parents as suggested. This part of the *Wolman* ruling is similar to the earlier *Meek* decision.

Prohibited by *Wolman* also is state aid for field trips for parochial schools. The Court commented that there is no restriction on the timing of the field trips or on the choice of the destination. These decisions will be made by nonpublic school teachers from a wide range of locations. Thus, the schools and not the pupils are the true recipients of the service. While the destination may be the same one chosen by the public school, it is the individual teacher who makes the field trip meaningful. This creates an unacceptable risk of fostering religion as an inevitable byproduct.

*Specific Supreme Court rulings: higher education cases.* The Higher Education Facilities Act of 1963, providing for the use of federal funds for construction of facilities at private institutions, was scrutinized by the Supreme Court in 1971. Grants had been approved for the construction of libraries, science buildings, and language laboratories. The issue was whether, even though the grants were for secular buildings, the fact that all the institutions were Roman Catholic barred such funding. The Court found the grants constitutional. It distinguished this case from *Lemon*, which it decided the same day, on the basis that there was a significant difference between church-related higher education institutions and parochial schools. The question posed was whether "religion so permeates the secular education provided by church-related colleges and universities that their religious and secular educational functions are in fact inseparable." The Court found that at these four higher education institutions, the secular program was independent of the religious program (*Tilton v. Richardson*, 1971).

In June 1976, following *Tilton*, the Supreme Court upheld a Maryland statute providing for noncategorized grants to private colleges and universi-ties. The lower court decision that the colleges were capable of separating secular and religious functions was affirmed (*Roemer* v. *Board of Public Works of Maryland*, 1976).

In December 1976, the Supreme Court again followed its reasoning in *Tilton* and let stand a decision of the supreme court of Missouri. It had ruled that state tuition grants to college students who attend certain approved public and private colleges do not violate the federal or state constitutions (*Americans United, Inc.* v. *Rogers*, 1976).

## FACILITIES

### Mandates of OSHA

Occupational Safety and Health Act of 1970 (OSHA) requires employ-ers to provide safe and healthful working conditions for employees. Safety usually refers to the condition of the building and equipment. Health has to do with such matters as the interaction of employees with chemical agents in the environment such as arsenic, asbestos, vinyl chloride, lead, DMCC, and kepone.

At educational institutions, safety and health translate into such mat-ters as safe stairways and electrical equipment, proper storage of flammable and combustible liquids, and properly functioning fire extinguishers. Person-nel operating procedures are involved, as well. Personnel must know how to operate and maintain equipment and facilities safely.

### State OSHAs To Supersede Federal OSHA

The aim of the federal OSHA is to encourage states to develop their own programs. State OSHAs must establish standards and mechanisms for enforcement at least as effective as that of the federal OSHA. Approved state OSHAs will then supersede the federal plan. About twenty-three states now have their own OSHAs. Private educational institutions are subject to the federal or state OSHA programs. Public institutions, as governmental agen-cies, are excluded from federal coverage but are covered by state plans as they become effective.

OSHA has created numerous questions. Some are purely legal in nature; others hinge on the philosophy of management.

### Search Warrants

Inspection without a search warrant is an example of how legal require-ments may interact with management philosophy. Proper inspections will take place, for the law requires them. But management has a Fourth Amend-ment right to object to the inspection as an unreasonable search and a breach of privacy. A search warrant then will have to be sought before the inspector may enter the premises (*Barlow's, Inc.* v. *Usery,* 1976). Management philosophy may be to regard inspections positively, as a way to provide the inspector immediately with management's views of the questioned working conditions. Or, management may regard the inspections negatively, and take the position that it is better to use every legal means possible to delay inspections on the theory that to do otherwise is to borrow trouble.

## Jury Trials

An employer may be cited for a violation and fined after an administrative hearing. A question has been asked regarding whether imposing such an administrative penalty without a jury trial is a violation of the Seventh Amendment. The Supreme Court let stand a lower court ruling that a jury trial was not required in the case of a civil penalty (*Atlas Roofing Co., Inc.* v. *Occupational Safety and Health Review Commission,* 1977).

## Common Law Right to Safe Working Conditions

A New Jersey court found that employees have a common law right to a safe working environment. This is in addition to the right created by the Occupational Safety and Health Act and state health laws.

The case in question involved a nonsmoking employee who had a severe allergic reaction to cigarette smoke. She alleged that her employer, the New Jersey Bell Telephone Company, caused her to work in an unsafe environment by refusing to ban smoking in the office where she was employed.

The court found that the office work area was in fact unsafe due to a preventable hazard which the court could stop. The court took judicial notice of the toxic nature of cigarette smoke and its well known association with emphysema, lung cancer, and heart disease. The court noted that the company already had in effect a rule that cigarettes were not to be smoked around telephone equipment because the machines were extremely sensitive and could be damaged by the smoke. The court went on to comment that human beings are also very sensitive and can be damaged by cigarette smoke. The court said, "A company that has demonstrated such concern for its mechanical components should have at least as much concern for its human beings."

The court held that "The employees' right to a safe working environment makes it clear that smoking must be forbidden in the work area. The employee who desires to smoke on his or her own time, during coffee breaks and lunch hours, should have a reasonably accessible area to smoke. Such a rule imposes no hardship upon the telephone company" (*Shimp* v. *New Jersey Telephone Company,* 1976).

## RECOMMENDATIONS

### Funding

Development officers should be as well informed as possible about new or changing sources of public and private funding. Indeed, better than keeping up is trying to look ahead a few years to see where funds for education will be increasing and decreasing. Public institutions, for example, may feel the effect of suits alleging that funds should be more equitably distributed to institutions than is now the case with reliance on local property taxes. Private institutions may be affected by changes in the tax laws regarding charitable contributions and bequests.

Academic officers may spare institutions a great deal of legal trauma by handling the curtailment or discontinuance of programs in an orderly and lawful fashion, giving appropriate notice and helping with retrenchment procedures. They also would do well to see the significance of proposed or new laws. The Rehabilitation Act, for example, offers an opportunity to develop training programs for special education teachers as mainstreaming of handicapped persons begins.

### Facilities

The Occupational Safety and Health Act has generated many lawsuits, and it is expected that the Rehabilitation Act will do likewise. Review of premises and safety conditions is essential and must be done on a regular basis. Questionable conditions should be brought to the attention of the institution's legal counsel. Handbooks of information and procedures for students and employees would be helpful.

Information about the Rehabilitation Act of 1973 appears in Appendix A and elsewhere in the book.

# Appendixes

# Appendix A: Twenty-Four Federal Statutes in Brief

ANNOTATED TABLE OF CONTENTS

Prohibits employment discrimination based on race, color, religion, sex, or national origin.

Public Law 94-553, effective January 1, 1978.
Limits use of copyrighted material, literary works, and music for teaching and library purposes. Sections 107 and 108 and Guidelines are reprinted in their entirety.

20 U.S.C. Sec. 1088b-1, Public Law 94-482, 90 Stat. 2081.
Regulations appear at 42 Fed. Reg. 61043 (December 1, 1977), 45 C.F.R. 178, and were effective January 14, 1978. Sec. 1070 requires full disclosure of financial and academic policies prior to payment of tuition.

20 U.S.C. Sec. 1681. Regulations appear at 45 C.F.R. Part 86 (1975). Amended 1976.
Prohibits sex discrimination in education, e.g. in admission to the institution and treatment thereafter, and as an employee of the institution.

As amended. Enacted as Sec. 6(d) of the Fair Labor Standards Act; 29 U.S.C. Sec. 206(d). Regulations appear at 29 C.F.R. Part 806 (1975).
Requires equal pay for equal work.

As amended by Executive Order 11375, 32 *Fed. Reg.* 14303: Revised Order No. 4, 41 C.F.R. Part 60-2. Implementing regulations appear at 41 C.F.R. Chapter 60. Uniform Guidelines on Employee Selection Procedures appear at 41 Fed. Reg. 29016 (July 14, 1976). Prohibits discrimination in employemnt based on race, color, religion, or national origin. Requires affirmative action if minorities and women are found to be underutilized in the work force.

29 U.S.C. Sec. 201. As amended.
Provides for minimum wages and maximum hours. However, state and locally supported institutions are not affected.

Public Law 93-380, Title IV, Sec. 438, as amended, 20 U.S.C. Sec. 1232(g) (Supp. IV, 1974).
Provides criteria for access by students and parents to students'

records, and requires consent of student or parent to release such data to others.

20 U.S.C. Sec. 1071 et seq. Regulations appear at 45 C.F.R. 177. Requires full disclosure of college's financial and academic programs to prospective students prior to taking out tuition loan.

45 C.F.R. 46. Effective July 1, 1974.
Protects rights of human subjects "at risk" in experiments, demonstration projects, teaching programs, or evaluations.

40 Fed. Reg. Sec. 3409 (Nov. 18, 1975), *Int. Rev. Bull.* 1975-49 (Dec. 8, 1975).
Private institutions without racially nondiscriminatory admissions policies cannot qualify as organizations exempt from federal income tax.

20 U.S.C. Sec. 651.
Sets safety and health standards in places of employment.

29 U.S.C. Sec. 1001. Public Law 93-406, 88 Stat. 829.
Sets standards for private pension plans.

5 U.S.C. Sec. 552a. Public Law 93-579. Regulations appear at 40 *Fed. Reg.* 47406 (Oct. 8, 1975).
Provides criteria for keeping personnel records by federal agencies. Affects use of social security number as identifier.

799 A and 845, 42 U.S.C. *Sec. 295h-9 (Supp. I, 1971), as amended (Supp. IV, 1974), and 298b-2 (Supp. I, 1971).* Regulations appear at 40 *Fed. Reg.* 28572 (July 7, 1975).
Prohibits sex discrimination in admissions to federally supported medical, nursing, and other schools providing health-related training.

29 U.S.C. Sec. 701 et seq. (Supp. III, 1973), as amended (Supp. IV, 1974). Public Law 93-112. Regulations appear at 45 C.F.R. Part 84, and were effective June 3, 1977.
Prohibits discrimination against handicapped persons in education and employment, and establishes a mandate to bring handicapped persons into the mainstream of American life. Affirmative action in employment is required by Section 503.

    Federal "Government in Sunshine Act of 1976," 5 U.S.C. Sec.
    552(b), was effective March 13, 1977. All 50 states now have "sun-
    shine laws" in force with similar provisions.
    Require public decision making to be done in open meetings and
    public records to be open to public scrutiny.
    38 U.S.C. Sec. 2012. Supp. IV, 1974.
    Regulations are at 41 *Fed. Reg.* 26386 (June 25, 1976).
    Provides equal employment opportunity and affirmative action to
    Vietnam veterans.

## 1. AGE DISCRIMINATION IN EMPLOYMENT ACT OF 1967

*Prohibits:*      Discrimination in employment against persons between the ages of 40 and 65. Age is not to be used as a basis for making decisions regarding hiring, classification of job categories, compensation, and employee benefit plans:

> It shall be unlawful for an employer (1) to fail or refuse to hire or to discharge any individual or otherwise discriminate against any individual with respect to his compensation, terms, conditions, or privileges of employment, because of such individual's age; (2) to limit, segregate, or classify his employees in any way which would deprive or tend to deprive any individual of employment opportunities or otherwise adversely affect his status as an employee, because of such individual's age; or (3) to reduce the wage rate of any employee in order to comply with this Act.

An exception to the act is a bona fide employee retirement plan that provides pensions. A court has found that the act permits retirement plans that provide for involuntary early retirement before age 65 if they result in no substantial monetary damage to the employee (*Rogers* v. *Exxon,* 1975).

*By:*      Employers of 20 or more persons.

*Affects:*      Hiring, promotion, compensation, retirement, etc.

*Example of violation:*      Refusal to hire a person within the protected age group who has all the qualifications required by the job description, and is refused employment solely on the basis of age.

*Remedies:*      Suit for damages by the Secretary of Labor. Suit for damages by the individual claimant, who must give the Secretary of Labor not less than 60 days notice of an intention to file such an action. If the Secretary of Labor files suit, the individual's right to a private suit is terminated. Time limit for filing suit is within 2 years after the alleged violation, or within 3 years in the case of a willful violation. State law may create state agencies for handling age discrimination. Suits may result in awards of damages for unpaid compensation owing because of the discrimination, punitive damages, injunctional remedies, and attorneys' fees.

*Case samples:*  May a court award damages for pain and suffering under the ADEA? Courts have given conflicting decisions.

In one case, the plaintiff had been forced illegally into early retirement. He experienced a syndrome of severe abdominal pain, vomiting, and impotency. Evidence clearly and persuasively demonstrated that the symptoms were the proximate result of the employer's illegal discrimination. A lower court found that the ADEA essentially established a new statutory tort, and that damages could be awarded for pain and suffering. An appellate court reversed this decision, finding that the act permitted only damages such as unpaid wages, overtime compensation, or liquidated damages (*Rogers* v. *Exxon*, 1977).

However, in a later case, a federal district court found that the act did permit damages for physical and mental suffering. Thus, there is conflict between jurisdictions as to whether a court may award damages for pain and suffering (*Bertrand* v. *Orkin Exterminating Co.*, 1977).

*Comments:*  Damage settlements and court awards have involved very large sums of money in some cases. Access to remedies by claimants is facilitated by availability of government agency to pursue violations, and by possible awards of attorneys' fees in private lawsuits. Many cases are based on a refusal to hire or on early involuntary retirement. Educational employers wishing to minimize risks of claims should review personnel policies, paying special attention to those regarding hiring and retirement.

*Further information:*  Wage and Hour Division, Employment Standards Administration, Department of Labor, Washington, D.C. 20210

## 2. AGE DISCRIMINATION ACT OF 1975

*Prohibits:* Discrimination in federally funded programs based upon age. Regulations are not yet developed.

*By:* Recipients of federal financial assistance.

*Affects:* Regulations will set forth more specifically how this act will affect educational institutions. It is expected to affect all phases of the institutional-student relationship, including recruitment, admissions, financial aid, treatment after matriculation, placement opportunities, and all other aspects of the operation of the institution regarding its students.

*Example of violation:* Regulations will probably indicate that a refusal to admit an otherwise qualified applicant solely on the basis of age will constitute a violation.

*Remedies:* Probably will include suspension or termination of federal financial assistance.

*Case sample:* No cases are available as yet. Hypothetically, a typical case would involve a person refused equal treatment at an institution based solely upon his or her age.

*Comments:* Institutions should begin to prepare now for implementation of regulations under the Age Discrimination Act. Review of present policies and procedures is necessary in order to assure that they do not disqualify a person from participation in institutional programs on the basis of age.

*Further information:* Department of Health, Education and Welfare, Washington, D.C. 20201.

## 3. CIVIL RIGHTS ACT OF 1866

*Prohibits:*          Racial discrimination in making contracts (covers whites as well):

All persons within the jurisdiction of the United States shall have the same right in every State and Territory to make and enforce contracts, to sue, be parties, give evidence and to the full and equal benefit of all laws and proceedings for the security of persons and property as is enjoyed by white citizens, and shall be subject to like punishment, pains, penalties, taxes, licenses, and exactions of every kind, and to no other.

*By:*                 Private individuals, or private or public institutions, associations, unions, agencies (whether or not under color of state law).

*Affects:*            Admissions, employment, sales, services, leases, loans, etc.

*Examples of*         Refusal to contract for sales or services because of race.
*violations:*         Refusal to admit to facilities, programs, or employment because of race.

*Remedies:*           Suit for damages or equitable relief in either federal or state court. Personal liability is possible. No prior administrative procedures are required. It is not yet clear what attorneys' fees may be available to complainants under the Civil Rights Attorneys' Fees Awards Act of 1976 or under 20 U.S.C. 1617.

*Case sample:*        *Runyon* v. *McCrary,* 49 L.Ed. 2d 415 (1976)
                      Blacks denied admission to segregated private schools may obtain equitable relief and compensatory damages against school proprietors under 42 U.S.C. Sec. 1981. This act prohibits private schools from rejecting an applicant who meets all academic and other qualifications except race. Such a rejection was found to violate the applicant's Fourteenth Amendment right to make contracts on the same basis as whites.

*Comments:*           Personal liability is possible. Measures to prevent claims include understanding which relationships are contractual in nature and assuring that refusals to contract are based on factors other than race. Insurance coverage should be considered.

## 4. CIVIL RIGHTS ACT OF 1871, 42 U.S.C. Sec. 1983

*Prohibits:* Depriving an individual of any civil rights guaranteed by the Constitution and Laws:

> Every person who, under color of any statute, ordinance, regulation, custom, or usage, of any State or Territory, subjects, or causes to be subjected, any citizen of the United States or other person within the jurisdiction thereof to the deprivation of any rights, privileges, or immunities secured by the Constitution and laws, shall be liable to the party injured in an action at law, suit in equity, or other proper proceeding for redress.

The action complained of must be taken "under color of state law," that is, by public officials. Officials at private institutions would be liable only if the institution were deemed to be involved in state action.

*By:* Public officials, such as educational institution administrators, trustees, faculty, school district and board members, and other similar public officials and their designated agents. *Note:* The public institution itself is not a "person." Its officials are persons. Therefore, it is the officials, not the institution, who are exposed to liability.

*Affects:* Almost all functions and activities carried on at public educational institutions.

*Examples of violations:* Deprivation of a property interest in a public education by suspending or expelling a student without due process. Deprivation of a liberty interest in one's good reputation by terminating an administrator or faculty member without due process under conditions which place a stigma on his or her reputation, adversely affecting future employment opportunities. Other examples would be deprivation of rights to equal protection, or to equal opportunity, or to First Amendment rights such as free press, speech, association, and religion. Deprivation of rights under statutes relating to handicaps, age, sex, or race also would be covered.

*Remedies:* Suit in either federal or state courts. Personal liability is possible (see example below). Relief both in law and equity are possible, such as compensatory and punitive damages, declaratory relief (declaring a rule or statute unconstitutional), injunctive relief (ordering an action stopped or started, and perhaps ordering records expunged), or reinstatement. It is not yet clear to what extent attorneys' fees may be available to complainants under the Civil Rights Attorneys' Fees Awards Act of 1976, or under 20 U.S.C. 1617. State statutes of limitations apply.

*Case sample:*     *Wood* v. *Strickland* (1975) involved expulsion of students from a public high school without notice or hearing. The students sued the institution and the officials personally for deprivation of their constitutional right to due process. The officials claimed they were shielded from personal liability because they had acted in good faith. Sovereign immunity of the state protected them, they alleged. The Supreme Court disagreed. It said that good faith included not only believing subjectively that one is acting correctly, but also knowing the unquestioned constitutional rights of students and safeguarding those rights. The decision of the Court was:

Therefore, in the specific context of school discipline, we hold that a school board member is not immune from liability for damages under Sec. 1983 if he *knew or reasonably should have known* that the action he took within his sphere of official responsibility would violate the constitutional rights of the students affected, or if he took the action with the malicious intention to cause a deprivation of constitutional rights or other injury to the student.

*Comments:*     Personal liability is possible. Preventive measures must include knowing what are clearly established constitutional rights and what constitutes appropriate due process. Insurance coverage should be considered. Presently courts tend to find that violations of constitutional rights have occurred but are reluctant to find that the law on constitutional rights is settled enough to assess personal liability. Educators are cautioned, however, that some law is clearly settled, and as time goes by, more will be. For further discussion of due process and personal liability, see Chapter 2.

## 5. CIVIL RIGHTS ACT OF 1871, 42 U.S.C. Sec. 1985(3)

*Prohibits:*     Conspiracy entered into to deprive an individual of equality in enjoyment of any rights secured by federal law:

If two or more persons in any State or Territory conspire or go in disguise on the highway or on the premises of another, for the purpose of depriving, either directly or indirectly, any person or class of persons of the equal protection of the laws, or for the purpose of preventing or hindering the constituted authorities of any State or Territory from giving or securing to all persons within such State or Territory the equal protection of the laws; or if two or more persons conspire to prevent by force, intimidation, or threat, any citizen who is lawfully entitled to vote, from giving his support or advocacy in a legal manner, toward or in favor of the election of any lawfully qualified person as an elector for President or Vice President, or as a Member of Congress of the United States; or to injure any citizen in person or property on account of such support or advocacy; in any case of conspiracy set forth in this section, if one or more persons engaged therein do, or cause to be done, any act in furtherance of the object of such conspiracy, whereby another is injured in his person or property, or deprived of having and exercising any right or privilege of a citizen of the United States; the party so injured or deprived may have an action for the recovery of damages, occasioned by such injury or deprivation, against any one or more of the conspirators.

*By:*           Two or more persons. Some courts interpret this act to cover only public officials or to require a discriminatory intent. Other courts do not.

*Affects:*      Most functions and activities in an educational institution.

*Examples of    A regulation prohibiting use of swimming pool by blacks at
violations:*    same time and under same conditions as enjoyed by whites.

*Remedies:*     Suit in either federal or state court. Personal liability is possible. These actions usually are not found to be within "one's official duties." Therefore, liability will be a personal liability for damages, with a right to a jury trial. Proof of conspiracy requires a showing of conscious and concerted action to violate equal protection. It is not clear yet to what extent attorneys' fees may be available to complainants under the Civil Rights Attorneys' Fees Awards Act of 1976 or under 20 U.S.C. 1617. No prior administrative procedures are required. State statutes of limitations apply.

*Case sample:* In *Tillman* v. *Wheaton-Haven Swimming Pool Association* (1973 and 1975), a group of blacks initially filed suit because they were denied membership in a private pool club in their community. The Supreme Court found that the swimming pool association had unlawfully discriminated against the black applicants for membership. The blacks then filed another suit, this time for damages against the individual directors personally. The directors alleged that their legal counsel had assured them that their exclusion of blacks was legal. They claimed exoneration from liability on the basis that they had acted with due diligence. The court hearing this subsequent case refused to accept such a defense. It pointed out that the directors fully intended to exclude blacks and their ignorance of the law, though engendered by their counsel, was not an acceptable defense.

*Comments:* Personal liability is possible. Obviously, participating in a conspiracy is not often found to fall within one's official duties. Administrators should disassociate themselves on the record from acts which may be interpreted as conspiracies. Insurance coverage should be considered.

## 6. CIVIL RIGHTS ACT OF 1964, TITLE VI

*Prohibits:*          Racial or ethnic discrimination in programs receiving feder-
                      al financial assistance:

                      No person in the United States shall, on the ground of
                      race, color, or national origin, be excluded from partici-
                      pation in, be denied the benefits of, or be subjected to
                      discrimination under any program or activity receiving
                      Federal financial assistance.

*By:*                 Any educational program or activity receiving federal finan-
                      cial assistance.

*Affects:*            Institution's responsibility to assure that all students are
                      given an equal opportunity to learn.

*Examples of*         Refusal to supply English language instruction to substan-
*violations:*         tial groups of non-English-speaking students.

*Remedies:*           Cutoff or deferral of federal financial assistance, broad
                      injunctive and declaratory relief, and specific organizational
                      plans to be followed by the individual institution or the sys-
                      tem. The federal government, as well as students and
                      parents, may file class action suits for violation of Title VI.
                      Attorneys' fees may be available to complainants under the
                      Civil Rights Attorneys' Fees Award Act of 1976 or under
                      20 U.S.C. 1617, though to what extent is not yet clear.
                      Personal liability is not possible.

*Case sample:*        In *Lau* v. *Nichols* (1974), about 1,800 non-English-speaking
                      Chinese students filed a class action suit against a school
                      district alleging unequal educational opportunity. The U.S.
                      Supreme Court found that a student who does not speak
                      English and is not afforded English language instruction is
                      prevented from participating equally with other students in
                      educational programs. The Supreme Court required the
                      schools to provide language instruction to the students.

*Comments:*           Loss of federal financial assistance by the institution is at
                      risk here. Administrators should be encouraged to develop
                      methods of forecasting enrollment of groups of students

who will need special educational services in order for them to participate fully in the learning experience.

*Further information:* Office for Civil Rights, Department of Health, Education and Welfare, Washington, D.C. 20201

## 7. CIVIL RIGHTS ACT OF 1964, TITLE VII

*Prohibits:*      Employment discrimination based on race, color, religion, sex, or national origin:

(a) It shall be an unlawful employment practice for an employer (1) to fail or refuse to hire or to discharge any individual, or otherwise to discriminate against any individual with respect to his compensation, terms, conditions, or privileges of employment, because of such individual's race, color, religion, sex, or national origin; (2) to limit, segregate, or classify his employees or applicants for employment in any way which would deprive or tend to deprive any individual of employment opportunities or otherwise adversely affect his status as an employee, because of such individual's race, color, religion, sex, or national origin.

(b) It shall be an unlawful employment practice for an employment agency to fail or refuse to refer for employment, or otherwise to discriminate against, any individual because of his race, color, religion, sex, or national origin, or to classify or refer for employment any individual on the basis of his race, color, religion, sex, or national origin.

*By:*             Any employer with 15 or more employees.

*Affects:*        All employment practices, including hiring, firing, classifying, promoting, or referring for employment on the basis of race, color, religion, sex, or national origin.

*Examples of*     Refusal to hire or promote blacks or females on same basis
*violations:*     as white males.

*Remedies:*       Complaint may be lodged against institutions and officials. Individual or class action complaint must first seek an administrative remedy before filing a lawsuit. The Equal Employment Opportunity Commission (EEOC) is the federal agency which initially handles these complaints. Ultimately, an individual complainant may commence an action in the federal court system, as may the EEOC or the U.S. Attorney General. The administrative and judicial procedural steps are as follows:

1. Complaint is filed with state or local fair employment law agency if a state law or local ordinance applies. EEOC defers to state or local agency if there is one. EEOC may proceed after 60 days. If state or local agency disposes of matter prior to 60 days, EEOC may move forward.

2. Complaint is filed with EEOC, either after or simultaneously with the state or local filing. The normal time limit for filing a complaint with EEOC is 180 days after the alleged discriminatory action. However, this time limit may be extended by having filed with a state or local agency, or by provision of a collective bargaining agreement, or if the complained of behavior constitutes a continuing violation.

3. EEOC remedies may consist of (a) an attempt to conciliate and reach a reasonable settlement, used by EEOC if its investigation produces "reasonable cause" to believe an illegal act of discrimination was committed; (b) an award of back pay for up to 2 years prior to the time the charge was filed, or up to 3 years if a willful violation has been proved.

4. Suit may be filed in federal district court by EEOC or individual complainant. (a) If conciliations fail, EEOC may itself file suit in a federal district court or notify the complainant of his or her right to commence legal action. (b) If EEOC finds no "reasonable cause," individuals may file suit within set time limit. (c) Suit may be filed to enjoin a "pattern or practice" of discrimination against a private employer by EEOC, or against a public sector employer by either the EEOC or the Attorney General.

5. Summary of possible remedies: (a) Injunctional awards, including hiring and promotional quotas, additional reporting requirements. (b) Damage awards, including back pay, but usually no punitive damages. Public institutions as well as private institutions are liable for back pay, in spite of the usual Eleventh Amendment bar to awards of public monies. This is because Congress authorized such awards, along with possible payment of attorneys' fees, in Title VII (see *Fitzpatrick* v. *Bitzer*, 1976). (c) Attorneys' fees may be awarded to prevailing party.

*Case sample:*  Louise Lamphere v. Brown University (proposed settlement, October 1977) was a class action suit brought by

female faculty members claiming sex discrimination resulting in unequal treatment regarding hiring, contract, renewal, promotion, and tenure. The investigation led to agreement for a consent decree which would provide monetary
and other relief to the women involved up to a maximum
of $400,000. It would provide also for the adoption of
specific criteria, standards, and procedures for hiring,
contract renewal, promotion, and tenure at the university.
In addition, provisions would be made for affirmative
action to be exercised in faculty employment and for goals
and timetables designed to increase the representation of
women on the faculty. A five-member Affirmative Action
Monitoring Committee would be established to implement
and enforce the provisions of the decree.

*Comments:*     This is one of the most active areas of employment litigation. Title VII specifically makes possible awards of attorneys' fees, which means that claims made under other laws
also may include a Title VII claim in order to recover costs
of legal representation. However, EEOC must be requested
to investigate violations before one may resort to a private
suit. Prevention of Title VII claims depends on the institutions' setting up and implementing nondiscriminatory employment practices. Consent decrees under this title have
involved millions of dollars and future monitoring of the
institution's employment practices over a period of years.

*Further*        Equal Employment Opportunity Commission, 2401 E.
*information:*    Street, N.W., Washington, D.C. 20506

## 8. COPYRIGHT REVISION ACT

*Prohibits:*   Section 106 (below) prohibits unauthorized use of copyrighted material for profit or public display without appropriate payment to or permission from the copyright proprietor.

Sec. 106 Exclusive rights in copyrighted works

Subject to sections 107 through 118, the owner of copyright under this title has the exclusive rights to do and to authorize any of the following:

(1) to reproduce the copyrighted work in copies or phonorecords;

(2) to prepare derivative works based upon the copyrighted work;

(3) to distribute copies or phonorecords of the copyrighted work to the public by sale or other transfer of ownership, or by rental, lease, or lending;

(4) in the case of literary, musical, dramatic, and choreographic works, pantomimes, and motion pictures and other audiovisual works, to perform the copyrighted work publicly; and

(5) in the case of literary, musical, dramatic, and choreographic works, pantomimes, and pictorial, graphic, or sculptural works, including the individual images of a motion picture or other audiovisual work, to display the copyrighted work publicly.

*Permits:*   Sections 107 and 108 (see pp. 221-224) permit educators and libraries to make "fair use" of copyrighted material. Section 107 specifically permits "reproduction in copies or phonorecords ... for purposes such as ... teaching (including multiple copies for classroom use), scholarship, or research. ..." To determine whether the use is a fair use the following factors are to be considered:

(1) the purpose and character of the use, including whether such use is of a commercial nature or is for nonprofit educational purposes;

(2) the nature of the copyrighted work;

(3) the amount and substantiality of the portion used in relation to the copyrighted work as a whole;

and
(4) the effect of the use upon the potential market
for or value of the copyrighted work.

Section 108 permits library employees to make and distribute copies of works as set forth in Section 107 and for
noncommercial purposes including making copies of unpublished works for purposes of preservation, making
copies of published works for purposes of replacement of
damaged copies, and making copies of out-of-print works
that cannot be obtained at a fair price. Libraries should
take care that copies made include a notice of copyright,
and that warnings are posted appropriately.

*By:*               Educators and libraries.

*Affects:*          Copyrighted works only. Does not affect works in the pub-
                    lic domain or works on which the copyright has expired.

*Examples of*       Making multiple copies of a copyrighted work and selling
*violations:*       them to students for a profit.

*Remedies:*         Injunctive relief; recovery of actual damages and profits;
                    statutory damages ranging from $250 to $10,000 for each
                    work infringed. However, if the infringer is an educator
                    who believed and had reasonable grounds for believing that
                    the use was a fair use, statutory damages will be forgiven;
                    see subsection 504(c)(2).

*Case sample:*      No cases are available at this writing since the revised law
                    only became effective on January 1, 1978. However, one
                    area of special concern which may result in litigation is
                    noteworthy: the use of copyrighted music performed at
                    halftime periods and the like at athletic events where an
                    admission fee is charged or monies are received from com-
                    mercial television or radio stations. The same concerns
                    exist for theater and music department productions where
                    there is an admission charge. The issue is whether such prac-
                    tices change the venture from an educational to a commer-
                    cial one.

*Caution:*          "Guidelines" of fair use by photocopying were agreed upon by certain groups of educational associations, publishers, and authors' groups. They dealt with photocopying of copyrighted material for use in research and classroom teaching, use in music teaching, and use by libraries in inter-library exchanges. These guidelines may bind the signatories of the agreements but do not bind other persons or groups, Congress, or the courts. Educational institutions may wish to consult the guidelines in setting their own policies. For that reason the guidelines are included below, along with Sections 107 and 108 of the Copyright Revision Act.

*Comments:* An individual or an institution may be liable for actual or statutory damages for *knowing* violations of the fair use doctrine. However, under an exception, educators who *reasonably* believe the use of a copyrighted work was a fair use probably are not culpable.

*Further information:* Register of Copyrights, Library of Congress, Washington, D.C. 20540.

## PUBLIC LAW 94-553, SECTION 107

### Sec. 107. Limitations on Exclusive Rights: Fair Use

Notwithstanding the provisions of section 106, the fair use of a copyrighted work, including such use by reproduction in copies or phonorecords or by any other means specified by that section, for purposes such as criticism, comment, news reporting, teaching (including multiple copies for classroom use), scholarship, or research, is not an infringement of copyright. In determining whether the use made of a work in any particular case is a fair use the factors to be considered shall include—

(1) the purpose and character of the use, including whether such use is of a commercial nature or is for nonprofit educational purposes.

(2) the nature of the copyrighted work;

(3) the amount and substantiality of the portion used in relation to the copyrighted work as a whole; and

(4) the effect of the use upon the potential market for or value of the copyrighted work.

PUBLIC LAW 94-553, SECTION 108

Sec. 108. Limitations on Exclusive Rights:
Reproduction by Libraries and Archives

(a) Notwithstanding the provisions of section 106, it is not an infringement of copyright for a library or archives, or any of its employees acting within the scope of their employment, to reproduce no more than one copy or phonorecord of a work, or to distribute such copy or phonorecord, under the conditions specified by this section, if—

(1) the reproduction or distribution is made without any purpose of direct or indirect commercial advantage;

(2) the collections of the library or archieves are (i) open to the public, or (ii) available not only to researchers affiliated with the library or archives or with the institution of which it is a part, but also to other persons doing research in a specialized field; and

(3) the reproduction or distribution of the work includes a notice of copyright.

(b) The rights of reproduction and distribution under this section apply to a copy or phonorecord of an unpublished work duplicated in facsimile form solely for purposes of preservation and security or for deposit for research use in another library or archives of the type described by clause (2) of subsection (a), if the copy or phonorecord reproduced is currently in the collections of the library or archives.

(c) The right of reproduction under this section applies to a copy or phonorecord of a published work duplicated in facsimile form solely for the purpose of replacement of a copy or phonorecord that is damaged, deteriorating, lost, or stolen, if the library or archives has, after a reasonable effort, determined that an unused replacement cannot be obtained at a fair price.

(d) The rights of reproduction and distribution under this section apply to a copy, made from the collection of a library or archives where the user makes his or her request or from that of another library or archives, of no more than one article or other contribution to a copyrighted collection or periodical issue, or to a copy or phonorecord of a small part of any other copyrighted work, if—

(1) the copy or phonorecord becomes the property of the user, and the library or archives has had no notice that the copy or phonorecord would be used for any purpose other than private study, scholarship, or research; and

(2) the library or archives displays prominently, at the place where orders are accepted, and includes on its order form, a warning of copyright in accordance with requirements that the Register of Copyrights shall prescribe by regulation.

(e) The rights of reproduction and distribution under this section apply to the entire work, or to a substantial part of it, made from the collection of a library or archives where the user makes his or her request or from that of another library or archives, if the library or archives has first determined, on the basis of a reasonable investigation, that a copy or phonorecord of the copyrighted work cannot be obtained at a fair price, if—

(1) the copy or phonorecord becomes the property of the user, and the library or archives has had no notice that the copy or phonorecord would be used for any purpose other than private study, scholarship, or research; and

(2) the library or archives displays prominently, at the place where orders are accepted, and includes on its order form, a warning of copyright in accordance with requirements that the Register of Copyrights shall prescribe by regulation.

(f) Nothing in this section—

(1) shall be construed to impose liability for copyright infringement upon a library or archives or its employees for the unsupervised use of reproducing equipment located on its premises: *Provided,* That such equipment displays a notice that the making of a copy may be subject to the copyright law;

(2) excuses a person who uses such reproducing equipment or who requests a copy or phonorecord under subsection (d) from liability for copyright infringement for any such act, or for any later use of such copy or phonorecord, if it exceeds fair use as provided by section 107;

(3) shall be construed to limit the reproduction and distribution by lending of a limited number of copies and excerpts by a library or archives of an audiovisual news program, subject to clauses (1), (2), and (3) of subsection (a); or

(4) in any way affects the right of fair use as provided by section 107, or any contractual obligations assumed at any time by the library or archives when it obtained a copy or phonorecord of a work in its collections.

(g) The rights of reproduction and distribution under this section extend to the isolated and unrelated reproduction or distribution of a single copy or phonorecord of the same material on separate occasions, but do not extend to cases where the library or archives, or its employee—

(1) is aware or has substantial reason to believe that it is engaging in the related or concerted reproduction or distribution of multiple copies or phonorecords of the same material, whether made on one occasion or over a period of time, and whether intended for aggregate use by one or more individuals or for separate use by the individual members of a group; or

(2) engages in the systematic reproduction or distribution of single or multiple copies or phonorecords of material described in subsection (d); *Provided,* That nothing in this clause prevents a library or archives from participating in interlibrary arrangements that do not have, as their purpose or effect, that the library or archives receiving such copies or phonorecords for distribution does so in such aggregate quantities as to substitute for a subscription to or purchase of such work.

(h) The rights of reproduction and distribution under this section do not apply to a musical work, a pictorial, graphic or sculptural work, or a motion picture or other audiovisual work other than an audiovisual work dealing with news, except that no such limitation shall apply with respect to rights granted by subsections (b) and (c), or with respect to pictorial or graphic works published as illustrations, diagrams, or similar adjuncts to works of which copies are reproduced or distributed in accordance with subsections (d) and (e).

(i) Five years from the effective date of this Act, and at five-year intervals thereafter, the Register of Copyrights, after consulting with representatives of authors, book and periodical publishers, and other owners of copyrighted materials, and with representatives of library users and librarians, shall submit to the Congress a report setting forth the extent to which this section has achieved the intended statutory balancing of the rights of creators, and the needs of users. The report should also describe any problems that may have arisen, and present legislative or other recommendations, if warranted.

\*   \*   \*

*The "fair use" section of the revised copyright law (PL 94-553) spells out the rights of teachers. This section of the law went into effect January 1, 1978. The guidelines below are from Report of the Judiciary Committee, House of Representatives, Hs. Rept. No. 94-1476, 94th Congress, 2d session, September 3, 1976, and Conference Report, Hs. Rept. No. 94-1733, September 29, 1976.*

\*   \*   \*

. . . the following statement of guidelines is not intended to limit the types of copying permitted under the standards of fair use under judicial decision and which are stated in Section 107 of the Copyright Revision Bill. There may be instances in which copying which does not fall within the guidelines stated below may nonetheless be permitted under the criteria of fair use.

## GUIDELINES

### I. Single Copying for Teachers

A single copy may be made of any of the following by or for a teacher at his or her individual request for his or her scholarly research or use in teaching or preparation to teach a class:

A. A chapter from a book;

B. An article from a periodical or newspaper;

C. A short story, short essay, or short poem, whether or not from a collective work;

D. A chart, graph, diagram, drawing, cartoon or picture from a book, periodical, or newspaper.

### II. Multiple Copies for Classroom Use

Multiple copies (not to exceed in any event more than one copy per pupil in a course) may be made by or for the teacher giving the course for classroom use or discussion; *provided that:*

A. The copying meets the tests of brevity and spontaneity as defined below; *and*

B. Meets the cumulative effect test as defined below; *and,*

C. Each copy includes a notice of copyright.

*Definitions:*

*Brevity—*

(*i*) Poetry: (a) A complete poem if less than 250 words and if printed on not more than two pages or, (b) from a longer poem, an excerpt of not more than 250 words.

(*ii*) Prose: (a) Either a complete article, story or essay of less than 2,500 words, or (b) an excerpt from any prose work of not more than 1,000 words or 10% of the work, whichever is less, but in any event a minimum of 500 words.

[Each of the numerical limits stated in "i" and "ii" above may be expanded to permit the completion of an unfinished line of a poem or of an unfinished prose paragraph.]

(*iii*) Illustration: One chart, graph, diagram, drawing, cartoon or picture per book or per periodical issue.

(*iv*) "Special" works: Certain works in poetry, prose or in "poetic prose" which often combine language with illustrations and which are intended sometimes for children and at other times for a more general audience fall short of 2,500 words in their entirety. Paragraph "ii" above notwithstanding such "special works" may not be reproduced in their entirety; however, an excerpt comprising not more than two of the published pages of such special work and containing not more than 10% of the words found in the text thereof, may be reproduced.

*Spontaneity—*

(*i*) The copying is at the instance and inspiration of the individual teacher, and

(*ii*) The inspiration and decision to use the work and the moment of its use for maximum teaching effectiveness are so close in time that it would be unreasonable to expect a timely reply to a request for permission.

*Cumulative Effect—*

(*i*) The copying of the material is for only one course in the school in which the copies are made.

(*ii*) Not more than one short poem, article, story, essay or two excerpts may be copied from the same author, nor more than three from the same collective work or periodical volume during one class term.

(*iii*) There shall not be more than nine instances of such multiple copying for one course during one class term.

[The limitations stated in "ii" and "iii" above shall not apply to current news periodicals and newspapers and current news sections of other periodicals.]

**III. Prohibitions as to I and II Above**

Notwithstanding any of the above, the following shall be prohibited:

(A) Copying shall not be used to create or to replace or substitute for anthologies, compilations or collective works. Such replacement or substitution may occur whether copies of various works or excerpts therefrom are accumulated or reproduced and used separately.

(B) There shall be no copying of or from works intended to be "consumable" in the course of study or of teaching. These include workbooks, exercises, standardized tests and test booklets and answer sheets and like consumable material.

(C) Copying shall not:

(a) substitute for the purchase of books, publishers' reprints or periodicals;

(b) be directed by higher authority;

(c) be repeated with respect to the same item by the same teacher from term to term.

(D) No charge shall be made to the student beyond the actual cost of the photocopying.

## GUIDELINES FOR THE EDUCATIONAL USES OF MUSIC

### A. Permissible Uses

1. Emergency copying to replace purchased copies which for any reason are not available for an imminent performance provided purchased replacement copies shall be substituted in due course.

2. (a) For academic purposes other than performance, multiple copies of excerpts of works may be made, provided that the excerpts do not comprise a part of the whole which would constitute a performable unit such as a section, movement or aria, but in no case more than 10% of the whole work. The number of copies shall not exceed one copy per pupil.

(b) For academic purposes other than performance, a single copy of an entire performable unit (section, movement, aria, etc.) that is, (1) confirmed by the copyright proprietor to be out of print or (2) unavailable except in a larger work, may be made by or for a teacher solely for the purpose of his or her scholarly research or in preparation to teach a class.

3. Printed copies which have been purchased may be edited or simplified provided that the fundamental character of the work is not distorted or the lyrics, if any, altered or lyrics added if none exist.

4. A single copy of recordings of performances by students may be made for evaluation or rehearsal purposes and may be retained by the educational institution or individual teacher.

5. A single copy of a sound recording (such as a tape, disc or cassette) of copyrighted music may be made from sound recordings owned by an educational institution or an individual teacher for the purpose of constructing aural exercises or examinations and may be retained by the educational institution or individual teacher. (This pertains only to the copyright of the music itself and not to any copyright which may exist in the sound recording.)

### B. Prohibitions

1. Copying to create or replace or substitute for anthologies, compilations or collective works.

2. Copying of or from works intended to be "consumable" in the course of study or of teaching such as workbooks, exercises, standardized tests and answer sheets and like material.

3. Copying for the purpose of performance, except as in A(1) above.

4. Copying for the purpose of substituting for the purchase of music, except as in A(1) and A(2) above.

5. Copying without inclusion of the copyright notice which appears on the printed copy.

## GUIDELINES FOR PHOTOCOPYING—
## INTERLIBRARY ARRANGEMENTS

1. As used in the proviso of subsection 108 (g)(2), the words ". . . such aggregate quantities as to substitute for a subscription to or purchase of such work" shall mean:

(a) with respect to any given periodical (as opposed to any given issue of a periodical), filled requests of a library or archives (a "requesting entity") within any calendar year for a total of six or more copies of an article or articles published in such periodical within five years prior to the date of the request. These guidelines specifically shall not apply, directly or indirectly, to any request of a requesting entity for a copy or copies of an article or articles published in any issue of a periodical, the pubication date of which is more than five years prior to the date when the request is made. These guidelines do not define the meaning, with respect to such a request, of ". . . such aggregate quantities as to substitute for a subscription to [such periodical]."

(b) With respect to any other material described in subsection 108(d), (including fiction and poetry), filled requests of a requesting entity within any calendar year for a total of six or more copies or phonorecords of or from any given work including a collective work during the entire period when such material shall be protected by copyright.

2. In the event that a requesting entity—

(a) shall have in force or shall have entered an order for a subscription to a periodical, or

(b) has within its collection, or shall have entered an order for, a copy or phonorecord of any other copyrighted work, material from either category of which it desires to obtain by copy from another library or archives (the "supplying entity"), because the material to be copied is not reasonably available for use by the requesting entity itself, then the fulfillment of such request shall be treated as though the requesting entity made such copy from its own collection. A library or archives may request a copy or photorecord from a supplying entity only under those circumstances where the requesting entity would have been able, under the other provisions of section 108, to supply such copy from materials in its own collection.

3. No request for a copy or phonorecord of any material to which these guidelines apply may be fulfilled by the supplying entity unless such request is accompanied by a representation by the requesting entity that the request was made in conformity with these guidelines.

4. The requesting entity shall maintain records of all requests made by it for copies or phonorecords of any materials to which these guidelines apply and shall maintain records of the fulfillment of such requests, which records shall be retained until the end of the third complete calendar year after the end of the calendar year in which the respective request shall have been made.

5. As part of the review provided for in subsection 108 (i), these guidelines shall be reviewed not later than five years from the effective date of this bill.

## 9. EDUCATION AMENDMENTS OF 1976
## (STUDENT CONSUMER INFORMATION)

*Provides:*           45 C.F.R. 178 sets forth additional regulations regarding full disclosure of academic and financial aid programs to all prospective and present students.

The Education Amendments are a compendium of federal legislative activity affecting elementary, secondary, and post-secondary educational institutions. They cover a wide range of topics such as community service, lifelong learning, basic grants, libraries, impact aid programs, construction, equal opportunity programs, vocational education, education of the handicapped, and guidance and counseling, to name but a few. This discussion focuses on only one of the new legal responsibilities: full disclosure of financial and academic policies prior to payment of tuition (Section 1070).

*By:*                 Educational institutions.

*Affects:*            As of July 1, 1977, an institution wishing to receive federal funds to cover cost of administering federal student financial aid must (1) disseminate information about the academic and aid programs through publications and mailings to prospective students and enrolled students; (2) provide full information about the institution, its academic programs, faculty, placement, etc.; and (3) designate someone or several persons, on a full-time basis, to assist students regarding financial aid.

*Example of*
*violation:*          Providing misinformation to prospective students.

*Remedies:*           Any institution providing "substantial misrepresentation" as to the "nature of its educational program, its financial charges, or the employability of its graduates" would be grounds for suspension or termination of the institution's eligibility under the student aid programs.

*Comments:*           Loss of eligibility of the institution to participate in student loan programs is at stake here. A specific person should be made accountable for complying with the notice and full disclosure requirements annually.

*Further information:*  Office of Education, Department of Health, Education and Welfare, Washington, D.C. 20201; or Education Commission of the States, Suite 300, 1860 Lincoln Street, Denver, Colorado 80203.

## 10. EDUCATION AMENDMENTS OF 1972: TITLE IX

*Prohibits:*     Sex discrimination in recruiting and admissions, financial aid, athletics, textbooks and curriculum, housing facilities, counseling for careers, insurance and health care, single-sex groups and programs, extracurricular activities, and employment.

No person in the United States shall, on the basis of sex, be excluded from participation in, be denied the benefits of, or be subjected to discrimination under any educational program or activity receiving Federal financial assistance.

*Note:* One court has declared that Title IX does not cover educational employees. This decision affects only Section 86.57 of Title IX and only in that court's jurisdiction (*Romeo Community School District* v. *HEW,* 1977). HEW is appealing this decision.

Also, compliance deadlines for athletics are July 21, 1976, for elementary schools and July 21, 1978, for secondary schools and higher education. The key is equal opportunity; dual departments are permitted.

*By:*            Educational institutions receiving federal financial assistance.

*Affects:*       (1) Admissions: Discrimination in admissions is prohibited only in vocational institutions (including high schools), graduate and professional schools, and public undergraduate coeducational institutions.
(2) Once admitted, female and male students at all educational institutions receiving federal financial assistance must be treated without discrimination.

*Examples of*    Recruiting only at male institutions, quotas limiting num-
*violations:*    ber admitted, using different criteria in assessing financial need of males and females, athletic scholarships for males only, unequal dormitory facilities (separate dorms are permitted, however), different age requirement for mandatory residence in dorms for males and females, encouraging stereotypes (e.g., counseling girls to be nurses and boys to

be doctors), not providing sterilization while providing vasectomies, not permitting males to enroll in women's studies courses, allowing only males to be members of organization which receives significant assistance from school, and refusal to treat pregnancy as a temporary disability.

*Note:* Prohibitions regarding textbooks and curriculum normally are not enforced because it may clash with the First Amendment.

*Exceptions to Title IX regulations:* Military and religious schools; social fraternities and sororities; Boy Scouts, Girl Scouts, Camp Fire, YMCA, YWCA, Boys' and Girls' States and Nations; father-son and mother-daughter events, so long as if event is held for one sex, comparable event is held for the other; scholarships to beauty pageant winners, where awards are based on appearance, poise and talent; single-sex scholarships provided to players on separate athletic teams, in proportion to number of students of each sex participating in interscholastic or intercollegiate athletics; and single-sex scholarships established by a foreign government or by a will, trust, etc. (*Note:* Women are now permitted to apply for Rhodes scholarships. The British Sex Discrimination Act of 1975 has eliminated the male-only rule.)

*Requires:* Self-study by the institution, modifications of sexually discriminatory practices, and "Assurance of Compliance" with Title IX. One person is to be made responsible for Title IX compliance and handling of grievances. Grievance procedures are to be set up for students and employees; there is no requirement that individuals use this procedure.

*Remedies:* Investigation of complaint and attempt at voluntary conciliation by Office of Civil Rights of HEW. Failure to settle appropriately may result in administrative hearing, followed by suspension or termination of federal funds. OCR may refer the complaint to the Department of Justice for court action. A court may order the institution to cease the discriminatory practices and provide equitable relief and take remedial actions.

Courts are divided on whether there is an individual right to sue under Title IX. A decision holding that an individual may not sue is *Cannon* v. *University of Chicago* (1977). However, another court has held that without recognition of a private cause of action under Title IX, individual litigants who suffered sex discrimination in educational activities (not related to employment) would be left with no remedy for personal injury (*Piascik* v. *Cleveland Museum of Art*, 1977).

It is not clear yet to what extent attorneys' fees may be available to complainants under the Civil Rights Attorneys' Fees Awards Act of 1976.

There is no apparent personal liability. Affirmative action is not required but may be undertaken voluntarily by the institution to overcome results of past sex discrimination.

*Comments:*       Loss of federal financial assistance by the institution is possible. A specific person should be responsible for complying with notice requirements, monitoring implementation, and handling grievances.

*Further*          Office for Civil Rights, Department of Health, Education
*information:*     and Welfare, Washington, D.C. 20201.

## 11. EQUAL PAY ACT OF 1963

*Prohibits:*  Discrimination on the basis of sex in pay for "equal" work:

Sec. 3(d)(1): No employer having employees subject to any provisions of this section shall discriminate, within any establishment in which such employees are employed, between employees on the basis of sex by paying wages to employees in such establishment at a rate less than the rate at which he pays wages to employees of the opposite sex in such establishment for equal work on jobs the performance of which requires equal skill, effort, and responsibility, and which are performed under similar working conditions, except where such payment is made pursuant to (i) a seniority system; (ii) a merit system; (iii) a system which measures earnings by quantity or quality of production; or (iv) a differential based on any other factor other than sex; Provided, That an employer who is paying a wage rate differential in violation of this subsection shall not, in order to comply with the provisions of this subsection, reduce the wage rate of any employee.

The text above defines "equal" work as "jobs the performance of which requires equal skill, effort, and responsibility, and which are performed under similar working conditions." Wage differentials are permitted based upon factors not having to do with sex, such as (1) a seniority system, (2) a merit system, (3) a system which measures earning by quantity or quality of production, or (4) other differentials based on any other factors other than sex.

*By:*  All employers, private and public.

*Affects:*  Virtually all jobs in an educational institution, including administrative, teaching, and other staff positions.

*Examples of violations:*  Payment of higher wages to male custodians than to female custodians who perform equal work.

*Remedies:*  The Department of Labor enforces the Equal Pay Act. If a violation is found, (a) the employer will be required to raise the salary to the highest rate in the classifications in dispute, rather than lowering the higher rate, in order to comply with the act; (b) the employer will be liable to pay back wages with interest to the underpaid employee subject to the statute of limitations.

Suit also may be brought by an individual or class of individuals in federal court, and in addition to the above remedy, such private suit may include a request for liquidated damages in an amount equal to the back wages due.

Liability under this act is both civil and criminal. Institutions, rather than individuals are exposed to civil liability. Individuals may be subject to a criminal penalty for willful violation, but such criminal penalties have seldom been invoked.

The statute of limitations for the recovery of unpaid wages by an individual or a Department of Labor is 2 years, with a 3-year period applicable in the event of a willful violation.

*Case sample:*   *Walker* v. *Columbia University* (1976), is an example of a university employer successfully proving that male custodians were doing "heavy" work that was sufficiently different from the "light" work done by females to establish that "unequal work" was being done. This permitted different rates of pay for male and female custodians.

*Comments:*   Civil and criminal liability are possible. Attorneys' fees may be awarded against employer. Wages should be monitored routinely to see that compensation relates to the job rather than to the gender of the job holder.

*Further*   Wage and Hour Division, Employment Standards Adminis-
*information:*   tration, Department of Labor, Washington, D.C. 20210

## 12. EXECUTIVE ORDER 11246,
## AS AMENDED BY EXECUTIVE ORDER 11375

| | |
|---|---|
| *Prohibits:* | Federal contractors from discriminating in employment on the basis of race, color, religion, sex, or national origin. Employment is to be on the basis of merit: |

> It is the policy of the United States Government to provide equal opportunity in Federal employment and in employment by Federal contractors on the basis of merit and without discrimination because of race, color, religion, sex or national origin.

Written affirmative action plans may be required of federal contractors and subcontractors with contracts of $50,000 or more and 50 or more employees. The contractor must determine whether minorities are "underutilized." If so, an affirmative action plan must be developed, including goals and timetables, to increase the employment and promotional opportunities for minorities and women. The contractor is required to make a good faith effort to reach the goals within the times which have been set. An affirmative action officer is to be named and given responsibility for implementing the plan.

| | |
|---|---|
| *By:* | All federal contractors and subcontractors having federal contracts in excess of $10,000, regardless of the number of employees. |
| *Affects:* | Employment throughout the institution. |
| *Examples of violations:* | Filling a position without a good faith search for qualified minorities and women who might be considered for the position along with other candidates. |
| *Remedies:* | The Office of Civil Rights of the U.S. Department of Health, Education and Welfare may recommend revocation of existing federal contracts and debarment from future federal contracts by noncomplying contractors or subcontractors. Suits by appropriate agencies may also be recommended to compel compliance. Individuals may file complaints regarding noncompliance. However, the OCR prefers large class action complaints which involve an overall |

pattern or practice of discrimination. No personal liability is involved.

*Case sample:*      *EEOC, U.S. Secretary of Labor and U.S. Department of Justice* v. *American Telephone and Telegraph* (1973): Allegations of sex discrimination at AT&T, the largest private employer of women in the United States, were investigated. Dual recruitment systems for women and men were found, with resulting dual tracks for jobs, wages, and promotions. The employer signed a consent decree in 1973 providing for substantial back pay and other affirmative remedial steps, to be in force over a 6-year period. This case was combined with a Title VII action.

*Comments:*      Loss of federal financial assistance by the institution may result. Costs of pursuing violators is borne generally by the government. Affirmative action is a highly emotional concept, but one simple to comply with in three steps: doing an inventory of the work force, setting goals and time-tables, and making good faith efforts to reach the goals. Stay out of the trap of confusing goals with quotas. Any football or hockey player can see the difference; so should any self-respecting administrator. If violations occur, however, quotas may be imposed as a penalty.

*Further information:*      Office for Civil Rights, Department of Health, Education and Welfare, Washington, D.C. 20201; or Office of Federal Contract Compliance Programs, Employment Standards Administration, Department of Labor, Washington, D.C. 20210.

## 13. FAIR LABOR STANDARDS ACT OF 1938

*Requires:*
Employees be compensated at no less than the minimum wage, presently $2.30 per hour, for hours worked per week up to 40 hours. All hours worked in excess of 40 hours within a work week are to be considered overtime and compensated at a rate not less than one and one half times the regular rate of pay.

*By:*
All employers except state agencies. Private educational institutions are covered by FLSA. State institutions are excluded from federal coverage, but may be covered by a state statute. Local public institutions, such as city or county, may be covered by FLSA or state or local provisions.

*Affects:*
All employees, except executives, administrators, and professionals who meet the specific provision of spending at least 50 percent of their time in a manner that their task can be labeled as such.

*Examples of violations:*
Paying less than the minimum wage per hour. Not paying overtime for work in excess of 40 hours per week. Not counting as hours worked certain work done at home; breaks of less than 20 minutes; certain time spent waiting for medical attention; time spent adjusting grievances; certain time spent attending lectures, meetings, or training programs; certain travel time.

*Remedies:*
Individuals or groups of employees may file suit for back pay. They may be entitled to liquidated damages, attorneys' fees, and court costs. The Secretary of Labor also may sue. Willful violations may result in fines or imprisonment.

*Case sample:*
*Bushwick Mills, Inc.* (1946): An employer found itself subject to three different wage laws: the Public Contracts Act, the FLSA, and the state minimum wage law. It sought a declaratory judgment as to which law applied. According to the public contracts administrator, the "legal minimum rate" is the highest minimum established by either federal or state law.

*Comments:*    Awards of back pay, fines, and imprisonment may result. Awards of attorneys' fees are possible in individual or class action suits. Simple accounting and monitoring systems should prevent most violations. In arcane situations, consult legal counsel.

*Further*        Wage and Hour Division, Employment Standards Adminis-
*information:*   tration, Department of Labor, Washington, D.C. 20210.

## 14. FAMILY EDUCATIONAL RIGHTS
## AND PRIVACY OF 1974 (BUCKLEY AMENDMENT)

*Prohibits:*    Student records being kept in a fashion which violates the privacy of students and their parents.

No funds shall be made available under any applicable program to any . . . institution of . . . education . . . which has a policy of denying . . . parents . . . the right to inspect and review any and all official records, files, and data directly related to their children.''

Parents of students (and students themselves who are over 18 or attending any postsecondary institution) have the right to inspect their children's records. Their consent must also be secured before information in a student's file may be released to others.

*By:*    Educational institutions receiving federal funds.

*Affects:*    Procedures for student record keeping, as follows. First, a parent or student has the right to inspect student records. If it appears they contain inaccurate material, a hearing must be held within a reasonable time before an impartial hearing officer to present the student's side of the story. An explanation may be inserted into the file by the student or parent. Second, written permission must be secured from the parent or student before information in the file is released to others.

If the student is 18 years of age or more, *or* is attending an institution of postsecondary education, these rights belong to the student only, not to the student's parents. An exception may be permitted by the institution for a parent who still is claiming a student as a dependent for income tax purposes.

Parents and students must be notified of their rights under the act to access, challenge, consent, and notice.

Exceptions do exist (but should be checked carefully with legal counsel) regarding the institution's security records, medical records, and certain private files.

The use of a social security number as a student identifier is highly questionable under this act and the Privacy

Act, discussed later.

Consent of the student or parent may be secured to waive rights to see confidential letters of recommendation placed in the student's file.

*Examples of violations:*

Refusal to allow a student or parent to inspect or challenge records which are alleged to be inaccurate, misleading, or otherwise inappropriate. Release of data in student's file to others without appropriate consent. Refusal to notify students of their rights under the act.

*Remedies:*

Investigation by Department of Health, Education and Welfare, possibly followed by termination of federal funding "under any applicable program." It is not clear whether a private cause of action also exists.

*Caution:*

A number of questions of interpretation of this act remain unanswered, including the manner of posting student grades and what information about a student may be released without the student's consent through publication in a student "directory."

*Comments:*

Loss of federal financial assistance is possible. A specific person should be made responsible for giving proper notice to students and parents, getting waivers to use personal data in student directories, getting waviers to permit confidential letters of recommendation, and getting consent to release data to others.

*Further information:*

Administrators and attorneys may seek assistance by calling the HEW School Records Task Force at (202) 245-7488 or writing to the Task Force at Room 5660, Department of HEW, 330 Independence Ave., S.W., Washington, D.C. 20201. Also, "A Guide to Postsecondary Institutions for Implementation of the Family Educational Rights and Privacy Act of 1974" is available for $4.00 from AACRAO, Suite 330, One Dupont Circle, Washington, D.C. 20036.

## 15. GUARANTEED STUDENT LOAN PROGRAM (GSLP)

The federal government encourages money lenders to make loans to students at postsecondary institutions by guaranteeing repayment. The GSLP is one of the largest sources of financial assistance available today. HEW estimates current loans outstanding at about $5 billion. These are private monies guaranteed by the federal government. It is clear then why the federal government is concerned about the rate of possible default. These loans pay for costs of postsecondary education. Repayment is deferred to a period after graduation or leaving the institution. Private parties and nonfederal agencies such as banks, savings and loan associations, insurance companies, state agencies, and educational institutions are typical lenders.

Defaults by student borrowers are reimbursed by the federal government to the agency lenders, directly or indirectly, for 80 to 100 percent of their losses. In some states the loans are guaranteed by the federal government directly. In other states the loans are guaranteed by state agencies, which in turn are reimbursed by the federal government for losses.

*Prohibits:*  Misuse or poor use of monies loaned to students under the GSLP. Experience has taught the federal government that there are two major concerns regarding monies lent. One is to make sure the funds are used appropriately by the institution. The other is to recognize the fact that most student borrowers have little or no experience handling large sums of money. They need to be assisted by having full information, before applying for a loan, regarding their proposed program of study and the placement possibilities upon completion of the program. They also benefit from having the loan proceeds made available in periodic payments, rather than in a lump sum.

*By:*  By colleges and universities, postsecondary vocational and correspondence schools.

*Affects:*  Standards of financial responsibility by the institution:
(1) Method of disbursement of loan proceeds, e.g., requires institution to return proceeds to lender if student

does not matriculate as planned. Also, requires that proceeds be sent to student in periodic payments rather than lump sum.

(2) Institution by requiring it to agree with the Office of Education to abide by laws and regulations of GSLP, thus recognizing that the institution, as well as the borrower and the lender, is an interested party to the loan transaction.

(3) Recordkeeping and reports by institution; e.g., institution is required to notify lender when the borrower has left school. Time to start repayment then begins. Institution is required to determine student's need for the loan and recommend a loan amount to the bank.

(4) Tuition refunds; e.g., institution must adopt a written policy setting forth some reasonable refund plan for students who withdraw before halfway point.

(5) Disclosure of information about institution to student prior to taking out loan; e.g., complete and accurate statement of current academic or training programs, faculties, and facilities. Regarding programs of study preparatory to a particular vocation, trade or career field, information shall be given on placement of graduates, including average starting salary and percentage of graduates who obtained employment. This does not apply to liberal arts programs.

(6) Default is preceded often by certain recognizable danger signals. Among these are an unusually large pattern of default already existing, a high dropout rate from the institution, too many loans at any one institution, and a general financial malaise in the operation of the institution. Prior to any action against the institution, an opportunity is provided for the institution to explain or eliminate the danger spots.

*Note:* GSLP regulations also permit the Office of Education to audit an institution's use of funds received through GSLs; and to limit, suspend, or terminate an institution's participation in the program for violations of regulations.

*Examples of violations:*

Not providing to an applicant to law school, before he or she takes out a loan, information on placement of recent graduates.

*Remedies:*   Loss of eligibility of institution to continue to participate in the program.

*Comments:*   Loss of eligibility of institution to participate in GSLP is possible. A specific person should be made responsible for giving notice annually and providing other required information. Effective in fall 1978, loans will no longer be guaranteed at colleges where the student default rate has been 15 percent or higher for 2 years. Effective in December 1977, the Office of Education may use private collection agencies in attempts to collect student debts.

*Futher
information:*   Office of Education, Department of Health, Education and Welfare, Washington, D.C. 20201.

## 16. HUMAN SUBJECTS RESEARCH REGULATIONS

*Prohibits:*  Research with human subjects at risk without prior informed consent and approval of an authorized Institutional Review Board. "No grant or contract involving human subjects at risk shall be made to an individual unless he is affiliated with or sponsored by an institution which can and does assume responsibility for the subjects involved." Selections from the regulations:

> It is the policy of the Department of Health, Education and Welfare that no activity involving human subjects be supported by DHEW grants or contracts shall be undertaken unless an Institutional Review Board has reviewed and approved such activity. . . . This review shall determine whether these subjects will be placed at risk, and if risk is involved, whether risk . . . is outweighed by benefit . . . subjects are adequately protected . . . legally effective informed consent will be obtained . . . risks to pregnant women and fetuses are avoided . . . IRB conducts review of the activity at timely intervals. Written assurance to DHEW is required.

*By:*  Any researcher carrying out research under the institution's auspices, whether or not government financed. Private consultation is not covered by these regulations.

*Affects:*  All research involving human subjects. A human subject is "at risk" who may be exposed to the possibility of injury, including physical, psychological, or social injury. In such situation, the Institutional Review Board must (1) ascertain that the risks are outweighted by the benefits and importance of the research; (2) that the rights and welfare of the subject will be protected; (3) that legally effective *informed consent* will be obtained; and (4) that the project is made subject to continuing review by the Board.

*Example of violation:*  Acquiring data from student records without getting informed consent of student or parent.

*Remedies:*  The secretary of DHEW may find that an institution has failed materially to comply with the terms of this policy.

The secretary then may terminate or suspend the grant or contract involved.

*Case sample:*    *State University of New York at Albany and New York State Health Department,* consent agreement entered into October 28, 1977. In this case, the institution was accused of violating federal and state regulations regarding research on human subjects. In the settlement, the institution admitted that members of its psychology department had violated the state's Protection of Human Subjects law in conducting a number of experiments. The violations included not obtaining the voluntary, informed, written consent of the participants; failing to make a fair explanation to the participants of the risks involved; failing to have the experiments approved by an authorized Institutional Review Board; and failing to supervise the experiment properly. The institution agreed to a 6-month period of monitoring to ensure compliance with the law. The institution also agreed to supply a policy statement to the effect that students at the institution will no longer be compelled to participate as subjects in human research by requiring that introductory psychology students either participate in experiments or alternatively write a term paper. Fines permissible under the state law were suspended and will not be assessed if the university stays in compliance with the law during the monitoring period. Fines levied by the state health department could have amounted to as much as $975,000 for the violations admitted. Federal officials from the National Institutes of Health also will require a separate assurance from the institution that the violations will not recur.

*Comments:*    Loss of federal grants or contracts is possible. State laws also may apply and may carry with them heavy fines for violations. Each institution should centralize responsibility for monitoring compliance with regulations regarding informed consent and approval by Institutional Review Boards.

*Further information:*    Department of Health, Education and Welfare, Washington, D.C. 20101

## 17. INTERNAL REVENUE PROCEDURE 75-50

*Prohibits:*            Private institutions which discriminate on the basis of race,
                        color, or national or ethnic origin from qualifying for
                        exemption from federal income tax under Section
                        501(c)(3) of the Internal Revenue Code of 1954 (Rev. Rul.
                        71-447, 1971–2 C.B. 230). Requires private institutions to
                        admit students of any race to all the rights, privileges, pro-
                        grams, and activities generally accorded or made available
                        to students at that institution. The institution may not dis-
                        criminate on the basis of race in administration of its edu-
                        cational policies, admissions policies, scholarship and loan
                        programs, and athletic and other school-administered pro-
                        grams. Selection of students on the basis of religious affili-
                        ation is permitted so long as membership in the religion is
                        open to all on a racially nondiscriminatory basis.

*By:*                   Private institutions applying for exemption or already
                        recognized as exempt from federal income tax.

*Affects:*              Admission to the institution and all subsequent treatment
                        at the school.

*Examples of*           Refusal to admit a student who is fully qualified, except
*violations:*           that he or she is black.

*Remedies:*             IRS refusal to grant exemption from federal income tax. It
                        is not clear yet to what extent attorneys' fees may be avail-
                        able under the Civil Rights Attorneys' Fees Awards Act of
                        1976.

*Comments:*             Loss of exemption from payment of federal income tax is
                        possible. Institution must make choice of being racially
                        nondiscriminatory in admissions or paying income tax. A
                        specific person should be charged with making sure such
                        notice of racially nondiscriminatory admissions policy is
                        disseminated fully according to IRS rules.

*Further*               Internal Revenue Service, Department of the Treasury,
*information:*          Washington, D.C.

## 18. OCCUPATIONAL SAFETY AND HEALTH ACT OF 1970 (OSHA)

*Requires:* Establishment of responsibility for OSHA compliance and establishment of a program for a standard of better operation of the institution as to safety and health of employees. There also are posting and reporting requirements. The act's purpose as stated in Section 651(b) is "to assure every man and woman in the nation safe and healthful working conditions and to preserve the nation's human resources."

*By:* All employers engaged in business affecting commerce. Private educational institutions are subject to federal or state OSHA programs. Public institutions such as governmental agencies are excluded from the federal program but will be covered by state programs as they become effective. Eventually the entire OSHA program is expected to be under the auspices of state agencies.

*Affects:* All facilities and plant, equipment. and materials, as well as personnel operating procedures.

*Examples of violations:* Violating standards for operation of electrical equipment, exit markings, clean and sanitary work areas, maintenance of portable fire extinguishers, marking aisles and passageways, stairway railings and guards, storage and use of flammable and combustible liquids, and use of personal protection equipment.

*Remedies:* Federal or state OSHA enforcement agency may issue citations for violations of standards found on inspection. Penalties include fines, injunctions, and possible criminal liability. Inspections without a search warrant may be resisted.

*Case sample:* *REA Exp., Inc.* v. *Brennan,* (1974): The employer permitted untrained employees to attempt to repair high voltage equipment on a wet concrete floor without protective equipment. A penalty was assessed by the trial court in the amount of $1,000. The appellate court found this amount was not excessive and that, in any event, it did not constitute an abuse of discretion by the trial court.

*Comments:*     Fines and orders to cease violations are possible. Government pays cost of pursuing violators. Development of a program of ongoing, in-house inspections is recommended. Handbook would be helpful for all employees setting forth basic principles and rules of procedure of institution for achieving safe and healthy working conditions. Goal is to be ready for inspection at any time. Additional discussion of OSHA appears in Chapter 7.

*Further
information:*     OSHA, Department of Labor, Washington, D.C. 20210.

## 19. PENSION REFORM ACT OR EMPLOYEE
## RETIREMENT INCOME SECURITY ACT OF 1974 (ERISA)

*Requires:* Private pension plans must meet specified standards as to length of service required before employee is covered, vesting of employees' rights in accrued benefits, funding of the plan, and fiduciary responsibility for establishment and operation of the plan. A plan administrator must be appointed who is responsible for preparing and filing summary plan descriptions, amnual reports, and terminal reports upon the dissolution of the plan. Reports must be filed with the Department of Labor, the Internal Revenue Service, the Pension Benefit Guaranty Corporation, and with those who participate in or benefit from the retirement plan.

It is hereby declared to be the policy of this Act to protect interstate commerce and the interests of participants in employee benefit plans and their beneficiaries, by requiring the disclosure and reporting to participants and beneficiaries of financial and other information with respect thereto, by establishing standards of conduct, responsibility, and obligation for fiduciaries of employee benefit plans, and by providing for appropriate remedies, sanctions, and ready access to the Federal courts.

It is hereby further declared to be the policy of this Act to protect interstate commerce, the Federal taxing power, and the interests of participants in private pension plans and their beneficiaries by improving the equitable character and the soundness of such plans by requiring them to vest the accrued benefits of employees with significant periods of service, to meet minimum standards of funding, and by requiring plan termination insurance.

*By:* All employee benefit plans established and maintained by private employers and employee organizations engaged in commerce are covered. Excluded are governmental plans, church plans, plans that exist solely for the purposes of complying with the applicable workmen's compensation laws or unemployment compensation or disability insurance plans, plans outside the United States that exist for nonresident aliens, and excess benefit plans that are un-funded.

*Affects:*          Employee benefit plans at private educational institutions.

*Examples of*       A fifth part of Subtitle I sets forth the rules for the admin-
*violations:*       tration and enforcement of the act. A violation of the act
                    may occur if the administrator fails to provide a participant
                    with a summary plan description and the secretary with an
                    annual report in accordance with the statute. The plan may
                    also be sued as an entity by a participant for past due bene-
                    fits. However, violations consisting of omissions of any of
                    the requirements of the general provisions will not cause
                    the administrator to be liable if he can prove a good faith
                    omission.

                    Part IV defines fiduciary responsibility and holds the fi-
                    duciary personally liable for any breach of that responsibili-
                    ty. The fiduciary must compensate any losses the plan has
                    suffered as a result of the breach of that responsibility.

*Remedies:*         Any person who willfully violates the act shall upon convic-
                    tion be fined not more than $5,000 or imprisoned for not
                    more than 1 year, or both. If the violation is committed by
                    an entity rather than a person, the fine may extend up to
                    $100,000. A participant may sue to recover benefits due, to
                    enforce his or her rights, or to clarify his or her rights to
                    future benefits. Remedy is therefore provided in both
                    monetary and declaratory relief. An administrator who fails
                    to comply with a request by the secretary for any informa-
                    tion shall be personally liable up to $100 for each day that
                    exceeds the 30 days allowed for compliance.

*Case sample:*      *U.S. Department of Labor* v. *Glen's, Inc.* (1976) was the
                    first suit initiated by the Labor Department itself under
                    ERISA. The suit charged former trustees of a restaurant's
                    retirement plan with violating their fiduciary responsibili-
                    ties under the law. Involved was a sale of stock to the plan
                    which was not solely in the interest of the plan's partici-
                    pants and beneficiaries. The suit asked for restitution of
                    funds and lost income resulting from the purchase of the
                    stock, removal of a present trustee, and a court order pro-
                    hibiting future violations.

*Comments:*      Personal liability is possible. Administrator of plan has fiduciary responsibilities and is held to highest level of care. Attorneys' fees may be awarded. Institution may be liable for penalties. Insurance should be considered.

*Further*      Office of Pensions and Welfare Benefit Program, Depart-
*information:*      ment of Labor, Washington, D.C. 20210.

## 20. PRIVACY ACT OF 1974

*Prohibits:*        Federal agencies from refusing to permit individuals to inspect and correct their own records kept by federal agencies. Also prohibits certain dissemination of personal information by federal agencies. The purpose of the act is "to assure that personal information about individuals collected by Federal agencies is limited to that which is legally authorized and necessary and is maintained in a manner which precludes unwarranted intrusions upon individual privacy."

*By:*               Federal agencies.

*Affects:*          Two parts of the Privacy Act particularly concern educational institutions. First, a question arose whether educational institutions "became" federal agencies subject to the act when they accepted federal research and other funding contracts. That question apparently has been answered in the negative. Therefore, institutional records are not subject to the Privacy Act, unless by the terms of the federal contract the institution actually *assumes a function* of a federal agency in developing and maintaining a system of records. Normally, the institution is an independent contractor, maintaining its own records, and is not subject to the act.

Second, the provision of the act regarding use of social security numbers does apply to public educational institutions because it specifically applies to *all* government agencies—federal, state, and local. It does not affect private institutions. Beginning January 1, 1975, a moratorium was placed on new uses of the social security number by government agencies. The purpose was to prevent intrusion on persons' privacy by eliminating the possible tracing of a person's identity through a social security number.

No public institution may deny one a right entitled by law because of a refusal to disclose one's social security number. For example, one could not be denied the right to apply or register at a public educational institution on the grounds that one refuses to disclose one's social security number.

The only exception exists when disclosure was specifically required by a statute or regulation adopted before January 1, 1975, or by a subsequent act of Congress. If such a requirement exists, the institution must give notice whether the disclosure is voluntary or mandatory, under what statute or regulation the request is authorized, and what uses will be made of the number. Social security numbers are required by law, for instance, to be disclosed to maintain records of amounts withheld from paychecks for income tax purposes. The Privacy Act permits a federal agency to disclose personal information without one's permission under the following circumstances: to employees of that agency who have a need for the record to perform their duties; as required by the Freedom of Information Act; for routine uses as announced in the *Federal Register;* to the Census Bureau, National Archives, Congress, or the General Accounting Office; pursuant to court order; in emergencies affecting health and safety; and to a law enforcement agency by written request of the agency head.

*Examples of violations:*     Posting grades; publicly using social security numbers as student identifiers.

*Remedies:*     Criminal penalties exist for knowingly and willfully disclosing information without permission.

*Comments:*     Criminal penalties exist for willful violations of the act. A specific person should be given responsibility for monitoring compliance with the law. Risks include misuse of computer data and information collected in research. Social security numbers should be discontinued as identifiers, and replaced with nonsense numbers.

*Further information:*     A federal agency must inform one, upon request, whether it has any record on one. A summary of information from federal agencies' Privacy Act notices appears in a publication called "Protecting Your Right to Privacy: Digest of Systems of Records." It is available in large libraries, or may be purchased for $5.00 from the Superintendent of Documents, Government Printing Office, Washington, D.C. 20402, or from GPO bookstores.

## 21. PUBLIC HEALTH SERVICE ACT

*Prohibits:*        Sex discrimination in admission to federally supported health-related training. Requires filing assurance of non-discrimination with Secretary of HEW.

*By:*               Schools of medicine, osteopathy, dentistry, veterinary medicine, optometry, pharmacy, podiatry, public health, allied health personnel, and nursing.

*Affects:*          Admissions policies and procedures.

*Examples of
violations:*        Refusal to admit qualified women to medical school.

*Remedies:*         HEW can recommend withdrawal of federal funds.

*Comments:*         Loss of federal financial assistance is possible. Admissions officer could be made responsible to comply with act, with cooperation of chief executive officer.

*Further
information:*       Office for Civil Rights, Department of Health, Education and Welfare, Washington, D.C. 20201.

## 22. REHABILITATION ACT OF 1973

*Prohibits:*  Discrimination against handicapped persons (students or employees). "Handicapped" includes physical or mental impariment which substantially limits one or more of such person's major life activities. Qualified handicapped individuals are those capable of learning, or being employed, with reasonable accommodation to his or her handicap. Persons handicapped by alcohol or other drugs are covered by this act; however, institutions may take the actual behavior of such individuals into account in deciding whether they are admissible or employable. Section 504 provides that "no otherwise qualified handicapped individual . . . shall, solely by reason of his handicap, be excluded from the participation in, be denied the benefits of, or be subjected to discrimination under any program or activity receiving federal financial assistance" from HEW.

*By:*  All institutions receiving funds from HEW; including elementary, secondary, and postsecondary institutions.

*Affects:*  Entire operation of institution beginning June 3, 1977. Programs and structures are to be made accessible. Mainstreaming is to be used, rather than separate facilities. The regulation does not require that every part of every building be accessible, *rather, programs as a whole are to be accessible.* Therefore, many institutions will be able to meet the requirements by reassigning classrooms or providing auxiliary aids for blind or deaf persons. Nonstructural changes are to be made within 60 days. Structural changes should be completed within 3 years.

  *Preschool, Elementary and Secondary, and Adult Education.* Effective immediately, each qualified handicapped child is entitled to a free appropriate education in the most normal setting possible. Complete compliance with this requirement must be achieved by September 1, 1978. Evaluation procedures must be improved to avoid inappropriate education due to misclassification. Parents and guardians must be provided with due process procedures to resolve disputes over placement of students. State and local educational agencies are to locate and identify unserved handicapped children. If a handicapped student is so disruptive that education of other students in the classroom is impaired, the student can be reassigned. Transportation must be arranged to and from educational programs. If placement in a public or private residential program is necessary, the school district has responsibility for the costs of the program, nonmedical care, room and board, and transportation.

*Postsecondary Education.* Recruitment, admissions, and treatment of qualified handicapped students must be free of discrimination. Preadmission inquiries about handicaps are generally not permitted. However, after admission, confidential inquiries about handicaps may be made to enable an institution to provide necessary services. An exception is made if the purpose of the preadmission inquiry is to take remedial action to correct past discrimination. Tests, including admissions tests, must be selected and administered so that the test results of students with impaired sensory, manual, or speaking skills are not distorted unfairly. Tests must measure the student's aptitude or achievement level, and not his or her disability. The director of the Office of Civil Rights of HEW has the burden of identifying alternate tests. Auxiliary aids must be provided, such as readers, tape recorders, and Braille material. This often may be done by assisting students to seek aid from state vocational rehabilitation agencies and from private charitable organizations. Academic requirements must be modified to ensure full opportunity. For example, an extension of time to complete degree requirements may be appropriate. Rules prohibiting tape recorders in class or dog guides on campus should be modified. Physical education, infirmary services, housing, financial assistance, counseling, placement services, and social organizations all must be accessible as a whole to qualified handicapped students.

*Employment Practices.* Institutions are prohibited from discriminating in employment in recruiting, hiring, compensation, job assignment and classification, and fringe benefits. Employers must make reasonable accommodations unless to do so would be an undue hardship, based on business necessity and cost. Simple adjustments are expected, such as modification of work schedules, use of ramps, and the shifting of some nonessential duties to other employees. Section 503 of the act requires affirmative action, similar to that under the Vietnam Veterans Readjustment Act, to seek out, hire, and advance in employment handicapped persons.

*Deadlines:* (1) By June 3, 1977, institutions with 15 or more employees must have designated a person to coordinate compliance efforts and to structure grievance procedures, including due process, for persons admitted or hired (but not for candidates for admission or employment).

(2) After June 3, 1977, new facilities or parts thereof must be designed to be readily accessible to and usable by handicapped persons. They must meet design standards of the American National Standards Institute for minimal accessibility.

(3) By July 5, 1977, institution must have returned Assurance of Compliance form to HEW.

(4) By August 2, 1977, institutions must function in existing facilities so that programs and activities, when viewed in their entirety, are readily accessible to handicapped persons.

*Education.* Consortia for handicapped only are not permitted; admissions tests must be modified; financial assistance (athletic scholarships) may be denied; courses and exams (requirements), including physical education, to be accessible; counseling and placement to be accessible; classroom aids, aides (readers, interpreters), tapes, special facilities to be provided; housing, infirmary, and other services to be accessible.

*Employment.* Employment tests and other selection criteria (medical exams), job restructuring, modified or part-time work schedules to be appropriate and accessible.

(5) By September 2, 1977, participants, beneficiaries, applicants, employees, and unions or professional organizations having agreements with the institution must have been notified that the institution does not discriminate in admission or access to, or treatment or employment in, its programs and activities.

(6) By December 2, 1977, institution must have developed a transition plan for making all structural changes.

(7) By June 2, 1978, the school must complete a self-evaluation of its policies and procedures, in consultation with handicapped persons.

(8) By September 1, 1978, all public preschool, elementary, secondary, and adult education schools are to provide each qualified handicapped student a free appropriate education.

(9) By June 2, 1980, all structural modifications must be complete, including housing.

*Examples of*   Refusing to accommodate wheelchair-bound student by
*violations:*    changing a class presently to be held in an inaccessible third-floor room to an accessible first-floor room.

*Remedies:*      Office of Civil Rights of HEW will investigate complaints and seek voluntary compliance with the law. If no resolution results, a hearing will be held. Ultimately, financial aid may be suspended, terminated, or not granted to the institution.

*Case samples:*  In *Barnes* v. *Converse College* (1977), a court ordered a college to find and compensate a qualified interpreter of its choosing for the purpose of assisting a deaf student.

*Comments:*      Loss of federal financial assistance is possible. A specific person is to be designated to oversee compliance with law, including affirmative action in employment practices.

*Further*        Director, Office for Civil Rights, Department of Health,
*information:*   Education and Welfare, Washington, D.C. 20201; or Wage and Hour Division, Employment Standards Administration, Department of Labor, Washington, D.C. 20210.

## 23. SUNSHINE ACTS

*Requires:*    Requirements vary from state to state. The federal act (below) requires public institutions to open to the public every portion of every meeting where governmental business is deliberated or determined.

It is hereby declared to be the policy of the United States that the public is entitled to the fullest practicable information regarding the decisionmaking processes of the Federal Government. It is the purpose of this Act to provide the public with such information while protecting the rights of individuals and the ability of the Government to carry out its reponsibilities.

Prior notice of such meetings is required, and transcripts or minutes of the meeting are to be made available to the public. Closed meetings are permitted only for specified stated purposes, such as prospective real estate transactions, certain personnel matters, some collective bargaining sessions, judicial deliberations, and particular law enforcement and national security matters.

*By:*    Public educational institutions. State sunshine laws, rather than the federal law, apply to most public institutions.

*Affects:*    Sunshine laws are so new that guidelines and interpretations still are being developed and tested in the courts. The language of most open meeting and open record laws appears fairly clear at first glance. However, immediate problems of interpretation arise. For example, precisely which governmental bodies are covered? Possible answers include meetings of the governor, boards of regents, school boards, faculty, students, and various other administrative bodies. Then, specifically which parts of such a body are covered? That is, does the law include subcommittees, advisory committees, staff meetings, department meetings, faculty evaluation committees, faculty senates, admissions committees, and student government committees? A third set of questions has to do with which gatherings of people constitute a "meeting" under the law. What about a telephone conversation between two people? Must there be a quorum present? Can there still be secret ballots? All of these questions are being litigated. In general, the trend appears to be toward more meetings being open than not.

*Examples of violations:* Failing to give proper notice prior to a meeting, failing to open a meeting to the public, and failing to make transcripts or minutes of the meeting available to the public after the meeting.

*Remedies:* Decisions made at improperly closed meetings may be declared void. The violation usually can be cured by a second, open, correctly held meeting. Suits may be filed seeking declaratory judgments, injunctions against future violations, and orders to make certain transcripts or records public. The burden usually is on the defendant institution to justify the closing of a meeting.

*Case sample:* Florida passed the first state sunshine act in 1905. Over the years it has been amended many times to let in more sunshine. Secret balloting, for example, was held to be a violation (*Bassett* v. *Braddock*, 1972).

*Comments:* In general, if a meeting involves making decisions that affect the public, it probably should be open to the public. However, it is essential that administrators familiarize themselves with the precise language and interpretation of their own state's open meeting and open record laws. Administrators then may wish to express their intention of abiding by all the requirements of the law. At the same time, it would be prudent to consult with legal counsel before making decisions as to which meetings should be open. Once a particular meeting becomes known as an open meeting, it is awkward to say it was all a mistake, and try to return it to its closed status. Open meetings do not necessarily require participation by the audience. Such participation would have to be clearly intended by the legislature.

*Further information:* Department of Justice, Washington, D.C. 20530.

## 24. VIETNAM ERA VETERANS' READJUSTMENT ASSISTANCE ACT OF 1974

*Prohibits:*   Discrimination in employment against qualified disabled Vietnam veterans.

All federal contracts and subcontracts in excess of $10,000 must require that contractor and subcontractor "take affirmative action to employ and advance in employment qualified disabled veterans and veterans of the Vietnam era."

A qualified disabled veteran is one who is capable of performing a particular job with reasonable accommodation to his or her disability.

*By:*   All educational institutions that are federal contractors and subcontractors with contracts in excess of $10,000.

*Affects:*   All "suitable" employment positions in the institution. These include openings compensated on a salary basis of less than $25,000 a year, and openings that are full time, temporary for more than three days, and part time.

*Requires:*   By November 23, 1976, affirmative action to have been taken "to employ and advance in employment qualified disabled veterans and veterans of the Vietnam era." An affirmative action officer should be designated. This program may be combined with or kept separate from other affirmative action programs. Regulations, for example, require each contractor to list with the appropriate local employment service officer all of its suitable employment openings. "Each such local office shall give such veterans priority in referral to such employment opening." Other recruiting requirements are set forth in the regulations.

*Examples of violations:*   Refusing to make a reasonable accommodation to the physical and mental limitations of the veteran. A reasonable accommodation is one which would not impose an undue hardship on the conduct of the employer's business. Factors taken into account in determining undue hardships include business necessity and financial cost and expenses.

*Remedies:*      Veterans may file complaints with Veterans' Employment
                 Service of the Department of Labor.

*Case sample:*   These regulations are relatively recent, and not many cases
                 exist. A typical violation at an educational institution
                 probably would involve a Vietnam veteran, mentally unim-
                 paired but physically requiring the use of a wheelchair, who
                 is qualified to teach but refused employment on the basis
                 of undue hardship to the institution. The installation of
                 ramps and use of first-floor classrooms would involve little
                 disruption of business activity and relatively minor cost in
                 most cases. Therefore, a complaint of discrimination
                 probably would be successful under those circumstances.

*Comments:*      The essence of this law, as of the Rehabilitation Act, is
                 accessibility and integration into normal employment situ-
                 ations. A specific person should be named to handle
                 compliance. An employer should make reasonable, good
                 faith efforts to accommodate qualified disabled veterans.
                 Records should be kept showing what efforts have been
                 made and the degree of success achieved.

*Further*        Veterans' Employment Service, Department of Labor,
*information:*   Washington, D.C. 20210.

# Appendix B: Professional Standards of Administrator and Faculty Organizations

## Professional Standards for Administrators in Higher Education
### American Association of University Administrators

### PREAMBLE

Just as academic freedom is the special hallmark of institutions of higher education, so, too, is academic responsibility the correlative of such freedom. Just as freedom to teach, learn, and research are inseparable attributes of academic freedom for faculty in universities and colleges, so is freedom to administer an inseparable part of academic freedom for university and college administrators. The correlative academic responsibility for administrators requires them to exercise academic freedom within the special service functions of higher education and within the objectives of the institution.

The administrative function in higher education exists to serve the educational community by facilitating the process of education and by the creation and maintenance of a milieu conducive to the teaching, learning, research, and service functions of higher education. The exercise of academic responsibility and academic freedom by administrators requires clearly understood conditions of employment, parameters of the operation of the office, career considerations, and personal responsibilities and rights.

© 1975, American Association of University Administrators.

Approved by AAUA Board of Directors on April 27, 1975. For further information, please write to the American Association of University Administrators, P.O. Box 6, Bidwell Station, Buffalo, New York 14222. Telephone: (716) 862-5132.

## A. THE RESPONSIBILITIES OF ADMINISTRATORS

### I. Conditions of Employment of the Administrator

1. An Administrator has the responsibility to carry out the duties of the office in such a way as to insure that race, sex, creed, national origin, or age do not enter into the formulation and execution of the policies of the institution.

2. An Administrator has the responsibility to carry out the duties of the office as noted in the written statement of the conditions of employment or in the job description published in an official handbook of the institution.

### II. The Administrator—The Operation of the Office

1. An Administrator has the responsibility to direct the utilization of the institution's resources in such a way as to implement the policy set by the governing board, to the extent these resources make possible such implementation.

2. An Administrator has the responsibility to utilize the institutional setting in such a way as to further its teaching, learning, research, and service functions.

3. An Administrator has the responsibility to participate, according to the nature and authority of the office, in the formulation and implementation of institutional policy.

4. An Administrator has the responsibility, according to the nature of the office and within limits set by the charter and governing board, to take appropriate action to develop, allocate, and preserve institutional resources.

5. An Administrator has the responsibility to act as official spokesman of the institution only according to the limits of the office held or by specific delegation.

6. An Administrator has the responsibility to create and sustain a milieu on campus such that each person can meet the responsibilities of office without disruption or harassment.

### III. The Administrator—Career Considerations

1. An Administrator has the responsibility to give the consideration to candidates within the institution for jobs that may become available.

2. An Administrator has the responsibility to improve professional and personal performance by attendance at appropriate meetings and by participation in the regular development programs of the institution, such as sabbaticals and leaves of absence.

3. An Administrator has the responsibility to be just and to avoid arbitrary or capricious actions regarding subordinates, especially in decisions

affecting continuation or termination of office.

4. An Administrator has the responsibility to participate in and assume responsibility for the regular and formal evaluation process of those under the Administrator's jurisdiction and to communicate to them in a timely fashion the results of the evaluation.

5. An Administrator has the responsibility to draw up and make available a written statement regarding the performance evaluation and the circumstances regarding the departure from the institution of those under the Administrator's supervision. The statement should be released only with the approval of the person who has departed from the institution.

6. An Administrator has the responsibility to seek actively new employment for a staff worker under the Administrator's jurisdiction whose employment was terminated solely due to a reallocation of resources.

## IV. Personal Responsibilities of the Administrator

1. An Administrator has the responsibility, when speaking as a private person regarding campus issues or issues that have no connection with the campus, to make clear that the Administrator is speaking in that capacity and not as a representative of the institution.

2. An Administrator has the responsibility to respect the right of privacy of others, particularly with regard to personal circumstances, including, but not limited to, financial information, religious beliefs, and political associations.

3. An Admininstrator has the responsibility to make clear to a subordinate that participation in associations and support of causes is undertaken as a private person and not as a representative of the institution, and that the only restraints are those imposed by the job description.

4. An Administrator has the responsibility to provide subordinates with the right of due process and to encourage and participate in the codification and promulgation of the institution's code of academic due process.

## B. THE RIGHTS OF ADMINISTRATORS

## I. Conditions of Employment of the Administrator

1. An applicant for an appointment as an Administrator has a right to consideration for employment without regard to race, sex, creed, national origin, or age.

2. An Administrator has a right to a written statement of the conditions of employment, including, but not limited to, statements on salary and fringe benefits, term of office, process of review, date of notification of action regarding renewal or continuance, and responsibilities of the position.

## II. The Administrator—The Operation of the Office

1. An Administrator has the right to resources consistent with the responsibility to implement policies set by the institution's governing board.

2. An Administrator has the right to a supportive institutional setting for the proper operation of the office held.

3. An Administrator has the right to adequate authority to the extent necessary to meet the responsibilities of the office.

4. An Administrator has the right to participate, according to the nature and authority of the office and within the limitations of the area of responsibility, in the formulation and implementation of institutional policy.

5. An Administrator, according to the nature of the office and within limits set by the charter and governing board, has the right to take appropriate action to develop, allocate, and preserve all resources of the institution, material and human.

6. An Administrator has the right to act as official spokesman for the institution only according to the limits of the office held, or by specific delegation.

7. An Administrator has the right to meet the responsibilities of the office held without disruption or harassment.

## III. The Administrator—Career Considerations

1. An Administrator has the right to be considered for career advancement opportunities within the institution.

2. An Administrator has the right to support for efforts undertaken to enhance personal growth and development by such means as attendance at professional meetings and by sharing in any regular staff development programs of the institution, such as sabbaticals and leaves of absence.

3. An administrator has the right to be free from arbitrary or capricious action on the part of the institution's administration or governing board, especially in those decisions affecting continuation or termination of office.

4. An Administrator has the right, under conditions established by the institution's board, to regular and formal evaluation of job performance, to participation in the evaluation process, and to receipt of timely knowledge of the results of such evaluation.

5. An Administrator has the right, when leaving an institution, to obtain written statements from the institution reflecting clearly and accurately job performance evaluation and the circumstances regarding departure. Such statements should be available for release upon request of the Administrator.

6. An Administrator has the right, in cases of termination of employment due to a reallocation of resources, to be assisted actively by the institution in seeking new employment.

## IV. Personal Rights of the Administrator

1. An Administrator has the right, conditioned only by specified limitations, to speak publicly and to express personal opinions regarding campus issues or issues that have no connection with the campus.

2. An Administrator has the right to privacy with regard to personal circumstances, including, but not limited to, financial information, religious beliefs, and political associations.

3. An Administrator has the right to participate in associations of his or her choice and to support causes, subject only to the constraints imposed by institutional responsibilities or conflict of interest considerations.

4. An Administrator has a right to due process. Such due process procedures should be codified, promulgated in writing, and communicated to the Administrator prior to appointment.

# 1940 Statement of Principles on Academic Freedom and Tenure

### American Association of University Professors and the American Association of Colleges

## STATEMENT OF PRINCIPLES

The purpose of this statement is to promote public understanding and support of academic freedom and tenure and agreement upon procedures to assure them in colleges and universities. Institutions of higher education are conducted for the common good and not to further the interest of either the individual teacher[1] or the institution as a whole. The common good depends upon the free search for truth and its free exposition.

Academic freedom is essential to these purposes and applies to both teaching and research. Freedom in research is fundamental to the advancement of truth. Academic freedom in its teaching aspect is fundamental for the protection of the rights of the teacher in teaching and of the student to freedom in learning. It carries with it duties correlative with rights. [1] [2]

Tenure is a means to certain ends, specifically: (1) freedom of teaching and research and of extramural activities and (2) a sufficient degree of economic security to make the profession attractive to men and women of ability. Freedom and economic security, hence, tenure, are indispensable to the success of an institution in fulfilling its obligations to its students and to society.

### Academic Freedom

(a) The teacher is entitled to full freedom in research and in the publication of the results, subject to the adequate performance of his other academic duties; but research for pecuniary return should be based upon an understanding with the authorities of the institution.

(b) The teacher is entitled to freedom in the classroom in discussing his

This statement is reprinted from *AAUP Policy Documents and Reports*, 1977 edition, published in Washington, D.C., by the AAUP.

For further information write to the American Association of University Professors, One Dupont Circle, Suite 500, Washington, D.C. 20036. Telephone: (202) 466-8050.

subject, but he should be careful not to introduce into his teaching controversial matter which has no relation to his subject. [2] Limitations of academic freedom because of religious or other aims of the institution should be clearly stated in writing at the time of the appointment. [3]

(c) The college or university teacher is a citizen, a member of a learned profession, and an officer of an educational institution. When he speaks or writes as a citizen, he should be free from institutional censorship or discipline, but his special position in the community imposes special obligations. As a man of learning and an educational officer, he should remember that the public may judge his profession and his institution by his utterances. Hence he should at all times be accurate, should exercise appropriate restraint, should show respect for the opinions of others, and should make every effort to indicate that he is not an institutional spokesman. [4]

## Academic Tenure

(a) After the expiration of a probationary period, teachers or investigators should have permanent or continuous tenure, and their service should be terminated only for adequate cause, except in the case of retirement for age, or under extraordinary circumstances because of financial exigencies.

In the interpretation of this principle it is understood that the following represents acceptable academic practice:

(1) The precise terms and conditions of every appointment should be stated in writing and be in the possession of both institution and teacher before the appointment is consummated.

(2) Beginning with appointment to the rank of full-time instructor or a higher rank, [5] the probationary period should not exceed seven years, including within this period full-time service in all institutions of higher education; but subject to the proviso that when, after a term of probationary service of more than three years in one or more institutions, a teacher is called to another institution, it may be agreed in writing that his new appointment is for a probationary period of not more than four years, even though thereby the person's total probationary period in the academic profession is extended beyond the normal maximum of seven years. [6] Notice should be given at least one year prior to the expiration of the probationary period if the teacher is not to be continued in service after the expiration of that period. [7]

(3) During the probationary period a teacher should have the academic freedom that all other members of the faculty have. [8]

(4) Termination for cause of a continuous appointment, or the dismissal for cause of a teacher previous to the expiration of a term appointment, should, if possible, be considered by both a faculty committee and the governing board of the institution. In all cases where the facts are in dispute, the accused teacher should be informed before the hearing in writing of the

charges against him and should have the opportunity to be heard in his own defense by all bodies that pass judgment upon his case. He should be permitted to have with him an adviser of his own choosing who may act as counsel. There should be a full stenographic record of the hearing available to the parties concerned. In the hearing of charges of incompetence the testimony should include that of teachers and other scholars, either from his own or from other institutions. Teachers on continuous appointment who are dismissed for reasons not involving moral turpitude should receive their salaries for at least a year from the date of notification of dismissal whether or not they are continued in their duties at the institution. [9]

(5) Termination of a continuous appointment because of financial exigency should be demonstrably bona fide.

*         *         *

## 1940 INTERPRETATIONS

At the conference of representatives of the American Association of University Professors and of the Association of American Colleges on November 7-8, 1940, the following interpretations of the 1940 *Statement of Principles on Academic Freedom and Tenure* were agreed upon:

1. That its operation should not be retroactive.

2. That all tenure claims of teachers appointed prior to the endorsement should be determined in accordance with the principles set forth in the 1925 Conference Statement on Academic Freedom and Tenure.

3. If the administration of a college or university feels that a teacher has not observed the admonitions of Paragraph (c) of the section on *Academic Freedom* and believes that the extramural utterances of the teacher have been such as to raise grave doubts concerning his fitness for his position, it may proceed to file charges under Paragraph (a) (4) of the section on *Academic Tenure*. In pressing such charges the administration should remember that teachers are citizens and should be accorded the freedom of citizens. In such cases the administration must assume full responsibility and the American Association of University Professors and the Association of American Colleges are free to make an investigation.

## 1970 INTERPRETIVE COMMENTS

*Following extensive discussions on the 1940* Statement of Principles on Academic Freedom and Tenure *with leading educational associations and with individual faculty members and administrators, a Joint Committee of the AAUP and the Association of American Colleges met during 1969 to reevaluate this key policy statement. On the basis of the comments received, and the discussions that ensued, the Joint Committee felt the preferable approach was to formulate interpretations of the Statement in terms of the experience gained in implementing and applying the Statement for over thirty years and of adapting it to current needs.*

*The Committee submitted to the two Associations for their consideration the following "Interpretive Comments." These interpretations were approved by the Council of the American Association of University Professors in April, 1970, and endorsed by the Fifty-sixth Annual Meeting as Association policy.*

In the thirty years since their promulgation, the principles of the 1940 *Statement of Principles on Academic Freedom and Tenure* have undergone a substantial amount of refinement. This has evolved through a variety of processes, including customary acceptance, understandings mutually arrived at between institutions and professors or their representatives, investigations and reports by the American Association of University Professors, and formulations of statements by that Association either alone or in conjunction with the Association of American Colleges. These comments represent the attempt of the two associations, as the original sponsors of the 1940 Statement, to formulate the most important of these refinements. Their incorporation here as Interpretive Comments is based upon the premise that the 1940 Statement is not a static code but a fundamental document designed to set a framework of norms to guide adaptations to changing times and circumstances.

Also, there have been relevant developments in the law itself reflecting a growing insistence by the courts on due process within the academic community which parallels the essential concepts of the 1940 Statement; particularly relevant is the identification by the Supreme Court of academic freedom as a right protected by the First Amendment. As the Supreme Court said in *Keyishian* v. *Board of Regents* 385 U.S. 589 (1967), "Our Nation is deeply committed to safeguarding academic freedom, which is of transcendent value to all of us and not merely to the teachers concerned. That freedom is therefore a special concern of the First Amendment, which does not tolerate laws that cast a pall of orthodoxy over the classroom."

The numbers refer to the designated portion of the 1940 Statement on which interpretive comment is made.

1. The Association of American Colleges and the American Association of University Professors have long recognized that membership in the academic profession carries with it special responsibilities. Both associations either separately or jointly have consistently affirmed these responsibilities in major policy statements, providing guidance to the professor in his utterances as a citizen, in the exercise of his responsibilities to the institution and stu-

dents, and in his conduct when resigning from his institution or when undertaking government-sponsored research. Of particular relevance is the *Statement on Professional Ethics*, adopted by the Fifty-second Annual Meeting of the AAUP as Association policy and published in the *AAUP Bulletin* (Autumn, 1966, pp. 290-291).

2. The intent of this statement is not to discourage what is "controversial." Controversy is at the heart of the free academic inquiry which the entire statement is designed to foster. The passage serves to underscore the need for the teacher to avoid persistently intruding material which has no relation to his subject.

3. Most church-related institutions no longer need or desire the departure from the principle of academic freedom implied in the 1940 Statement, and we do not now endorse such a departure.

4. This paragraph is the subject of an Interpretation adopted by the sponsors of the 1940 Statement immediately following its endorsement which reads as follows:

> If the administration of a college or university feels that a teacher has not observed the admonitions of Paragraph (c) of the section on Academic Freedom and believes that the extramural utterances of the teacher have been such as to raise grave doubts concerning his fitness for his position, it may proceed to file charges under Paragraph (a) (4) of the section on Academic Tenure. In pressing such charges the administration should remember that teachers are citizens and should be accorded the freedom of citizens. In such cases the administration must assume full responsibility and the American Association of University Professors and the Association of American Colleges are free to make an investigation.

Paragraph (c) of the 1940 Statement should also be interpreted in keeping with the 1964 *"Committee A Statement on Extramural Utterances" (AAUP Bulletin*, Spring, 1965, p. 29) which states inter alia: "The controlling principle is that a faculty member's expression of opinion as a citizen cannot constitute grounds for dismissal unless it clearly demonstrates the faculty member's unfitness for his position. Extramural utterances rarely bear upon the faculty member's fitness for his position. Moreover, a final decision should take into account the faculty member's entire record as a teacher and scholar."

Paragraph V of the *Statement on Professional Ethics* also deals with the nature of the "special obligations" of the teacher. The paragraph reads as follows:

As a member of his community, the professor has the rights and obligations of any citizen. He measures the urgency of these obligations in the light of his responsibilities to his subject, to his students, to his profession, and to his institution. When he speaks or acts as a private person he avoids creating the impression that he speaks or acts for his college or university. As a citizen engaged in a profession that depends upon freedom for its health and integrity, the professor has a particular obligation to promote conditions of free inquiry and to further public understanding of academic freedom.

Both the protection of academic freedom and the requirements of academic responsibility apply not only to the full-time probationary as well as to to the tenure teacher, but also to all others, such as part-time and teaching assistants, who exercise teaching responsibilities.

5. The concept of "rank of full-time instructor or a higher rank" is intended to include any person who teaches a full-time load regardless of his specific title.[3]

6. In calling for an agreement "in writing" on the amount of credit for a faculty member's prior service at other institutions, the Statement furthers the general policy of full understanding by the professor of the terms and conditions of his appointment. It does not necessarily follow that a professor's tenure rights have been violated because of the absence of a written agreement on this matter. Nonetheless, especially because of the variation in permissible institutional practices, a written understanding concerning these matters at the time of appointment is particularly appropriate and advantageous to both the individual and the institution.

7. The effect of this subparagraph is that a decision on tenure, favorable or unfavorable, must be made at least twelve months prior to the completion of the probationary period. If the decision is negative, the appointment for the following year becomes a terminal one. If the decision is affirmative, the provisions in the 1940 Statement with respect to the termination of services of teachers or investigators after the expiration of a probationary period should apply from the date when the favorable decision is made.

The general principle of notice contained in this paragraph is developed with greater specificity in the *Standards for Notice of Nonreappointment*, endorsed by the Fiftieth Annual Meeting of the American Association of University Professors (1964). These standards are:

Notice of nonreappointment, or of intention not to recommend reappointment to the governing board, should be given in writing in accordance with the following standards:

(1) *Not later than March 1 of the first academic year of service*, if the appointment expires at the end of that year; or if a one-year appoint-

ment terminates during an academic year, at least three months in advance of its termination.

(2) *Not later than December 15 of the second academic year of service,* if the appointment expires at the end of that year; or if an initial two-year appointment terminates during an academic year, at least six months in advance of its termination.

(3) At least twelve months before the expiration of an appointment after two or more years in the institution.

Other obligations, both of institutions and individuals, are described in the *Statement on Recruitment and Resignation of Faculty Members,* as endorsed by the Association of American Colleges and the American Association of University Professors in 1961.

8. The freedom of probationary teachers is enhanced by the establishment of a regular procedure for the periodic evaluation amd assessment of the teacher's academic performance during his probationary status. Provision should be made for regularized procedures for the consideratiom of complaints by probationary teachers that their academic freedom has been violated. One suggested procedure to serve these purposes is contained in the *Recommended Institutional Regulations on Academic Freedom and Tenure,* prepared by the American Association of University Professors.

9. A further specification of the academic due process to which the teacher is entitled under this paragraph is contained in the *Statement on Procedural Standards in Faculty Dismissal Proceedings,* jointly approved by the American Association of University Professors and the Association of American Colleges in 1958. This interpretive document deals with the issue of suspension, about which the 1940 Statement is silent.

The 1958 Statement provides: "Suspension of the faculty member during the proceedings involving him is justified only if immediate harm to himself or others is threatened by his continuance. Unless legal considerations forbid, any such suspension should be with pay." A suspension which is not followed by either reinstatement or the opportunity for a hearing is in effect a summary dismissal in violation of academic due process.

The concept of "moral turpitude" identifies the exceptional case in which the professor may be denied a year's teaching or pay in whole or in part. The statement applies to that kind of behavior which goes beyond simply warranting discharge and is so utterly blameworthy as to make it inappropriate to require the offering of a year's teaching or pay. The standard is not that the moral sensibilities of persons in the particular community have been affronted. The standard is behavior that would evoke condemnation by the academic community generally.

## NOTES

[1] The word "teacher" as used in this document is understood to include the investigator who is attached to an academic institution without teaching duties.

[2] Bold-face numbers in brackets refer to Interpretive Comments which follow.

[3] For a discussion of this question, see the "Report of the Special Committee on Academic Personnel Ineligible for Tenure," *AAUP Bulletin*, Autumn, 1966, pp. 280-282.

# Professional Standards:
# National Education Association
# and American Federation of Teachers

The National Education Association's professional standards are found in its constitution, its resolutions, and its code of ethics. For further information, please write to NEA Executive Office, 1201 16th Street N.W., Washington, D.C. 20036. Telephone: (202) 833-4000.

Professional standards of the American Federation of Teachers are found in its constitution and in its various publications and agreements. For further information, please write to American Federation of Teachers, AFL-CIO, 1012 14th Street N.W., Washington, D.C. 20005. Telephone: (202) 797-4400.

# Index of Cases